The Great Book of
Mediterranean
Cuisine

The Great Book of
Mediterranean
Cuisine

More than 400 recipes from the sunny Mediterranean

By
STELLA DONATI

Translated by
ANDREA JOURDAN

**CHARTWELL
BOOKS, INC.**

Editorial coordinator: Valeria Camaschella
Project and graphic coordination: Marco Volpati

Editorial collaboration: Tiziana Campana
Graphic design: Gianfranco Fiori
Jacket: Marco Volpati

*Research into iconography by the Centro Iconografico at the
Istituto Geografico De Agostini directed by Maria Serena Battaglia*
Photos: Archivio I.G.D.A. (N. Banas, L. Chiozzi, G. Cigolini,
D. Dagli Orti, M. Del Comune, K. Kissov, G. Losito, R. Marcialis,
P. Martini, G. Pisacane, F. Reculez, M. Sarcina, F. Tanasi,
G. Ummarino, Visual Food, Zanchi-St. Novak)

First published in Italy by Istituto Geografico De Agostini
under the title:
Il Grande libro della Cucina Mediterranea

Copyright © 2000 Istituto Geografico De Agostini, Novara, Italy.

This edition published in 2001 by
Chartwell Books, Inc.
A Division of Book Sales, Inc.
114 Northfield Avenue
Edison, New Jersey 08837

ISBN 0-7858-1368-3

Printed in Italy.

Mediterranean cuisine, known as "the healthiest in the world," is now recognized internationally as the cuisine with the most flavors and aromas, as well as being light and healthy, low in fat and rich in fibers and vitamins, and perfectly in tune with all the modern trends in terms of nutrition.

This book is intended as a guide to the "cuisine of the sun," by offering the best: more than 400 recipes have been chosen, all delicious and nutritious, yet healthy and without too many calories (to emphasize this concept, an approximate calorie count is indicated for every recipe). The recipes are carefully explained often with illustrations of the various operations necessary to follow the recipe step by step. Even for beginners, the recipes should be easy to follow.

Following the introduction, which illustrates the characteristics of the Mediterranean diet, the recipes are arranged in a most practical way: Antipasti, First courses (pasta, rice, soups); Pizza, Focaccia & Savory Pies; Fish (including seafood); Meat (especially white meats); Sweets & Desserts (mostly with fruits). From the delicious Crostini *with spicy mussels to the superb* Rice and zucchini pie *or the* Spicy fish soup *to the sweet* Fruit aspic, *you need only choose from among hundreds of delicious recipes.*

Summary

8
Introduction

12
ANTIPASTI

40
PIZZA, FOCACCIA & SAVORY PIES

72
FIRST COURSES

166
FISH

234
MEAT

262
VEGETABLES

340
SWEETS & DESSERTS

376
Index

380
Index by section

Introduction

Since the 70's, long and detailed research has proven that to live a healthy life, the Mediterranean diet had to be introduced in a daily regimen. A varied alimentation, adapted to all stages of life, from infancy to the golden age, helps reduce the risk of almost all illnesses known in our time. The term "Mediterranean" does not define only Italy but all countries around the Mediterranean basin, blessed by the same climate and united by the elements of their cuisine.

Forgotten by Western Civilization for a long period, the resurgence in the interest for Mediterranean food really took place with the establishment of serious links between nutrition and certain important illnesses such as obesity, diabetes, arteriosclerosis, high blood pressure, cardiovascular problems and others. In order to protect our health, it is important, above all, to balance calorie consumption among proteins, carbohydrates and fats, as well as the right proportion of saturated fats (primarily animal) and unsaturated fats (almost all vegetal) and of simple carbohydrates (sugar, sweets, caramel, marmalades) and complex carbohydrates (starches, especially those of pasta, rice, and bread).

The Mediterranean traditions

Mediterranean cuisine is particularly rich in natural fibers; it includes few simple sugars, it helps to avoid excessive calories, because it is rich in vegetables and it is amply satiating; using typical flavors like spices, herbs, pepper, garlic, onions and tomatoes results in appetizing and flavorful dishes while reducing fat as well as salt in cooking; and on top of that, there is less use of animal fat.

It is very easy to apply this model: one need only to follow the Mediterranean traditional recipes which are readily available and which can be prepared in the simple and tasty ways that are well popularized and which can be made by following this book… One of the major characteristics of this cuisine is the copious use of vegetables, above all, cereals and their derivatives: pasta, rice, bread, polenta and other less used products. Another characteristic is the important use of pulses. Herbs, vegetables and fruit also provide an ample quantity of fiber without having to get them through pharmaceutical products.

Not only fruits and vegetables

Meat is also present in Mediterranean cuisine, but in small quantities. Chicken, veal and lean pork are important elements. Fish, of course, has always been a staple of all countries around the Mediterranean Basin.

A few simple rules to be remembered: every day should start with a good breakfast. The two principal meals in the morning and the afternoon should be separated by small, light snacks of fruit juice or tea. This helps the digestive process and uses the nutritional values of food in a better, more efficient way.

Often, a meal should consist of only cooked and raw vegetables and fruits. Extra virgin olive oil should be an ever present element of all meals. Fresh fish should also be consumed regularly: tasty, with high nutritional value and a non negligible liquid content, it is a very important part of a balanced diet.

Why pasta and rice

In the Mediterranean diet, rice and pasta should be the main part of one of the daily meals. The old idea that they are high calorie food is absolutely wrong and needs to be removed from our minds. It is the heavy sauces that are sometimes served with rice or pasta that increase the calorie count. Every 3 oz of pasta or rice give about 360 calories;

2 1/2 oz are generally enough for a portion and give about 280 calories. Countless varieties of pasta – dried, fresh, short, long, filled, etc. – are all designed to absorb different sauces. Sauces made with meat, fish, shellfish, as well as vegetables can be used with rice.

It is best to use certain elements with moderation: butter, lard, margarine and cream should be abandoned to the benefit of simple condiments made of tomatoes, herbs and fresh olive oil. Being a polyunsaturated fat, extra virgin olive oil is easy to digest; it helps digest other fats and, of course, is an incredibly delicious way to flavor dishes.

Regularly eating fish, particularly anchovies, sardines and mackerel, which are typical of the Mediterranean, offers many advantages: wonderful flavor, high nutritive value and a certain quantity of moisture.

Balanced diet

Obviously, all meals should include fresh vegetables and fresh fruits: carrots, zucchini, squash, spinach, peppers, lettuce, apricots, melons - all rich in vitamin A; tomatoes, cauliflower, broccoli, citrus fruit, strawberries – all full of vitamin C. To avoid losing precious nutritional values and vitamins, it is better to cook vegetables in minimum amounts of water and to reuse these "cooking liquids" for soup or to cook rice.

Other important products to use are cheeses. The variety is enormous: whether from cow's, goat's, or sheep's milk, young or aged, they all have a place on the table and in every meal. Of course, wine is also a prime player. Used in moderation and in the right way, in harmony with the right food, it can be beneficial to your health. It can help digestion and reduce certain types of cholesterol.

The real secret is in the balance of the food. In a perfect world, a meal should supply the body with all the natural nutrients it requires to function without ever needing foreign non-natural additives.

At a recent convention of the Italian Culinary Academy, it was suggested to consider food as one would consider a soccer team: pulses as the goalkeeper; fish, dairy, and vegetables as the defense; meat, eggs, cheese, fruits as the center players; extra virgin olive oil, wine, and cereals as the offense; and rice, corn, tomatoes, as the reserve players, ready to jump in and replace similar products. As referee, remains the potato: rich in calories, poor in protein and full of minerals; because of its qualities, it dispenses traditional values and intrinsic merits.

Cholesterol

The effect of cholesterol on health remains one of the most controversial aspects of contemporary medicine. Often there is confusion about alimentary cholesterol and cholesterol in our blood; the former is present in food, the latter is carried by blood to all parts of our body.

Eggs, especially the yolks, are rich in cholesterol; anyone who has high cholesterol should limit their use without totally eliminating such an important natural product. Other foods rich in cholesterol are animal innards like giblets which also should be avoided by anyone suffering from gout.

Butter, other animal fats, fatty meat, sweets rich in fat should be consumed in moderation to avoid increasing cholesterol count. On the contrary, whole wheat bread and pasta, fresh vegetables, including onions and garlic, pulses and fresh fruit are foods that, regularly consumed, can reduce cholesterol. All these ingredients are the base of the Mediterranean cuisine: we invite you to enjoy our recipes.

Antipasti

Difficulty **easy**
Preparation time **1 hour**
Calories **310**

Ingredients *for 4 servings*

Day-old Italian-style bread *12 thick slices*

Potatoes *1/2 lb*

Grated carrots *3 tablespoons*

Egg whites *1*

Corn meal or corn flour *1 tablespoon*

Chopped parsley *3 tablespoons*

Sesame seeds *1 tablespoon*

Salt *to taste*

Potato crostini

● Rinse and brush the potatoes; boil in salted water. When cooked, peel the potatoes and pass through a potato ricer. In a large bowl, mix the mashed potatoes, carrots, salt, corn flour and egg white. Mix well and spread equally on the bread slices.

● In a small bowl, mix the sesame seeds with the chopped parsley. Cover each potato-bread slice with this mixture, pressing lightly so it sticks to the potato spread. Place the bread slices into a preheated oven at 375°F until golden. Remove from oven, place on a large plate and garnish with thin slices of green pepper. Serve immediately.

Shrimp antipasto

Difficulty **easy**
Preparation time **30 minutes**
Calories **160**

Ingredients *for 4 servings*

Small shrimp *1 lb*
Tomatoes *2*
Garlic *2 cloves*
Mild paprika *2 teaspoons*
Extra virgin olive oil *4 tablespoons*
Salt *a pinch*

● Rinse peel and devein the shrimp; remove the black thread. Peel the garlic cloves, remove the green sprout and chop finely. Drop the tomatoes in boiling water for a few seconds. Remove, immerse in cold water and peel tomatoes. Cut them in half and press lightly to remove seeds and liquid. Dice finely.

● In a small bowl, with a fork, mix the sweet paprika with 2 tablespoons of extra virgin olive oil, half the chopped garlic and a pinch of salt. Set aside.

● In a pan, heat the extra virgin olive oil. Add the shrimp and cook for 3 minutes. Transfer to a large bowl; carefully mix in the chopped tomatoes and the paprika sauce. Set aside in the refrigerator for 20 minutes before serving. Serve with fresh crusty bread.

Shrimp with avocado & egg sauce

Difficulty **easy**
Preparation time **30 minutes**
Calories **410**

Ingredients *for 4 servings*

Large shrimp *1 lb*
Avocado *1 small*
Shallot *1*
Dry sherry *2 teaspoons*
Cayenne pepper *a pinch*
Lettuce *a few leaves*
Extra virgin olive oil *2 teaspoons*
Salt *a pinch*

For the sauce

Egg yolk *1*
Dijon mustard *1 teaspoon*
Ketchup *2 teaspoons*
Plain yogurt *1 tablespoon*
Extra virgin olive oil *2 tablespoons*
Salt *a pinch*

● Peel the shrimp, remove the black thread, rinse shrimp and dry them on paper towels. Peel, rinse, dry and finely chop shallot.

● In a large pan, heat the oil lightly. Add chopped shallot and cook until transparent; add shrimp and sauté for 2 minutes; add sherry and let reduce for 5 minutes on medium heat, mixing with a wooden spoon. Remove from the heat, drain shrimp, salt them lightly and set aside. When cool, place in a bowl and refrigerate. Keep cooking juices in a separate bowl.

● To prepare the sauce: In a medium bowl, whisk egg yolk incorporating the extra virgin olive oil drop by drop. When the sauce has thickened, add the filtered cooking juices, mustard, ketchup, yogurt, a pinch of salt, and mix well. Refrigerate until ready to serve.

● Rinse the lettuce leaves, dry well and place in 4 bowls. Peel the avocado, remove the nut and dice it. Add this to the shrimp. Divide mixture into the 4 bowls. Add a dash of hot pepper to each plate and cover with the prepared sauce.

Spicy mussels on toast

Difficulty **easy**
Preparation time **30 minutes**
Calories **210**

Ingredients *for 4 servings*

Day-old bread *4 slices*
Mussels *1 lb*
Red bell peppers *2*
Onion *1*
Hot red peppers *2*
Extra virgin olive oil *4 teaspoons*
Salt *to taste*

● Rinse the peppers; cut in half, remove seeds and white parts and cut in thin slices. Peel onion and slice thinly. Set aside. Rinse mussels and brush them carefully to remove any sand or filaments. Place them in a large pan with 2 tablespoons of extra virgin olive oil; cover the pan and cook, shaking the pan from time to time, until all mussels are opened. Remove from heat. Remove mussels from shells and place in a bowl. (Discard any shell that has not opened.) Filter the cooking liquid and set aside.

● In a saucepan, add 2 tablespoons of extra virgin olive oil, peppers, onion, and 4 tablespoons of cooking liquid. Cook on medium heat, mixing often, until almost all liquid has evaporated. Pass remaining vegetables through a food mill into a large bowl.

● Dice the mussels and place in a pan with 1 tablespoon of extra virgin olive oil, and crushed red peppers. Cook on medium heat for 5 minutes, mixing often.

● Cut bread slices in 4 and toast in preheated oven at 400°F for 5 minutes, turning the bread once. Spread with the pepper sauce and cover with the hot mussels. Serve immediately.

(Note that this meal can also be eaten cold.)

Eggplant & pepper antipasto

Difficulty **easy**
Preparation time **30 minutes**
Calories **150**

Ingredients *for 4 servings*

Eggplant *1, about 1/2 lb*
Bell peppers *1*
Onion *1/2*
Raisins *2 teaspoons*
Pine nuts *1 tablespoon*
Capers in vinegar *1 tablespoon*
Extra virgin olive oil *4 tablespoons*
Salt *to taste*

● In a small bowl, soak the raisins in warm water for 15 minutes. During this time, peel the onion and slice it very thinly. Rinse the eggplant and remove both ends, but do not peel. Dice it. Rinse, dry and cut pepper in half. Remove seeds and dice.

● In a pan, heat 1 tablespoon of extra virgin olive oil; add onion and cook for 1 minute on medium heat. Add the pepper and eggplant; cook for 15 minutes, mixing well.

● Drain the raisins carefully and add to the pan. Cook for 5 minutes. Add pine nuts, caper and remaining oil. Mix well. Remove from the heat and transfer to a bowl. Serve immediately with bread.

Difficulty **easy**
Preparation time **40 minutes**
Calories **410**

Lemon rice balls

Ingredients *for 4 servings*

Rice (carnaroli *or* **baldo)** *1/2 lb*

Lemons *4*

Garlic *1 clove*

Parsley *1 small bunch*

Capers in vinegar *1 teaspoon*

Grated parmigiano *4 oz*

Extra virgin olive oil *4 tablespoons*

Salt *&* **pepper** *to taste*

● Peel the garlic and remove the green sprout. Rinse and dry the parsley and chop it finely with the garlic. In a large saucepan, cook the rice in abundant salted water. Drain the rice and transfer to a large bowl. Set aside to cool.

● During this time, in a small bowl, whisk together the juice from 1 lemon, a pinch of salt, pepper, the parsley-garlic mixture and grated peel of 1 lemon, until emulsified.

● Pour the sauce on the cold rice, add the grated parmigiano cheese and mix gently but thoroughly with a wooden spoon. With the rice mixture, make little balls the size of a walnut.

● Cut the leftover lemons in thin slices and place them decoratively on a large plate. On each lemon slice, place one rice ball and decorate with capers. Serve immediately.

Artichoke & carrot salad

Difficulty **easy**
Preparation time **1 hour**
Calories **390**

Ingredients *for 4 servings*

Artichokes *4*

Carrots *2*

Mayonnaise *1 cup*

Dijon mustard *1 teaspoon*

Lemons *3*

Black olives *12*

Arugula *1 bunch*

Cloves *2-3*

Bay leaves *1*

White wine vinegar *1 tablespoon*

Extra virgin olive oil *1 tablespoon*

Salt *&* pepper *to taste*

● Prepare the artichokes by removing the hard exterior leaves, the stems and the tips. Place them in a large bowl filled with water and 2 tablespoons of lemon juice (so they do not turn black) for 30 minutes. In a large pot filled with boiling water, add the white wine vinegar, cloves, bay leaf and drained artichokes.

● Cook them for 15-20 minutes. Drain and dry on paper towels. Slice them in long strips, removing the chokes. Peel the carrots, rinse, dry and cook them until al dente. Slice them. In a bowl, mix the mayonnaise with mustard, extra virgin olive oil, lemon juice, a pinch of salt and a little fresh ground pepper.

● Transfer the carrot slices and artichokes to a large bowl. Mix in the prepared sauce until all vegetables and covered. Divide the preparation into 4 individual bowls. Rinse, dry and shred the arugula; decorate each bowl with a few leaves. Add the olives, a few thin slices of lemon and serve.

1 *Trim the artichokes by removing the hardest leaves and cutting the spiny tips.*

2 *Slice the artichokes and cut the carrots transversely.*

3 *Put into a bowl in which you have already prepared the mayonnaise, oil, Dijon mustard, lemon juice, salt and pepper.*

Difficulty **average**
Preparation time **40 minutes**
Calories **150**

Ingredients *for 4 servings*

Calamari *1/2 lb*

Lamb's lettuce *1/4 lb*

Tomatoes *2, small*

White wine vinegar *2 teaspoons*

Soy sauce *2 teaspoons*

Extra virgin olive oil *5 tablespoons*

Salt *&* **pepper** *to taste*

Lamb's lettuce & calamari salad

● If fresh, clean the calamari. Discard any cartilage, empty them, remove eyes, mouth and skin. Remove the triangular spines and open the sac, cutting it lengthwise; cut the resulting triangle into three parts, then, with a sharp knife, make horizontal and vertical incision in each. Slice the tentacles in half, lengthwise. (If frozen, buy them already cleaned and sliced.)

● In abundant boiling water, drop the tomatoes for 30 seconds. Drain, peel and press lightly to remove seeds. Dice the tomatoes. Rinse and dry the lamb's lettuce and place it in a large salad bowl with the diced tomatoes.

● Brush a cookie sheet with 1 tablespoon of extra virgin olive oil. Place the calamari on the sheet and brush them with extra virgin olive oil. Place in a preheated oven at 390°F for 20 to 25 minutes. Remove from oven and add to the salad bowl.

● In a small bowl, whisk the pepper in the vinegar; add the soy sauce and the remaining extra virgin olive oil and whisk until well blended. Pour over the salad and toss gently. Serve.

Difficulty **easy**
Preparation time **45 minutes**
Calories **280**

Ingredients *for 4 servings*

Tomatoes *4*

Anchovies *4*

Unsalted bread *1/2 lb*

Garlic *1 clove*

Parsley *1 small bunch*

Extra virgin olive oil *5 tablespoons*

Salt *to taste*

Tomato baskets

● Slice the bread in small cubes. Rinse the anchovies under running water to remove all traces of salt and debone them. Peel the garlic cloves and remove the green sprout. Rinse, dry and finely chop the parsley with 1 garlic clove.

● In a pan, lightly heat one garlic clove in 4 tablespoons of extra virgin olive oil. Before it browns, remove the garlic and add the anchovies to the pan. Remove from heat. Press them with a wooden spoon so they melt in the oil. Add the bread and return pan to medium heat. Toss the bread.

● Rinse the tomatoes, dry them and cut in half. With a small spoon, remove all seeds. Fill the tomato cavities with the toasted bread cubes and drizzle with the remaining pan juices. Place tomatoes on an oiled cookie sheet and put in a preheated oven at 420°F for about 20 minutes. Remove from oven and serve immediately.

Difficulty **easy**
Preparation time **45 minutes**
Calories **180**

Ingredients *for 4 servings*

Mussels *8*
Zucchini *1*
Eggplant *1 small*
Bell peppers *1/2*
Diced tomato *4 oz*
Garlic *1 large clove*
Capers *1 tablespoon*
Pitted olives *4 oz*
Oregano *1 teaspoon*
Hot red pepper flakes *a pinch*
Day-old bread *2 large slices*
Extra virgin olive oil *3 tablespoons*
Salt *to taste*

Crostini with mussels & vegetables

● Brush well and rinse the mussels. Place in a pan with one tablespoon of extra virgin olive oil and, on medium heat, shake the pan until the mussels are open. Remove from heat. Remove mussels from the shell and set aside. (Discard any unopened shells.) Cut each bread slice in 4 and toast in a preheated oven at 375°F for 5 minutes. (Turn bread after 2 minutes.)

● Peel the garlic, remove the green sprout and chop finely. Rinse, dry and dice the eggplant, pepper and zucchini. Rinse the capers under running water. Chop the olives.

● In a large pan, pour in the remaining extra virgin olive oil. Add the vegetables, capers, olives and a little salt. Cook on medium heat for 3 minutes. Add 2 to 3 tablespoons of water, cover the pan and reduce to low heat. Cook for 15 minutes. Cut the mussels in large pieces and add to the pan with the oregano, hot pepper flakes and cook for another 5 minutes. Place the toasted bread on a serving plate. Distribute the mussels and vegetable mixture on the bread and serve at once.

Difficulty **average**
Preparation time **30 minutes**
Calories **120**

Ingredients *for 4 servings*

Fresh anchovies *1 lb*
Parsley *1 bunch*
Garlic *2 cloves*
Lemons *2, the juice*
Extra virgin olive oil *2 tablespoons*
Salt *& pepper to taste*

Fresh anchovies

● Peel the garlic, remove the sprout and slice it thinly. Scale the anchovies, remove the heads, empty the fish and remove the bones; rinse under running water and dry delicately on paper towels.

● In a saucepan filled with boiling water, add the juice of 1 lemon and dip in the fish for 1 minute. Drain and dry on a kitchen towel. Set aside to cool.

● Brush a large serving plate with extra virgin olive oil; on it, place the butterflied anchovies. Sprinkle with salt and fresh ground pepper, chopped parsley and the sliced garlic. Drizzle with extra virgin olive oil and leftover lemon juice. Serve immediately.

Difficulty **easy**
Preparation time **40 minutes**
Calories **490**

Ingredients *for 4 servings*

Friselle *8*

Mussels *3/4 lb*

Clams *1/2 lb*

Small shrimp *1/4 lb*

Bell peppers *2*

Saffron *1/4 teaspoon*

Garlic *2 cloves*

Chopped parsley *3 tablespoons*

Shallot *1*

Dry white wine *4 oz*

Extra virgin olive oil *5 tablespoons*

Salt *&* pepper *to taste*

Andrea's note: Generally from the Apulia region, friselle are a particular donut-shaped bread that has been dried. They need to be very briefly soaked in water before using.

Friselle alla marinara

● Rinse the clams and leave them in abundant cold water for a few hours. Brush and rinse the mussels under running water. Drain the clams and place them, with the mussels in a large pan. Drizzle with 2 tablespoons of extra virgin olive oil; add 1 garlic clove, peeled and crushed, and a little parsley. Add the wine and cook on high heat, shaking the pan, until the clams and mussels are all open.

● Remove from heat. Remove clams and mussels from the shells and set aside in a bowl. (Discard any unopened shells.) Filter the cooking juices and set aside. Peel and rinse the shrimp. Rinse the peppers and remove any white pith; then dice. Peel shallot and chop finely.

● In a large pan, add 2 tablespoons of extra virgin olive oil and cook the shallots on medium heat for 1 minute. Add the diced peppers and cook until tender. Dissolve the saffron in the reserved cooking liquid and add to the pan. Add salt and pepper; continue cooking for a few minutes. Add mussels and clams and the remaining chopped parsley; cook for 3 minutes.

● During this time, rapidly soak the friselle in cold water. Peel and cut the garlic in half; rub garlic on the friselle. Brush friselle with remaining extra virgin olive oil. Remove mussels and clam mixture from heat and distribute over the friselle. Serve immediately.

Mediterranean skewers

Difficulty **average**
Preparation time **30 minutes**
Calories **300**

Ingredients *for 4 servings*

Mussels *16*
Razor shells *8*
Shrimp *8*
Scallops *4*
Sea snails *4*
Parsley *1 small bunch*
Breadcrumbs *4 oz*
Extra virgin olive oil *4 tablespoons*
Salt *&* **pepper** *to taste*

● Soak the razor shells and the sea snails for 40 minutes. Rinse and peel the shrimp and devein. Rinse the scallops. Brush and rinse the mussels under running water; remove any hair or filaments. Rinse and dry the parsley; chop finely.

● In a large pan, heat one tablespoon of extra virgin olive oil. Add the scallops and the shrimp; when cooked, remove from heat and set aside on a plate. In the same pan, add one more tablespoon of extra virgin olive oil and cook the mussels, the razor shells and sea snails on medium heat. Shake often until mussels are open. Remove from heat.

● Soak 4 skewers in water for 5 minutes. Drain. On each skewer, place one of each in the following order: mussel, razor shell, sea snail, shrimp, scallop, mussel, shrimp and mussel.

● Brush each with the remaining extra virgin olive oil. Roll in breadcrumbs and place all skewers on a cookie sheet. Put in a preheated oven, at 375°F, for 5 to 7 minutes. (Turn after 4 minutes.) Remove from oven, place on a serving dish and serve very hot.

Small whitefish with zucchini

Difficulty **easy**
Preparation time **30 minutes**
Calories **200**

Ingredients *for 4 servings*

Small whitefish *10 oz*
Zucchini *1/2 lb*
Tomatoes *3, ripe and firm*
Garlic *1 clove*
Chervil *1 bunch*
Parsley *a small bunch*
Tarragon *a small bunch*
Lemon juice *3 tablespoons*
Extra virgin olive oil *5 tablespoons*
Salt *&* **pepper** *to taste*

● Rinse and dry the chervil and the parsley; chop separately. In boiling water, blanch the tomatoes for 1 minute. Drain, peel and press them gently to remove all seeds. Chop finely.

● In a bowl, whisk the lemon juice with a pinch of salt and pepper. Add the extra virgin olive oil slowly until the sauce thickens. Peel and chop the garlic clove; add to the sauce with the diced tomatoes, the chervil and parsley; mix well.

● Place the small white fish in a colander. Rinse well; drain and cook in a steamer for 2 to 3 minutes. Rinse, dry and cut the zucchini in julienne; steam them for 3 minutes. On a serving dish, alternate the small white fish and the zucchini. Cover with the prepared sauce and serve immediately.

Andrea's note: This is a recipe originally made for bianchetti, baby anchovies or sardines only a few days old, mostly famous in the region of Liguria. Any small whitefish can be used.

Triumph salad

Difficulty **easy**
Preparation time **40 minutes**
Calories **220**

Ingredients *for 4 servings*

Large shrimp *12*

Pineapple *1/2*

Pink grapefruit *1*

Oranges *1*

Apples *1*

Pears *1*

Lemons *1*

Orange juice *2 tablespoons*

Walnuts *2 oz*

Onion *1/2*

Leek *1/2*

Parsley *3 small bunches*

Thyme *1 small bunch*

Bay leaves *1*

Yogurt *5 tablespoons*

Dry white wine *4 oz*

Salt *&* **peppercorns** *to taste*

● Peel, rinse, dry and slice the onion. Rinse, dry and slice the leek. In a large saucepan, place the onion, leek, 2 bunches of parsley, the thyme and bay leaf. Cover with 4 cups of water, the wine, a few peppercorns and a pinch of salt. Bring to a boil, reduce heat and cook for 10 minutes.

● Rinse the shrimp; add to the broth and cook 3 minutes. Remove from heat and cool in the broth. Press the lemon into a small bowl and set aside a large piece of lemon peel. Peel the grapefruit and orange; remove the pith and detach segments; place the segments in a salad bowl.

● Peel the pineapple and remove the core. Dice and mix with the oranges and grapefruits. Peel the apple and pear; remove core, dice and drizzle with lemon juice. Add to the other fruits.

● Slice the lemon peel in thin julienne; blanch in boiling water for a minute, drain and cool before adding to the other ingredients. Drain the shrimp. Add shrimp and coarsely chopped walnuts to the other ingredients.

● In a bowl, mix the yogurt, orange juice, a pinch of salt and a pinch of pepper, until well blended. Pour over the salad and toss delicately. Sprinkle with the leftover parsley and serve at once.

Asparagus with warm baby cuttlefish

Difficulty **average**
Preparation time **30 minutes**
Calories **110**

Ingredients *for 4 servings*

Baby cuttlefish *1 lb*

Asparagus *1 lb*

Shallot *1*

Dry white wine *4 oz*

Extra virgin olive oil *3 tablespoons*

Salt *&* **pepper** *to taste*

● Clean the baby cuttlefish; remove the skin and rinse; set aside to dry. Remove the end of the stem of the asparagus; peel them with a potato peeler; rinse and dry them. Slice the stems and leave the heads whole.

● Peel the shallot and slice it thinly. In a pan, heat the oil and cook the shallot; add the cuttlefish and sauté for 3 minutes on medium heat. Add the wine, turn up the heat and let it evaporate, mixing often with a spoon. Add salt and pepper. Drain the cuttlefish and keep warm between two plates.

● In the same pan, add the asparagus with a little salt and pepper, and cook for 6 to 7 minutes on medium heat, mixing often. Return the cuttlefish to the pan and cook for 5 minutes. Transfer onto a serving plate and serve.

Orange & carrot salad

Difficulty **easy**
Preparation time **20 minutes**
Calories **160**

Ingredients *for 4 servings*

Carrots *8*

Oranges *1 large*

Apples *1*

Parsley *1 small bunch*

Extra virgin olive oil *5 tablespoons*

Salt *to taste*

● Rinse and dry the parsley; finely chop it. Peel the carrots carefully; rinse and dry them. Grate thinly and set aside in a large bowl.

● Peel the apple and dice it. Add to the carrots, mixing well. Press the orange into a small bowl; slowly add the extra virgin olive oil, whisking continuously. Add a pinch of salt and mix well.

● Pour the prepared sauce over the carrots; toss well. Sprinkle with the chopped parsley and serve as a starter for a fresh summer lunch.

Timbal of shrimp, peppers & eggplant

Difficulty **average**
Preparation time **40 minutes**
Calories **250**

Ingredients *for 4 servings*

Shrimp *1 3/4 lb*

Eggplant *1*

Bell peppers *1*

Tomatoes *2, ripe and firm*

Shallot *1*

Garlic *1 clove*

Basil *1 bunch*

Parsley *a few sprigs*

Extra virgin olive oil *8 tablespoons*

Salt *&* **pepper** *to taste*

● Rinse, dry and dice the eggplant. Cut the sweet peppers; remove all seeds and white parts; dice. Blanch the tomatoes in boiling water; drain, peel and press gently to remove all seeds; set aside in a colander. Slice the shallot.

● Peel the shrimp; rinse, dry and de-vein them. Brush 4 molds with a little extra virgin olive oil. Press the shrimp around the edges of the molds. Add a little salt and pepper. In a pan, heat 2 tablespoons of extra virgin olive oil and cook the eggplant on moderate heat until lightly golden. Set aside.

● In another pan, heat 2 tablespoons of extra virgin olive oil and cook the shallot until just transparent. Add the diced pepper with a pinch of salt. Cook for 5 minutes. Remove from heat, add the eggplant mixture, one diced tomato and the chopped basil; toss well. Fill the shrimp molds with the vegetable mixture and place in a pre-heated oven at 400°F for 10 minutes.

● Chop the garlic; dice the tomatoes and place both in a bowl. Add the remaining extra virgin olive oil, a few leaves of basil, salt and pepper. Mix well. Remove molds from the oven, set aside to cool in 2 minutes, turn onto serving plates. Serve warm with a few tablespoons of the garlic-tomato mixture and a few sprigs of parsley.

1 *Prepare the eggplant and the pepper: rinse, dry and dice them.*

3   *Cook the pepper, add the eggplant and a tomato.*

2 *Brush the molds with oil and line with the shrimp.*

4   *Fill the molds with the cooked vegetable mixture.*

Scampi & asparagus salad

Difficulty **average**
Preparation time **40 minutes**
Calories **170**

Ingredients *for 4 servings*

Asparagus *16*

Scampi *1 lb*

Celery *1 small branch*

Carrots *1*

Onion *1, small*

Bay leaves *1*

Mesclun mix *1/2 lb*

Lemon juice *2 tablespoons*

Extra virgin olive oil *4 tablespoons*

Salt *&* **pepper** *to taste*

● Peel and chop the celery, carrot and onion. Place them in a large saucepan with 5 cups of water and the bay leaf. Bring to boil, add salt and pepper; cook for 15 minutes. Rinse the scampi and add to the broth; cook for 4 minutes. Remove from heat; drain the scampi and set aside to cool. Peel and devein the scampi.

● Remove hard parts of the asparagus stems. Peel asparagus, cut heads and slice stems diagonally. Steam asparagus for 6 to 7 minutes, until al dente. Transfer to a non-stick pan to dry them, on low heat for 3 minutes.

● Rinse and delicately dry the mesclun mix. Transfer to a large serving dish. Add the scampi and the asparagus heads; place slices of asparagus in the center.

● In a bowl, whisk a pinch of salt into the lemon juice; add a pinch of pepper and, slowly pour in the extra virgin olive oil. Mix until well blended. Pour the sauce over the salad and serve immediately.

1 *Add the scampi to the boiling vegetable broth.*

2 *Remove the hard ends of the asparagus. Peel with a potato peeler.*

3 *After steaming them, dry the asparagus in a non-stick pan.*

Difficulty **average**
Preparation time **30 minutes**
Calories **360**

Shrimp & fruit salad

Ingredients *for 4 servings*

Small shrimp *1 lb*
Avocado *1*
White grapes *1/2 lb*
Orange juice *3 tablespoons*
Mayonnaise *4 oz*
Yogurt *4 oz*
Lemon juice *3 tablespoons*
Salt *&* **pepper** *to taste*

● Rinse, peel and devein the shrimp. Cook for 5 minutes in abundant salted water. Drain and cool completely.

● In a bowl, mix the mayonnaise, yogurt, orange juice, a pinch of salt and a generous pinch of pepper. Mix with a fork until all ingredients are well blended. Set aside.

● Cut the avocado in half; remove the nut and the peel. Dice the avocado and mix with the lemon juice; set aside. Rinse and carefully dry the grapes.

● Stir in the diced avocado, grapes and shrimp to the sauce bowl. Toss delicately and serve in 4 individual bowls.

Difficulty **easy**
Preparation time **30 minutes + resting time**
Calories **270**

Panzanella

Ingredients *for 4 servings*

Day-old Italian-style bread *10 slices*
Tomatoes *6, ripe and firm*
Onion *1*
Basil *1/4 cup of leaves*
Parsley *a few sprigs*
White wine vinegar *1 tablespoon*
Extra virgin olive oil *5 tablespoons*
Salt *&* **pepper** *to taste*

● Soak the bread in cold water for 5 minutes. Press it lightly to remove excess water and shred it in small pieces. Set aside in a large salad bowl.

● Peel, rinse, dry and slice the onion thinly. Rinse and dry the parsley and basil. Chop parsley and tear the basil. Rinse and peel the tomatoes, press gently to remove seeds and dice.

● Place onions, basil, parsley and tomatoes in salad bowl; toss with bread. Add a generous pinch of salt and pepper. Drizzle with the vinegar and extra virgin olive oil. Toss well.

● Set aside for at least 2 hours in a cool place. Serve as a starter for a country-style meal.

Harlequin antipasto

Difficulty **easy**
Preparation time **30 minutes**
Calories **230**

Ingredients *for 4 servings*

Quail eggs *8*

Tuna (in water) *7 oz*

Green apples *2*

Oranges *2*

Celery *4 stalks*

Lemons *1, the juice*

Pine nuts *1 oz*

Extra virgin olive oil *4 tablespoons*

Salt *to taste*

● Peel the apple and the orange; slice them very thinly and set aside in a bowl. Drain the tuna from its liquid and crush it with a fork. Rinse, peel and slice the celery thinly. Add tuna and celery to the sliced fruits.

● Fill a small saucepan with water, bring to a boil and add the quail eggs; cook for 2 to 3 minutes. Drain the eggs, peel them and slice in two; add to the salad bowl.

● In a small bowl, dilute a pinch of salt in the lemon juice; whisk in the oil, drop by drop. Pour the sauce over the salad and toss delicately. Divide the salad onto serving dishes; decorate with pine nuts and serve with fresh bread.

Sweet pepper & anchovy crostini

Difficulty **easy**
Preparation time **30 minutes**
Calories **140**

Ingredients *for 4 servings*

Day-old Italian-style bread *2 large slices*

Yellow bell peppers *1*

Anchovy filets *4*

Garlic *2 cloves*

Extra virgin olive oil *3 tablespoons*

Salt *to taste*

● Rinse and dry the pepper; cut and remove seeds and white parts; slice thinly. Rinse the anchovies under running water; dry and finely chop. Peel the garlic cloves; remove the green sprout and chop finely.

● Toast the bread slices in a preheated oven (at 390°F) for 5 minutes. Remove from oven and cut each slice in 4 pieces.

● In a pan, heat one tablespoon of extra virgin olive oil and garlic; do not let the garlic brown. Remove from heat; add the anchovy filets and mash them into the oil so they melt. Transfer the preparation to a small bowl and keep warm.

● In the same pan, heat the remaining oil; add the pepper and a pinch of salt. Cook for 10 minutes, mixing often. Pour the anchovy sauce, equally, on the slices of bread. Cover with the cooked peppers. Serve very hot.

Shrimp, arugula & carrot salad

Difficulty **average**
Preparation time **20 minutes**
Calories **150**

Ingredients *for 4 servings*

Small shrimp *1 lb*
Carrots *1 1/4 lb*
Arugula *1/2 lb*
Lemon juice *1 tablespoon*
Orange juice *1 tablespoon*
Extra virgin olive oil *3 tablespoons*
Salt *&* **pepper** *to taste*

● Peel and devein the shrimp; rinse well under running water and dry. Transfer to a saucepan filled with salted boiling water and cook for 3 minutes. Set aside.

● Peel the carrots, rinse and dry. Cut in julienne. Pick and rinse and dry the arugula. Tear it and place on a round serving plate.

● Place the shrimp and the carrots in a bowl. Add the extra virgin olive oil, the orange juice, lemon juice, a pinch of salt and pepper. Toss very well and transfer the mixture onto the bed of arugula. (You can decorate the sides of the plate by alternating slices of lemon and orange.) Cover the plate with plastic wrap and refrigerate for at least 45 minutes before serving.

Scampi with green sauce

Difficulty **average**
Preparation time **30 minutes**
Calories **190**

Ingredients *for 4 servings*

Scampi *2 1/4 lbs*
Thyme *a few sprigs*
Parsley *a few sprigs*
Bay leaves *2*
Salt *&* **white peppercorns** *to taste*

For the sauce

Chopped parsley *2 tablespoons*
Extra virgin olive oil *6 tablespoons*
Salt *to taste*

● Rinse and dry the thyme, parsley and bay leaves. In a large saucepan, bring to boil 3 cups of water. Add a generous pinch of salt, thyme, parsley, bay leaves, a few white peppercorns and the scampi. Cook for 5 minutes.

● Drain the scampi; peel and devein them. Transfer to a plate. To keep warm, place the plate over a saucepan filled with boiling water.

● To prepare the sauce, place the extra virgin olive oil, the salt and chopped parsley in a food processor. Mix until well blended. Remove the plate of scampi from the saucepan and pour the green sauce over the scampi. Serve immediately.

Difficulty **average**
Preparation time **1 hour 20 minutes**
Calories **340**

Potato & herb soufflé

Ingredients *for 6 servings*

Potatoes *2 1/2 lbs*

Asparagus *6*

Yogurt *1 tablespoon*

Eggs *3*

Chopped parsley *2 teaspoons*

Chopped tarragon *1 teaspoon*

Chopped chives *1 teaspoon*

Baking powder *1 teaspoon*

Grated Emmenthal *2 oz*

Breadcrumbs

Extra virgin olive oil *3 tablespoons*

Salt *&* **pepper** *to taste*

● Cook the potatoes in abundant salted water. Steam the asparagus. Drain the potatoes, peel them and mash through a potato ricer into a large bowl. Slice asparagus tips and purée stems in a food processor.

● In a large pan, place the potato purée, the asparagus purée and the asparagus tips. Stirring with a wooden spoon, let the mixture dry on medium heat, for a few minutes. Add 2 tablespoons of extra virgin olive oil, yogurt, grated Emmenthal, chopped herbs, a pinch of salt and pepper. Set aside to cool. Add the eggs, one at a time, whipping. Stir in the baking powder. Mix well.

● Brush 6 individual soufflé molds with extra virgin olive oil and sprinkle with breadcrumbs. Divide potato mixture in the molds. Cook in a preheated oven at 375°F for 30 minutes. Remove from the oven. Turn onto serving dishes and serve at once. (Can also be served warm.)

Difficulty **average**
Preparation time **1 hour**
Calories **220**

Green bean & calamari antipasto

Ingredients *for 4 servings*

Small calamari *14 oz*

Green beans *12 oz*

Potato *1*

Garlic *1 small bunch*

Parsley *1 small bunch*

White wine vinegar *1 tablespoon*

Extra virgin olive oil *6 tablespoons*

Salt *a pinch*

● Clean the calamari. Remove eyes and mouth; empty them. If frozen, just rinse and dry. Cut the ends of the green beans and remove the central string; rinse. Peel the potato; rinse and cut in small cubes. In a saucepan, bring 4 cups of salted water to boil. Add the beans and cook until just tender. Drain and keep warm.

● In a pan, heat 1 tablespoon of extra virgin olive oil. Add the calamari, a pinch of salt and pepper. Cook for 20 minutes. Remove from the pan and keep warm. In the same pan, add a tablespoon of extra virgin olive oil and sauté the diced potato.

● Rinse and dry the parsley. Peel the garlic and chop finely with the parsley. Transfer to a bowl. Add the vinegar and the remaining extra virgin olive oil; whisk until all ingredients are blended.

● Transfer the calamari, the green beans and potatoes to a deep dish. Pour parsley sauce in the bowl and toss well. Taste and add salt if necessary. Serve warm.

Toast with clams & eggs

Difficulty **average**
Preparation time **30 minutes**
Calories **300**

Ingredients *for 4 servings*

Clams *2 1/2 lbs*

Day-old Italian-style bread *8 slices*

Eggs *1*

Egg yolks *2*

Garlic *2 cloves*

Shallot *1*

Parsley *a few sprigs*

Dry white wine *4 tablespoons*

White wine vinegar *1 tablespoon*

Extra virgin olive oil *3 tablespoons*

Salt *&* **pepper** *to taste*

● Soak the clams in water for 3 to 4 hours. Peel the garlic and shallot. Chop shallot finely. Rinse, dry and chop parsley. Drain the clams; place in a large pan with garlic, one tablespoon of extra virgin olive oil and a pinch of parsley. On high heat, shake the pan until the clams open.

● Remove pan from heat. Remove clams from shells and place in a bowl. (Discard any unopened clams.) Filter the cooking liquid and set aside. In a pan, heat the remaining extra virgin olive oil lightly; add the shallot and cook until just transparent. Add the clams and cook for a few minutes.

● Place the egg and the two egg yolks in a small saucepan. Add the vinegar, the white wine, 4 tablespoons of the clam cooking liquid, a pinch of salt and pepper. Place the saucepan on low heat and whisk until the sauce has doubled in volume. Remove from heat and add clams. Toast the slices of bread. Rub the toasts with remaining garlic. Pour clam sauce over the bread, sprinkle with remaining parsley and serve.

Eggplant paté

Difficulty **easy**
Preparation time **30 minutes**
Calories **130**

Ingredients *for 4-6 servings*

Round eggplants *2*

Garlic *1 clove*

Dried oregano *1/2 teaspoon*

Chili pepper *1 small*

Extra virgin olive oil *5 tablespoons*

Salt *to taste*

● Rinse the eggplant; dry, peel and cut in large cubes. Peel the garlic, remove the sprout and chop finely.

● In a pan, heat 2 tablespoons of extra virgin olive oil. Add the garlic and chili pepper. Sauté for a minute; do not let the garlic brown. Add the eggplant and a pinch of salt. Mix well and cook for about 15 minutes.

● Remove from heat. Mash the eggplant with a potato masher (or a fork) to obtain a creamy purée. Add the oregano and extra virgin olive oil. Mix well and transfer the preparation to a serving bowl. Serve with toasts.

Endives with ricotta

Difficulty **easy**
Preparation time **20 minutes**
Calories **120**

Ingredients *for 4 servings*

Endives *2*
Ricotta *1/2 lb*
Yogurt *6 tablespoons*
Pine nuts *2 oz*
Basil *about 10 leaves*
Salt *&* **pepper** *to taste*

● Remove and discard the exterior leaves of the endives. Detach the next 12 leaves. Rinse and dry them delicately. Clean the basil leaves with a humid towel. Chop the basil with the pine nuts.

● In a bowl, relax the ricotta with a wooden spoon until creamy. Stir in the yogurt, chopped basil and pine nuts. Add a generous pinch of pepper.

● Divide the ricotta mixture to fill the bottom part of the 12 endive leaves. Place the filled leaves on a serving plate. Serve with grissini or melba toasts.

Difficulty **easy**
Preparation time **15 minutes**
Calories **200**

Mediterranean 'crostoni'

Ingredients *for 4 servings*

Day-old Italian-style bread *4 slices*
Tomato purée *4 teaspoons*
Mozzarella *4 slices*
Anchovy filets in oil *4*
Garlic *1 clove*
Capers *1 teaspoon*
Oregano *1 teaspoon*
Extra virgin olive oil *2 tablespoons*

● Heat the oven to 400°F. Toast the bread in the oven for 5 minutes, turning it after 3 minutes. Remove from the oven. Rub the bread with peeled and cut garlic clove.

● On each piece of bread, spread a teaspoon of tomato purée; place a slice of mozzarella, one anchovy filet, a few capers and a pinch of oregano. Drizzle with extra virgin olive oil and return to the oven for a few minutes.

● When the mozzarella is melted, the "crostoni" are ready. Remove from oven, transfer to serving plates and serve immediately.

Pizza, Focaccia & Savory Pies

Difficulty **average**
Preparation time **1 hour 20 minutes**
Calories **450**

Ingredients *for 4 servings*

Bread dough *12 oz*

Unbleached flour *1/2 cup*

Tomato paste *2 cups*

Anchovies *8*

Onions *2, large*

Black olives *4 oz*

Basil *a few leaves*

Extra virgin olive oil *4 tablespoons*

Salt *&* **pepper** *to taste*

Pizza all'Andrea

● Mix the flour with the bread dough, adding 2 tablespoons of extra virgin olive oil. Cover the dough with a kitchen towel and set aside in a warm place for 30 minutes. Brush a pizza dish with olive oil. Roll dough and, with your fingers, press it onto the dish. Let the dough hang over the sides of the dish and bring it back in to make a thick border.

● Peel the onion and slice it thinly. Rinse the anchovies to remove salt; debone and cut in small pieces. In a large pan, lightly heat the remaining oil; add the onion. Cook until just transparent. Add the tomato paste, a pinch of salt and pepper. Rinse, dry and tear the basil; add to pan.

● Cook on very low heat until the sauce thickens lightly. Add the anchovies, turn off the heat and mix well. Pour the sauce on the prepared dough and spread. Place the olives on the sauce. Cook in a preheated oven at 400°F for about 30 minutes, or until the dough is fully cooked. Remove from oven, cut and serve.

Anchovy focaccia

Difficulty **average**
Preparation time **1 hour + raising time**
Calories **500**

Ingredients *for 4 servings*

For the dough

Unbleached flour *10 oz*

Yeast *1 teaspoon*

Extra virgin olive oil *3 tablespoons*

Salt *to taste*

For the topping

Tomato paste *10 oz*

Anchovies *4-5*

Caciocavallo cheese *4 oz*

Onion *1*

Garlic *1 clove*

Oregano *a pinch*

Extra virgin olive oil *3 tablespoons*

Salt *&* **pepper** *to taste*

● Dissolve the yeast in 1/2 cup of warm water. Sift the flour on a work surface; make a whole in the center. Pour the dissolved yeast in the middle and add to half the flour. Add the extra virgin olive oil and a pinch of salt. Mix all ingredients and work the dough until it becomes elastic. Form a ball and place in a large bowl. Cover with a kitchen towel and let raise in a warm place for at least one hour.

● Peel, rinse, dry and thinly slice the onion. In a pan, cook the onion in 2 tablespoons of extra virgin olive oil until just transparent. Add the tomato sauce, a pinch of salt and fresh ground pepper. Cook for 15 minutes. Set aside. Rinse the anchovies to remove salt; debone and finely chop. Remove the outer crust from the caciocavallo and dice.

● Punch down the dough. Transfer to a work surface and knead for a minute. Divide dough in 4 pieces; roll with a rolling pin until thin. Cover dough with the prepared sauce, the diced cheese, the pieces of anchovy; sprinkle with oregano and drizzle with extra virgin olive oil. Cook in a preheated oven at 415°F for 20 to 30 minutes. Remove from oven and serve immediately.

Escarole pizza

Difficulty **easy**
Preparation time **1 hour
+ raising time**
Calories **450**

Ingredients *for 4 servings*

Bread dough *1 lb*

Escarole *4 heads*

Pitted black olives *6 oz*

Anchovies *6*

Raisins *1 tablespoon*

Capers *1 tablespoon*

Pine nuts *1 tablespoon*

Extra virgin olive oil *4 tablespoons*

Salt *to taste*

● Soak the raisins in warm water. Clean the escarole. Blanch it in abundant salted water for about 5 minutes. Drain and press to remove any excess water. Rinse the capers and the anchovies under running water to remove salt. Debone anchovies.

● In a pan, lightly heat 3 tablespoons of extra virgin olive oil with the anchovies; press the anchovies with a wooden spoon so they melt in the oil.

Add the olives and the capers and cook, on low heat, for a few minutes. Add the escarole.

● Brush a pizza pan with oil. Roll the dough and press into the pan. Cover with the prepared sauce. Sprinkle the drained raisins and the pine nuts. Drizzle with remaining olive oil. Place in preheated oven at 450°F for about 25 minutes. Serve very hot.

Beet green & chili pepper calzone

Difficulty **easy**
Preparation time **50 minutes**
Calories **470**

Ingredients *for 4-6 servings*

Bread dough *1 lb*

Beet greens *14 oz*

Pitted black olives *4 oz*

Chili pepper *1*

Extra virgin olive oil *6 tablespoons*

Salt *to taste*

● Pick, rinse well and dry the beet greens. Slice beet greens in strips and set aside in a salad bowl. Chop the pitted olives and add to the greens. Add the chopped pepper, a pinch of salt and 2 tablespoons of extra virgin olive oil. Mix all ingredients well.

● To the bread dough, add 2 tablespoons of extra virgin olive oil and work the dough until well blended. Roll the dough, with a rolling pin, very thinly. Cut as many 6-inch circles as you can.

In the middle of every dough circle, place a large dollop of beet greens mixture. Fold the dough to make large half moons and press well to close the calzone.

● With a fork, prick the top of each calzone. Place them on an oiled cookie sheet. Brush every calzone with the remaining extra virgin olive oil and bake in a preheated oven at 425°F until they are lightly browned. Serve hot or cold.

Tomato & onion focaccia

Difficulty **average**
Preparation time **1 hour 10 minutes + raising time**
Calories **670**

Ingredients *for 4 servings*

For the dough

Unbleached flour *1 lb*

Yeast *1 teaspoon*

Milk *5 tablespoons*

Extra virgin olive oil *4 tablespoons*

Salt *to taste*

For the topping

Onions *2*

Tomato sauce *16 oz*

Anchovies *3*

Black olives *2 oz*

Garlic *8 cloves*

Basil *8 leaves*

Oregano *a pinch*

Extra virgin olive oil *4 tablespoons*

● Sift the flour on a work surface. Dissolve the yeast in the warmed milk; add to the flour. Add salt, the extra virgin olive oil and enough warm water to make a soft dough.

● Work the dough vigorously, beating it on the counter, until it is elastic. Cover the dough with a kitchen towel and let it rise until doubled.

● Peel, rinse and dry the onions; slice thinly. Rinse, dry and chop anchovies. In a pan, cook onions in the oil on low heat, until transparent. Add the tomato sauce and the basil. Cook the sauce until reduced by half and add the anchovies.

● Punch the dough and flatten with a rolling pin. Spread the dough on a large cookie sheet brushed with oil. (The dough should about 1/2 inch thick.)

● Pour the sauce over the dough. Peel the garlic and remove the sprout; place on top of the sauce with the olives. Sprinkle with oregano and place in the oven at 450°F for about 30 minutes. Serve very hot.

Pizza napoletana

Difficulty **easy**
Preparation time **45 minutes**
Calories **510**

Ingredients *for 4 servings*

Bread dough *14 oz*

Tomatoes *3*

Garlic *2 cloves*

Basil *6 leaves*

Oregano *1/2 teaspoon*

Extra virgin olive oil *3 tablespoons*

Salt *to taste*

● Blanch the tomatoes in boiling water. Drain, peel and press gently to remove excess water. Slice the tomatoes in thin strips and set aside in a bowl. Peel and crush the garlic. Rinse, dry and tear the basil leaves. Add garlic, basil, oregano and a pinch of salt to the tomatoes. Mix well.

● Roll the dough with a rolling pin. Brush one large or several small cookie sheets with extra virgin olive oil. Spread the tomato mixture on the dough, leaving the sides empty. Drizzle with extra virgin olive oil. Bake in a preheated oven at 450°F for about 20 minutes. Remove from the oven and serve immediately.

Pizza margherita

Difficulty **average**
Preparation time **1 hour + raising time**
Calories **550**

Ingredients *for 4 servings*

For the dough

Unbleached flour *1 lb*
Yeast *2 teaspoons*
Extra virgin olive oil *2 teaspoons*
Salt *to taste*

For the topping

Tomato sauce *14 oz*
Mozzarella *5 oz*
Basil *a few leaves*
Extra virgin olive oil *4 tablespoons*
Salt & **pepper** *to taste*

● Dissolve the yeast in 2 tablespoons of warm water and mix with 2 tablespoons of flour. Cover with a kitchen towel and set aside to rise in a warm place until doubled in volume. Sift the flour on a work surface and make a well in the middle. Pour the yeast mixture in the well; add a pinch of salt, 2 tablespoons of oil and work the dough. Knead until dough is smooth and elastic.

● Knead vigorously for a few minutes; place in a floured bowl. Cover with a kitchen towel and set aside in a warm place. When doubled in volume, punch down and return dough to the work surface. Knead for another 5 minutes. Divide dough in 4 pieces; roll out to very thin circles. Brush a large cookie sheet with oil and place circles of dough on it.

● Brush every circle with tomato sauce; drizzle with olive oil and season with salt and pepper. Bake in a preheated oven at 450°F for 15 minutes. Remove from oven. Sprinkle each pizza with diced mozzarella and basil leaves. Return to the oven for about 10 minutes. Serve hot.

Sun-dried tomato & vegetable tart

Difficulty **average**
Preparation time **1 hour + raising time**
Calories **710**

Ingredients *for 4 servings*

For the dough

Unbleached flour *18 oz*
Yeast *2 teaspoons*
Extra virgin olive oil *5 tablespoons*
Salt *to taste*

For the filling

Beet greens *1 1/4 lbs*
Sun-dried tomatoes in olive oil *6*
Powdered chili pepper *a pinch*
Extra virgin olive oil *5 tablespoons*
Salt *to taste*

● Dissolve the yeast in 4 ounces of warm water; set aside until frothy. On a work surface, sift 16 ounces of flour with a generous pinch of salt. Make a well in the middle and add the yeast and enough warm water to make a smooth but dense dough. Flatten dough, roll in the remaining flour and cover with a kitchen towel. Set aside to rise for at least one hour.

● Punch down dough. Knead on an oiled surface, gradually adding the 5 tablespoons of olive oil, until well incorporated. Divide the dough in 2 pieces. Roll out each piece to thin circles, making one slightly larger than the other. Brush a large pie plate with olive oil; flour the plate. Place the largest circle of dough in the pie plate.

● Rinse and dry the greens; slice thinly and place in a bowl. Cut the tomatoes in pieces and add to the greens. Add the hot chili pepper. Season with salt and pepper; drizzle with extra virgin olive oil. Toss well. Place this mixture into the dough; cover with the second circle of dough and close tightly around the edges. Prick the pie with a fork. Place in a preheated oven at 450°F for about 30 minutes. Remove the pie from the oven and cool briefly before serving.

Difficulty **average**
Preparation time **1 hour**
Calories **360**

Vegetable calzone

Ingredients *for 4 servings*

Unbleached flour *1/2 lb*

Raised bread dough *2 oz*

Beet greens *12 oz*

Raisins *2 teaspoons*

Crushed pepper flakes *a pinch*

Extra virgin olive oil *5 tablespoons*

Salt *to taste*

● Sift the flour on a work surface. Make a well in the middle. Break the raised dough in little pieces and place in the well with 2 tablespoons of extra virgin olive oil and a pinch of salt. Work the flour with the other ingredients until dough is elastic. Add warm water if necessary. Form a ball with the dough and set aside, covered with a kitchen towel to rise.

● Soak the raisins in warm water for 5 minutes. Rinse and dry the beet greens in a salad spinner. Slice in thin strips and set aside in a bowl. Drain the raisins and add to the greens. Add one tablespoon of oil, a pinch of salt and the pepper flakes. Mix well.

● Roll dough with a rolling pin into a large and very thin sheet. Place it on a cookie sheet brushed with oil. Spread the vegetable mixture on half of the dough. Fold the other half over and press the sides to close well. Brush the calzone with the remaining oil. Bake in a preheated oven at 400°F for about 25 minutes. Remove from oven and serve.

Difficulty **average**
Preparation time **1 hour**
Calories **480**

Wild herb tart

Ingredients *for 4 servings*

Bread dough *1 lb*

Wild herbs *3/4 lb (borage, nettles, chicory, dandelion, etc.)*

Ricotta *4 oz*

Garlic *1 clove*

Eggs *2*

Egg yolks *1*

Raisins *1 tablespoon*

Pine nuts *1 tablespoon*

Sugar *1 tablespoon*

Grated grana cheese *2 tablespoons*

Extra virgin olive oil *5 tablespoons*

Salt *&* **pepper** *to taste*

● Soak the raisins in a bowl filled with warm water. Pick the wild herbs, rinse well and cook in abundant salted water for 5 minutes. Drain the herbs and press to remove any water. In a pan, heat lightly 2 tablespoons of extra virgin olive oil with the peeled garlic clove. Add the herbs and cook for a few minutes. Drain the herbs and set aside in a bowl.

● To the herbs, add the drained raisins, the eggs, the egg yolks, the ricotta, sugar and grana cheese, salt and pepper. Mix well. Toast the pine nuts on a cookie sheet in a preheated oven at 450°F for a few minutes. Stir into the herb mixture. Brush a pie dish with oil. Cover with 2/3 of the bread dough and fill with the mixture.

● With the remaining dough, form a circle and cover the pie. With your fingers, close the pie tightly. Remove any excess dough from the sides. With a fork, prick the pie and brush it with the remaining oil. Bake in a preheated oven at 450°F for about 30 minutes. Remove from oven and serve hot or cold.

Vegetable tart

Difficulty **average**
Preparation time **1 hour**
Calories **380**

Ingredients *for 4 servings*

Carrots *3/4 lb*

Green beans *3/4 lb*

Fresh green peas *3/4 lb*

Eggs *6 large*

Basil *1 bunch*

Milk *4 tablespoons*

Breadcrumbs *4 tablespoons*

Grated grana cheese *6 tablespoons*

Extra virgin olive oil *2 tablespoons*

Salt *&* **pepper** *to taste*

● Peel the carrots. Cut the ends of the beans and remove thread. Dice carrots and cut beans in small pieces. Rinse, dry and tear the basil. In abundant salted water, cook the carrots and the beans separately. Drain and set aside in a bowl.

● In a small bowl, whisk the eggs, the milk and the grated grana cheese. Mix into the vegetables; add the bread-crumbs, basil, a pinch of salt and pepper.

● Brush a 12-inch pie plate with oil. Pour in the egg and vegetable preparation. Bake in a preheated oven at 400°F, for about 20 minutes until golden on the top. Remove from oven and set aside to cool. Turn onto a serving plate, cut in pieces and serve warm.

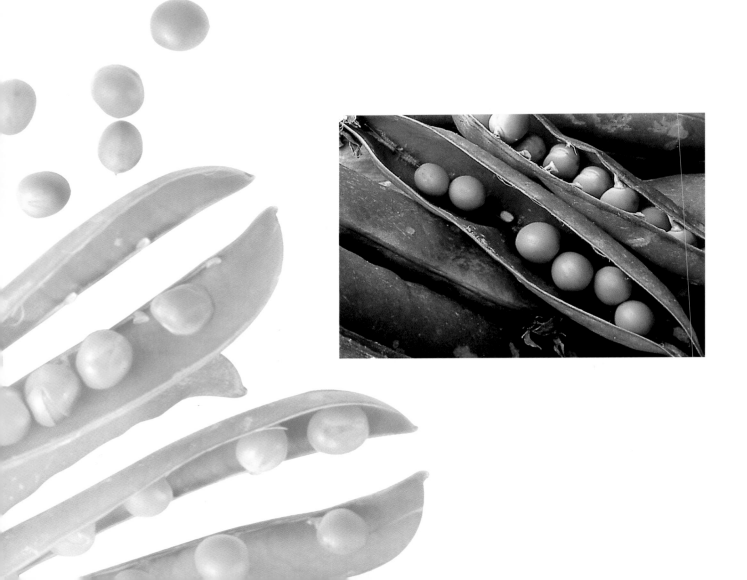

Difficulty **average**
Preparation time **1 hour 30 minutes**
Calories **820**

Ingredients *for 4 servings*

Frozen puff pastry *14 oz*

Eggplants *2*

Tomatoes *4*

Emmenthal cheese *7 oz*

Garlic *1 clove*

Eggs *3*

Basil *a few leaves*

Oregano *a pinch*

Extra virgin olive oil *2 tablespoons*

Salt *&* **pepper** *to taste*

Crostata Teresa

● Peel the eggplants; dice and place in a colander. Season with salt and set aside, over a bowl, and let the juices. Drain for about 30 minutes. Rinse the eggplants and dry on paper towels. Peel the garlic, remove the sprout and rinse. Rinse and dry tomatoes; quarter and press delicately to remove the seeds; set aside to drain in a colander.

● In a large pan, heat the oil and garlic. When garlic is lightly golden, remove it. Add the eggplants, a pinch of salt, pepper and oregano. Cook on low heat for about 12 minutes. Beat the eggs and add to the eggplants; mix well. Turn off the heat and mix in the diced Emmenthal cheese. Cover and set aside.

● Roll out the pastry dough (thawed at room temperature) and use it to line a pie dish. Pour the eggplants and egg mixture into the pie. Delicately dry the tomato quarters on paper towels and place them, like a crown on top of the pie. Bake in a preheated oven at 400°F for about 30 minutes. Remove the pie from the oven, decorate with basil leaves and serve at once.

Artichoke rolls

Difficulty **average**
Preparation time **1 hour**
Calories **540**

Ingredients *for 4 servings*

For the dough

Unbleached flour *14 oz*
Extra virgin olive oil *4 tablespoons*
Salt *to taste*

For the filling

Artichokes *8 small*
Parsley *1 small bunch*
Lemons *1, the juice*
Garlic *1 clove*
Breadcrumbs *2 tablespoons*
Grated grana cheese *2 tablespoons*
Extra virgin olive oil *5 tablespoons*
Salt *to taste*

● Prepare the artichokes: Remove stems and hard exterior leaves. Cut off the prickly tips and slice them thinly, removing any central chokes. Place in a large bowl; cover with water and the lemon juice (to prevent them from blackening). Peel the garlic. Rinse and dry the parsley. Finely chop the parsley and garlic together.

● In a pan, heat 4 tablespoons of extra virgin olive oil with the parsley mixture for a few minutes. Add the artichokes. Season with salt, cover and cook on low heat for about 20 minutes. (Add a little water if necessary.) When cooked, sprinkle with breadcrumbs.

● Blend the flour, salt and oil with enough warm water to make an elastic yet compact dough. Knead for a few minutes, then roll it with a rolling pin until dough is quite thin. Spread the cooked artichoke mixture on the dough.

● Roll the dough with the artichokes and press the sides to close the roll well. Place the roll on an oiled cookie sheet. Bake in a preheated oven at 400°F for 20-25 minutes. Remove from oven, slice in thick pieces; place the "rolls" on a serving dish and serve hot or slightly cool.

Radicchio pizza

Difficulty **average**
Preparation time **1 hour + raising time**
Calories **410**

Ingredients *for 4 servings*

For the dough

Unbleached flour *10 oz*
Yeast *1 teaspoon*
Salt *& pepper to taste*

For the topping

Red radicchio *2 1/4 lbs*
Capers *2 tablespoons*
Large black olives *10*
Garlic *1 clove*
Eggs *1*
Extra virgin olive oil *4 tablespoons*
Salt *& pepper to taste*

● Dissolve the yeast in a little warm water. Sift the flour onto a work surface. Add a pinch of salt and pepper. Add the dissolved yeast and mix well, adding enough warm water to make the dough elastic. Knead briefly and form a large ball; cover with a kitchen towel and set aside until doubled in volume.

● Rinse and dry the radicchio leaves; slice in large strips. In a large pan, cook the radicchio and garlic clove in 4 tablespoons of extra virgin olive oil. Season with salt and pepper. Cover, reduce heat to low and continue cooking until radicchio is tender and dried.

● Divide dough in 2 pieces, one slightly larger than the other. Roll the larger ball of dough in a very thin sheet. Transfer to an oiled pizza oven sheet. Spread the cooked radicchio on top of dough; remove garlic clove. Sprinkle with the rinsed and dried capers and the pitted black olives.

● Roll out the second ball of dough and cover the pizza; close the sides well. Brush the dough with the beaten egg. Bake in a preheated oven at 400°F for about 25 minutes. Remove from oven, transfer to a serving dish and serve immediately.

Clam pizza

Difficulty **easy**
Preparation time **1 hour**
+ raising time
Calories **440**

Ingredients *for 4 servings*

Bread dough *1 lb*
Clams *2 1/4 lbs*
Tomatoes *1 lb, ripe and firm*
Chopped parsley *1 tablespoon*
Oregano *a pinch*
Extra virgin olive oil *5 tablespoons*
Salt & pepper *to taste*

● Rinse the clams and set aside, covered with water for at least 3 hours. Drain well and transfer to a large pan. Cook on high heat shaking the pan, until all clams are open. Remove from heat. Remove clams from shells and set aside in a bowl. (Discard any clams that have not opened.)

● Blanch the tomatoes rapidly in boiling water. Drain, peel and press lightly to remove all seeds. Dice tomatoes and place in a saucepan with 2 tablespoons of olive oil. Season with salt and fresh ground pepper; add a pinch of oregano and half the chopped parsley. Cook on medium heat.

● Add 2 tablespoons of extra virgin olive oil to the dough; knead well and roll out with a rolling pin. Brush a large pie dish with oil and cover with dough. Spread tomatoes on dough and bake in a preheated oven at 415°F for about 20 minutes. Remove from oven and place clams on the pizza. Sprinkle with remaining chopped parsley and return to oven for 5 minutes. Serve extremely hot.

Rice & zucchini pie

Difficulty **average**
Preparation time **1 hour 10 minutes**
Calories **390**

Ingredients *for 4 servings*

For the dough

Unbleached flour *7 oz*
Extra virgin olive oil *3 tablespoons*
Salt *to taste*

For the filling

Zucchini *1/2 lb*
Rice *4 oz*
Onions *1*
Eggs *1 extra large*
Grated grana cheese *2 tablespoons*
Extra virgin olive oil *2 tablespoons*
Salt & pepper *to taste*

● Cook the rice in abundant salted boiling water, until just al dente. Drain well and set aside. Rinse and dry the zucchini; slice in julienne. Set aside. Peel, rinse, dry and finely chop the onion. Add to the zucchinis. In a large bowl, mix zucchini, chopped onion, rice, grated cheese and oil. Season with salt and pepper; mix in the egg.

● To prepare the dough, place the flour in a bowl. Add a pinch of salt, 2 tablespoons of extra virgin olive oil and enough warm water to make a soft and elastic dough. Brush a pie dish with oil; divide dough in 2 pieces. Roll into 2 thin circles, one slightly larger than the other. With the larger piece, cover the dish. Pour the zucchini mixture in the dough and press down delicately. Cover with the second circle of dough.

● Press the sides to close the pie well. Brush the dough with remaining olive oil. Bake in a preheated oven at 400°F for about 30 minutes. Remove from oven and serve warm.

Difficulty **average**
Preparation time **1 hour 10 minutes**
Calories **380**

Onion & sweet pepper pie

Ingredients *for 4 servings*

For the dough

Unbleached flour *1/2 cup*

Unsalted butter *2 tablespoons*

Salt *to taste*

For the filling

Onions *12 oz*

Red bell peppers *1*

Yellow bell peppers *1*

Eggs *2*

Milk *1/4 cup*

Extra virgin olive oil *2 tablespoons*

Salt *&* **pepper** *to taste*

● In a food processor, place the flour and butter, cut in small pieces. Add a pinch of salt and mix, adding enough cold water, drop by drop, to make a firm dough. Mix until dough forms a ball. Wrap dough in plastic or cover with a kitchen towel. Refrigerate for at least 30 minutes.

● Peel the onion and slice thinly. Cut the peppers in half; remove all seeds and white parts; slice thinly. In a large pan, heat the oil and cook onion until just tender. Transfer to a bowl and set aside. In the same pan, cook the peppers for 5 minutes. Drain and add to the onions.

● In a small bowl, mix the eggs, the milk, a pinch of salt and fresh ground pepper, with a fork. Add to the onion and pepper mixture; mix well.

● Remove dough from refrigerator. Roll out to 1 1/4-inch thick. Brush a pie dish in the oil and line with dough. Prick the bottom of the pie with a fork. Fill with the prepared eggs and vegetable mixture. Bake the pie in a preheated oven at 400°F for 30 minutes or until top of pie is golden. Remove from oven and cool for a few minutes. Carefully transfer to a serving dish and serve. (Can also be served cold.)

1 Cook the thinly sliced onions in a pan until transparent.

2 Mix the eggs and milk with the cooked onions and peppers.

3 Fill the pie crust with the prepared vegetable mixture.

Difficulty **easy**
Preparation time **1 hour**
Calories **300**

Ingredients *for 4 servings*

Ready-made pie dough *1/2 lb*

For the filling

Small zucchini *14 oz*

Tomatoes *1/2 lb, ripe and firm*

Mozzarella *6 oz*

Basil *1 bunch*

Grated grana cheese *4 oz*

Breadcrumbs *1 tablespoon*

Unbleached flour *1 tablespoon*

Extra virgin olive oil *3 tablespoons*

Salt *&* **pepper** *to taste*

Zucchini, mozzarella & tomato pie

● Rinse, dry and slice the zucchini. In a large pan, cook the zucchini with 2 tablespoons of extra virgin olive oil. Season with salt and pepper; remove from heat and set aside.

● Blanch the tomatoes in boiling water. Drain, peel and press lightly to remove all seeds. Slice thinly. Slice the mozzarella. Rinse, dry and tear the basil in small pieces.

● Roll out the dough very thinly. Brush a large pie plate with a little oil; cover with rolled dough and prick the dough with a fork. Cover with half the zucchini, then add half mozzarella. Sprinkle with a little grated grana cheese and cover with the tomato slices. Season with salt, pepper and the basil.

● Continue alternating layers of mozzarella, grated grana and zucchini. Mix the remaining grated grana with the breadcrumbs and sprinkle over the last layer of zucchini. Drizzle with remaining extra virgin olive oil. Bake in preheated oven at 400°F for 30 minutes. Remove from oven, place on a serving plate and serve immediately.

1 *Cover the prepared pie dough with half of the cooked zucchini.*

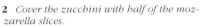

2 *Cover the zucchini with half of the mozzarella slices.*

3 *Place the sliced tomatoes over the mozzarella.*

Four seasons pizza

Difficulty **easy**
Preparation time **30 minutes**
Calories **230**

Ingredients *for 1 pizza*

Bread dough *7 oz*
Clams *8-10*
Mussels *15-20*
Chopped black olives *12-15*
Anchovy filets *4*
Artichokes in oil *6-7*
Unbleached flour *for work surface*
Extra virgin olive oil *2 tablespoons*

● Rinse mussels and clams well. Place them in a large pan, on high heat, shaking the pan from time to time. As the clams and mussels open, remove from shells and set aside. Flour a work surface and roll out the bread dough in a large circle. Brush a pizza sheet with oil and cover with the dough. With the back of a knife blade, make a cross on the dough so it is marked in four equal parts.

● Cover each part with a different ingredient. In the first, place the clams; in the next, the olives and anchovy filets; in another, the artichokes, sliced; and in the last one, the mussels. Bake in a preheated oven at 415°F for 15 to 20 minutes. Remove and drizzle with extra virgin olive oil before serving.

Mushroom pizza

Difficulty **average**
Preparation time **1 hour**
+ raising time
Calories **450**

Ingredients *for 4 servings*

For the dough

Unbleached flour *14 oz*
Yeast *1 1/4 teaspoons*
Salt *to taste*

For the topping

Mushrooms *14 oz*
Garlic *2 cloves*
Parsley *1 small bunch*
Extra virgin olive oil *4 tablespoons*
Salt *to taste*

● Prepare the dough. Dissolve the yeast in half a cup of warm water. Place the flour on a work surface, make a well in the middle and pour in the yeast, a pinch of salt and a little warm water.

● Gently work the ingredients with a fork, until all incorporated. Knead vigorously until soft and elastic. For a ball, place it in a floured bowl and cover with a kitchen towel. Set aside until risen or about 2 hours at room temperature.

● In a pan, heat 3 tablespoons of extra virgin olive oil. Add mushrooms and parsley mixture. Mix well and cook, on medium heat, for 10 minutes or until the mushrooms will have rendered all their water. Season with a pinch of salt.

● Roll out dough in a large circle. Brush a large cookie sheet with oil; cover with dough. Spoon the mushrooms onto the dough, leaving the edges empty. Bake in a preheated oven at 450°F for 20 minutes. Remove from oven and serve immediately.

Focaccia with green olives

Difficulty **average**
Preparation time **40 minutes**
+ raising time
Calories **610**

Ingredients *for 4 servings*

Unbleached flour *15 oz*

Yeast *1 teaspoon*

Pitted green olives *1 cup*

Sparkling water *14 cup*

Extra virgin olive oil *5 tablespoons*

Salt *to taste*

● Dissolve the yeast in half a cup of warm water. Sift the flour and salt into a large bowl; make a well in the middle. Gradually pour in the yeast, the sparkling water and 3 tablespoons of extra virgin olive oil. Mix to make a smooth dough. Knead for 8-10 minutes.

● Place dough in a bowl and set aside to rise until doubled in volume. Add 3/4 of chopped olives and knead again. Roll out dough to 1/2-inch thick. Brush a cookie sheet with oil and cover with the dough. Drizzle with the remaining olive oil; season with salt and remaining olives. Bake in a preheated oven at 425°F for about 20 minutes or until golden and crisp.

Spinach pie

Difficulty **average**
Preparation time **1 hour 40 minutes**
+ raising time
Calories **580**

Ingredients *for 4 servings*

For the dough

Unbleached flour *1/2 lb*

Butter *2 oz*

Salt *to taste*

For the filling

Spinach *or* **chard** *2 1/4 lb*

Grated grana cheese *6 oz*

Chopped parsley *2 tablespoons*

Garlic *1 clove, chopped*

Eggs *1*

Extra virgin olive oil *5 tablespoons*

Salt *&* **pepper** *to taste*

● Make the dough. Sift the flour and salt into a large bowl. Make a well in the center. Add the butter, softened and cut in small pieces. Mix, adding enough warm water to form a soft and smooth dough. Cover with a kitchen towel and set aside for 30 minutes, in a cool place.

● Rinse the spinach several times. Cook in abundant salted water until just al dente. Drain well and chop. In a large pan, heat 3 tablespoons of extra virgin olive oil. Add the spinach with the parsley and garlic. Cook until all water is evaporated. Remove from heat; add egg, grated grana and fresh ground pepper. Mix well.

● Roll out dough in two circles, one slightly larger than the other. Brush a pie dish with oil and line with the larger circle of dough. Fill with the spinach mixture. Cover with the second circle.

● Close the edges. Brick the top of the pie with a fork. Brush with oil. Bake in a preheated oven at 400°F for about 45 minutes. Serve warm or cold.

Eggplant & pepper pie

Difficulty **easy**
Preparation time **1 hour 10 minutes**
Calories **510**

Ingredients *for 4 servings*

Bread dough *1 1/2 lbs*
Eggplants *2*
Red bell peppers *1*
Onion *1*
Grated parmigiano *3 tablespoons*
Extra virgin olive oil *4 tablespoons*
Salt *&* **pepper** *to taste*

● Peel, rinse, dry and slice the onion. Rinse and dry the sweet pepper; remove seeds and slice thinly. Rinse and dry the eggplants; dice. In a large pan, heat 3 tablespoons of extra virgin olive oil. Add the onion and cook until transparent. Add the pepper slices and the diced eggplants. Season with salt and cook over medium heat for about 20 minutes. Remove from heat and mix in the grated parmigiano.

● Divide the dough in two. Roll out into 2 circles, one larger than the other. Brush a pie plate with oil. Line the pie plate with the larger circle of dough. Fill with the vegetable mixture and cover with the remaining dough circle. Close the edges carefully. Bake in a preheated oven at 400°F for about 30 minutes. Remove from oven and serve hot or warm.

Rosemary focaccia

Difficulty **easy**
Preparation time **45 minutes + raising time**
Calories **370**

Ingredients *for 4 servings*

Unbleached flour *9 oz*
Chopped rosemary *2 teaspoons*
Yeast *1 teaspoon*
Extra virgin olive oil *5 tablespoons*
Salt *to taste*

● Dissolve the yeast in 3 tablespoons of warm water. Sift the flour in a large bowl and make a well in the middle. Pour yeast in the flour, with 3 tablespoons of extra virgin olive oil, the chopped rosemary and a pinch of salt. Slowly mix in all ingredients, adding 6 tablespoons of warm water. Knead for about 10 minutes, until dough is smooth and elastic. Cover with a kitchen towel and set aside to rise for about 30 minutes, in a warm place.

● Knead again and roll out the dough to 1/2-inch thick. Brush a cookie sheet with oil and line with dough. Brush dough with 1 tablespoon of extra virgin olive oil. Set aside to rise for 30 minutes. Bake in a preheated oven at 400°F for about 20 minutes. Remove from heat, transfer to a wooden board, slice and serve hot or cold.

Vegetable pie

Difficulty **average**
Preparation time **1 hour 10 minutes**
Calories **420**

Ingredients *for 4 servings*

Bread dough *14 oz*

Chard *14 oz*

Spinach *14 oz*

Onions *2*

Capers *1 teaspoon*

Pitted green olives *3 oz*

Anchovy filets *4*

Milk *1 1/4 cup*

Eggs *1*

Garlic *1 clove*

Extra virgin olive oil *3 tablespoons*

Salt *&* **pepper** *to taste*

● Peel, rinse and dry the onions and garlic; chop finely. In a large pan, heat 2 tablespoons of oil and cook onions and garlic until onions are transparent. Add anchovies and mix until dissolved. Add spinach and chard; cook briefly. Add the olives and rinsed capers. Season with salt and pepper. Cook on low heat until all water has evaporated and vegetables are soft. Remove from heat, transfer to a bowl and set aside.

● Roll out the dough thinly. Brush a pie dish with oil and line with dough. Cut out excess dough and set aside. In a bowl, whisk the egg, milk, a pinch of salt and pepper; add to vegetable mixture. Fill the pie with mixture. Roll out the excess dough and cut into strips; criss-cross over the pie. Bake in a preheated oven at 400°F for about 30 minutes. Serve hot or warm.

Eggplant & mushroom strudel

Difficulty **average**
Preparation time **1 hour**
Calories **200**

Ingredients *for 6 servings*

Bread dough *14 oz*

Eggplant *10 oz*

Mushrooms *1/4 lb*

Black olives *3 oz*

Garlic *2 cloves*

Parsley *1 bunch*

Lemons *1, the juice*

Extra virgin olive oil *4 tablespoons*

Salt *&* **pepper** *to taste*

● Peel, rinse, dry and finely chop the eggplant. Remove ends of stems from the mushrooms; rinse, dry and chop. Rinse the parsley and blanch it in boiling water; drain, rinse under cold water, drain again, dry and chop finely.

●In a pan, heat 2 tablespoons of extra virgin olive oil. Add eggplants and mushrooms. Cook, stirring from time to time, until all liquid has evaporated. Season with a pinch of salt and fresh ground pepper. Add the parsley, olives and chopped garlic. Mix well and re-move from heat. Add the lemon juice and set aside to cool.

● Over a large towel or sheet that has been floured, roll out dough very thinly. You should get a rectangle 20 inch x 24 inch. Brush with oil. Cover with eggplant and mushroom mixture, leaving edges free. Roll the strudel, helping yourself with the sheet. Close the edges carefully. Brush with remaining extra virgin olive oil and bake in a preheated oven at 400°F for about 30 minutes. Serve hot or cool.

Plain pizza

Difficulty **average**
Preparation time **50 minutes + raising time**
Calories **490**

Ingredients *for 4 servings*

For the dough

Unbleached flour *14 oz*

Yeast *1 1/4 teaspoons*

Salt *to taste*

For the topping

Tomatoes *6 small*

Garlic *4 cloves*

Oregano *a pinch*

Extra virgin olive oil *5 tablespoons*

Salt *&* **pepper** *to taste*

● Dissolve the yeast in half a cup of warm water. Sift the flour on a work surface; make a well in the middle. Pour in the yeast with a pinch of salt. Mix the ingredients and knead until dough is smooth and firm. Cover with a kitchen towel and set aside until dough has doubled.

● Rinse, peel and slice the tomatoes in half. Press gently to remove all seeds. Peel the garlic; cut in half and remove green sprout. Knead the dough again. Brush a pizza pan with oil and line with dough, pressing dough with your fingers to fill the pan.

● Poke the dough all over with a finger to make large dimples in the surface. In the dimples, place tomato halves and garlic clove halves. Drizzle with the remaining olive oil; season with salt and oregano. Bake in a preheated oven at 450°F for about 20 minutes.

Savory pie with yellow squash

Difficulty **average**
Preparation time **2 hours**
Calories **860**

Ingredients *for 4 servings*

Frozen puff pastry dough *14 oz*

Rice *4 oz*

Yellow squash *14 oz*

Chard *7 oz*

Eggs *3*

Onion *1*

Garlic *1 clove*

Grated grana cheese *3 tablespoons*

Nutmeg *a pinch*

Dried marjoram *a pinch*

Extra virgin olive oil *3 tablespoons*

Salt *&* **pepper** *to taste*

● Peel the squash and remove all seeds and filaments; slice and place on a non-stick cookie sheet. Bake in a preheated oven at 350°F for 25 to 30 minutes, until squash is dry and soft. Cook the rice in abundant salted water until al dente; drain well. Rinse chard and cook in a little salted water. Drain very well.

● Chop the chard and the squash together; place in a large bowl. Mix in the rice. Peel and chop onion and garlic. In a pan, heat 3 tablespoons of extra virgin olive oil; cook the onion and garlic for a few minutes. Add to the pumpkin mixture. Season with nutmeg, marjoram, salt and grated grana cheese. Mix well. When mixture is cool, mix in 2 eggs.

● Roll out the thawed dough in 2 circles, one larger than the other. Sprinkle water on a pie dish. Line with the larger piece of dough. Fill with the squash mixture. Cover with the second piece of dough; seal the edges carefully. Beat the remaining egg and brush onto the pie. Bake the pie in a preheated oven at 400°F for about 40 minutes. Remove from oven and serve at once.

Difficulty **average**
Preparation time **1 hour**
Calories **400**

Potato pizza

Ingredients *for 4 servings*

Unbleached flour *5 oz*

Potatoes *1 lb*

Peeled tomatoes *1 lb*

Mozzarella *4 oz*

Grated pecorino *2 oz*

Oregano *a pinch*

Extra virgin olive oil *2 tablespoons*

Salt *to taste*

● Brush the potatoes well; rinse under running water. Cook the potatoes, unpeeled, in a pressure cooker or steam them. Slice the mozzarella thinly. When the potatoes are cooked, peel them and mash through a potato ricer. Place in a large bowl. Sift the flour into the potatoes; season with salt and mix well until all ingredients are blended.

● Brush a round tart pan with oil. Fill with the potato mixture. Dice the tomatoes and place on top of potato mixture. Sprinkle with grated pecorino. Cover with sliced mozzarella; season with a pinch of salt and oregano. Drizzle with 1 1/2 tablespoons of extra virgin olive oil. Bake in a preheated oven about 20 minutes. Remove from oven and serve immediately.

Pizza capricciosa

Difficulty **average**
Preparation time **45 minutes**
+ raising time
Calories **530**

Ingredients *for 4 servings*

For the dough

Unbleached flour *9 oz*
Yeast *1 teaspoon*
Extra virgin olive oil *1 tablespoon*
Salt *to taste*

For the topping

Peeled tomatoes *1/4 lb*
Mozzarella *4 oz*
Small artichokes in oil *5*
Small mushrooms in oil *2 oz*
Anchovy filets in oil *3*
Pitted black olives *2 oz*
Capers *10*
Extra virgin olive oil *4 tablespoons*
Salt *to taste*

● Dissolve the yeast in 1/2 cup of warm water. Sift the flour in a large bowl; make a well in the center. Add yeast and blend slowly; add salt, extra virgin olive oil and enough warm water to make a soft elastic dough. Knead the dough vigorously into a small loaf; cover with a kitchen towel and set aside, in a warm place, for 1 hour.

● Dice the mozzarella. Chop the tomatoes; place in a bowl with 2 tablespoons of extra virgin olive oil and a pinch of salt. Mix delicately. Punch down and roll out dough. Press with your fingers, from the center out, and form a thick border around the edges.

● Brush a pizza pan with oil and line with dough. Cover with the tomatoes, leaving the edges empty. Add the sliced artichokes, chopped anchovy filets, mushrooms, olives, capers and mozzarella. Drizzle with the remaining olive oil. Bake in a preheated oven at 425°F for about 20 minutes. Remove from oven and serve at once.

Onion focaccia

Difficulty **easy**
Preparation time **45 minutes**
Calories **300**

Ingredients *for 4 servings*

Bread dough *9 oz*
Red onions *1 lb*
Sugar *a pinch*
Extra virgin olive oil *5 tablespoons*
Salt *& pepper* *to taste*

● Peel the onions and slice thinly. In a non-stick pan, heat 2 tablespoons of extra virgin olive oil. Add the onions, cover and cook on low heat until just transparent. Season with salt and fresh ground pepper. Set aside.

● Knead the dough briefly, adding 2 tablespoons of extra virgin olive oil. Press the dough into an oiled tart pan. With the palm of your hand, push dough to flatten and cover the pan. Bake in a preheated oven at 425°F for about 15 minutes.

● Remove the focaccia from the oven; cover with the cooked onion and sprinkle with sugar. Return to oven for 5 to 8 minutes. Remove from oven and gently transfer to a serving dish. Can be served hot or cool.

Sardine pizza

Difficulty **average**
Preparation time **1 hour**
+ raising time
Calories **755**

Ingredients *for 4 servings*

For the dough

Unbleached flour *1 lb*

Yeast *1 1/2 teaspoons*

Extra virgin olive oil *1 tablespoon*

Salt *to taste*

For the topping

Fresh sardines *2 lbs*

Cherry tomatoes *10 oz*

Garlic *2 cloves*

Oregano *1 teaspoon*

Extra virgin olive oil *3 tablespoons*

Salt *& pepper to taste*

● Dissolve the yeast in 1/4 cup of warm water. Sift the flour in a large bowl; make a well in the center. Add the yeast, salt and olive oil. Mix in the flour and add more water, if needed, to make a smooth dough. Cover with a kitchen towel and set aside to rise for 30 minutes, in a warm place. Knead the dough for 3 minutes and let it rise again for about 10 minutes.

● During this time, peel the garlic, remove the green sprout and slice finely. Rinse and dry cherry tomatoes; slice in quarters. Rinse the sardines; remove heads and debone; butterfly, rinse and dry carefully. Season with salt on both sides.

● Roll out dough with a rolling pin into a circle. Brush a pizza pan with oil; line with dough. Place the sardines in rays over the dough; sprinkle with garlic and oregano. Cover with the tomatoes. Season with salt and drizzle with the remaining extra virgin olive oil. Bake in a preheated oven at 425°F for about 20 minutes. Serve very hot.

Garlic & oregano pizza

Difficulty **average**
Preparation time **1 hour 10 minutes**
+ raising time
Calories **345**

Ingredients *for 4 servings*

Unbleached flour *9 oz*

Yeast *1 teaspoon*

Oregano *1 teaspoon*

Garlic *3 cloves*

Extra virgin olive oil *4 tablespoons*

Salt *a pinch*

● Dissolve the yeast in 1/4 cup of warm water. Sift the flour onto a work surface; make a well in the center. Add the yeast and a pinch of salt. Mix, adding enough warm water to make a soft dough. Knead vigorously, until dough feels elastic, and form a ball. Place in a floured bowl, cover with a kitchen towel and let rise, in a warm place, until doubled.

● Return dough to work surface and knead for a few minutes, adding 2 tablespoons of extra virgin olive oil. Roll out dough and place in a pizza pan. Brush with extra virgin olive oil. Peel garlic and slice thinly. Sprinkle the dough with garlic and oregano. Prick with a fork all over. Bake in a preheated oven at 420°F for 20 to 30 minutes. Carefully remove from pan; cool on a rack for a few minutes and serve. Can also be served cold.

Difficulty **average**
Preparation time **1 hour**
Calories **600**

Ricotta & vegetable tart

Ingredients *for 4 servings*

Flaky dough *1/2 lb*

Chard *14 oz*

Mushrooms *4 oz*

Dried porcini mushrooms *4 or 6, presoaked*

Onion *1*

Anchovies *3*

Marjoram *a pinch*

Eggs *2*

Ricotta *6 oz*

Grated Emmenthal *3 tablespoons*

Extra virgin olive oil *4 tablespoons*

Salt *&* **pepper** *to taste*

● Rinse, drain and chop chard. Brush the mushrooms; clean with a humid towel and slice thinly. Drain and chop dried mushrooms; reserve the soaking liquid. Rinse the anchovies under running water to remove salt, then chop. Peel the onion and finely chop.

● In a large pan, heat the extra virgin olive oil; cook the onions until softened. Add the anchovies and cook until dissolved; mix in the chard, marjoram, dried and fresh mushrooms, and 2 tablespoons of soaking water from the dried mushrooms. Season with salt and pepper. Cover and cook 10 to 12 minutes. Remove cover and let any remaining liquid evaporate on high heat.

● Remove from heat and set aside to cool. Add the eggs, ricotta, grated Emmenthal, a pinch of salt and pepper; mix well. Roll out dough thinly. Brush a pie plate with oil; line with the dough. Prick the border of the dough with a fork. Fill with the prepared vegetable mixture. Bake the tart in a preheated oven at 400°F for about 30 minutes. Remove from oven and serve while extremely hot.

Difficulty **easy**
Preparation time **45 minutes**
Calories **510**

Ingredients *for 4 servings*

Bread dough *1 lb*
Peeled tomatoes *10 oz*
Cooked ham *4 oz*
Mozzarella *4 oz*
Artichokes in oil *3 oz*
Oregano *a pinch*
Extra virgin olive oil *4 tablespoons*
Salt *& pepper to taste*

Pizza regina

● Knead the dough, adding 2 tablespoons of extra virgin olive oil. Cover with a kitchen towel and set aside while you prepare the rest of the ingredients. Remove seeds from tomatoes and dice. Chop the cooked ham. Slice the mozzarella. Cut the artichokes in quarters.

● Brush a pizza pan with extra virgin olive oil. Roll out dough in a thin circle and place on the pan. Cover with the tomatoes, chopped ham, mozzarella and artichokes. Season with oregano, salt and pepper. Drizzle with remaining extra virgin olive oil. Bake in a preheated oven at 450°F for 20 to 25 minutes. Serve extremely hot.

Difficulty **average**
Preparation time **1 hour
+ raising time**
Calories **690**

Ingredients *for 4 servings*

For the dough

Unbleached flour *14 oz*
Yeast *1 1/4 teaspoons*
Salt *to taste*

For the topping

Tomatoes *1 1/2 lb, ripe and firm*
Tuna in olive oil *6 oz*
Pitted black olives *3 oz*
Capers in salt *1 oz*
Anchovies in salt *1 oz*
Egg yolks *2*
Garlic *1 large clove*
Extra virgin olive oil *6 tablespoons*
Salt *& pepper to taste*

Stuffed focaccia

● Dissolve the yeast in 1/4 cup of warm water. Sift the flour in a large bowl; make a well in the center. Add the yeast and salt. Mix the ingredients and add enough warm water to make a soft and elastic dough. Knead into a ball, flour lightly and place in a bowl; cover with a kitchen towel and let rise, in a warm place, until doubled.

● Peel the tomatoes; press lightly to remove seeds; chop and place in a saucepan. Add 2 tablespoons of extra virgin olive oil, peeled garlic and cook for 20 minutes. Remove from heat and transfer to a bowl to cool. Rinse the anchovies and capers. Debone anchovies if necessary and chop. Chop olives. Crumble tuna.

● Punch down the dough and knead vigorously, mixing in a pinch of fresh ground pepper, 3 tablespoons of extra virgin olive oil and 2 beaten egg yolks. (Set aside 1 tablespoon to brush the dough.) Divide the dough in 2 parts, one larger than the other. Brush a deep pie dish with extra virgin olive oil. Roll out dough and line the pie dish with the larger circle of dough. Mix the tomatoes with tuna, anchovies, capers and olives. Transfer mixture to pie.

● With the remaining circle of dough, cover the filling; press around the edges of the pie with your fingers to seal well. Brush pie with beaten egg yolk. Cover with a damp cloth and let rise for 30 minutes. Bake in a preheated oven at 450°F for about 20 minutes. Remove from oven and serve at once.

Difficulty **easy**
Preparation time **45 minutes**
Calories **320**

Ingredients *for 4 servings*

Bread dough *1 lb*
Fresh anchovies *10 oz*
Garlic *4 cloves*
Oregano *a generous pinch*
Extra virgin olive oil *3 tablespoons*
Salt *&* **pepper** *to taste*

Anchovy pizza

● Clean anchovies. Remove head and debone. Rinse them under running water and dry carefully on paper towels. Butterfly them and remove filets.

● Brush a pizza pan with extra virgin olive oil. Roll out the bread dough and line the pan with it. Place the anchovy filets in rays on the dough. Peel the garlic, remove the green sprout and slice thinly. Sprinkle the pizza with the garlic, oregano, salt and a generous pinch of fresh ground pepper. Drizzle with remaining olive oil.

● Bake the pizza in a preheated oven at 425°F for about 15 minutes. Remove from oven and carefully transfer to a serving dish. Serve extremely hot.

Difficulty **easy**
Preparation time **1 hour**
Calories **470**

Ingredients *for 6 servings*

Bread dough *1 lb*
Onions *1 lb*
Pitted green olives *2 oz*
Tomatoes *1 1/4 lb, ripe and firm*
Capers *1 teaspoon*
Anchovies *4*
Oregano *a pinch*
Extra virgin olive oil *5 tablespoons*
Salt *&* **pepper** *to taste*

Rustic onion & olive pie

● Blanch the tomatoes in abundant boiling water; drain, press lightly to remove seeds and dice. Rinse anchovies under running water; debone and chop finely. Peel onion and chop. In a pan, heat 3 tablespoons of extra virgin olive oil. Add onions and cook on low heat, until just softened. Add tomatoes and cook on high heat for 10 minutes. Season with salt and pepper.

● With a rolling pin, roll out 2/3 of the dough in a thin sheet. Brush a pie plate with oil and line with rolled dough; prick with a fork all over the dough. Pour in the onions and tomato mixture; cover with chopped anchovies, olives, capers and oregano.

● Roll out the leftover dough and place on top of the pie. Close the edges firmly and prick the pie with a fork. Brush with remaining extra virgin olive oil. Bake in a preheated oven at 425°F for about 30 minutes. Remove from oven, place on a plate and cool slightly before serving.

First Courses

Beet tagliatelle with leek sauce

Difficulty **average**
Preparation time **1 hour**
Calories **480**

Ingredients *for 4 servings*

Unbleached flour *11 oz*

Eggs *2*

Cooked beet *1 small*

Leeks *1 lb*

Ricotta *4 oz*

Grated grana cheese *2 tablespoons*

Dry white wine *1/4 cup*

1% milk *2 or 3 tablespoons*

Extra virgin olive oil *3 tablespoons*

Salt *&* **pepper** *to taste*

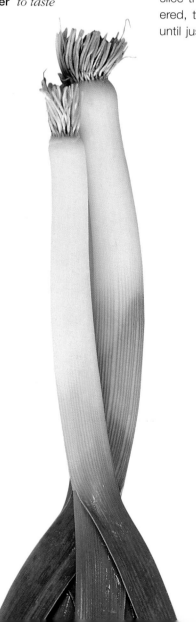

● Peel the beet, chop and blend in a food processor. Mix the sifted flour, the eggs, beet and a pinch of salt to make a soft smooth dough. Roll out the dough very thinly; flour lightly and roll dough onto itself. With a sharp knife, cut in tagliatelle. Set aside to dry briefly.

● Clean leeks, removing the darker green leaves; rinse, dry carefully and slice thinly. In a large pan, cook, covered, the leeks in extra virgin olive oil, until just tender. Season with salt and generous fresh ground pepper. Add the wine and let evaporate completely. Mix ricotta with 2 or 3 tablespoons of milk to make a very soft cream; add to the leeks and cook on low heat for a few minutes until the mixture is hot.

● During this time, cook tagliatelle in abundant salted water, until al dente. Drain well and toss with leek sauce. Transfer to a warm serving bowl. Sprinkle with grated grana and serve immediately.

Bavette with avocado

Difficulty **easy**
Preparation time **30 minutes**
Calories **565**

Ingredients *for 4 servings*

Bavette *12 oz*

Avocado *1*

Tomatoes *4, ripe and firm*

Black olives *2 oz*

Parsley *1 bunch*

Basil *1 bunch*

Lemons *1, the juice*

White wine vinegar *1 tablespoon*

Extra virgin olive oil *5 tablespoons*

Salt *&* **pepper** *to taste*

● Pit the olives, slice and cut in half. Rinse and dry the parsley and basil. Chop parsley finely. Slice the basil in strips. Rinse the tomatoes; press delicately to remove seeds, dice and place in a colander to drain.

● In a small bowl, mix the white wine vinegar, a pinch of salt and a generous pinch of pepper. Whisk until salt is dissolved. Add the oil slowly and continue whisking until sauce is emulsified.

● In a large bowl, mix the tomatoes, olives, chopped parsley and basil. Add the prepared sauce and toss well.

● Peel the avocado; remove nut; slice thinly and toss with lemon juice. In a large pan, cook the bavette in abundant boiling salted water until al dente. Drain well and transfer to the tomato mixture; toss with the avocado slices delicately. Serve at once.

Whole wheat spaghetti with anchovies

Difficulty **easy**
Preparation time **30 minutes**
Calories **460**

Ingredients *for 4 servings*

Whole wheat spaghetti *12 oz*

Anchovies *4 oz*

White onions *4*

Grated pecorino *to taste*

Extra virgin olive oil *6 tablespoons*

Salt *&* **pepper** *to taste*

● Rinse the anchovies under running water to remove salt; debone, dry on paper towels and chop. Peel onions, rinse, dry and slice very thinly.

● In a large pan, heat 4 tablespoons of oil. Add onions and cover; cook on very low heat, until transparent and dry. Season with salt. Add chopped anchovies and mash with a fork. Pour in the remaining olive oil and a generous pinch of fresh ground pepper. Cook for another 3 minutes.

● During this time, cook the spaghetti in abundant salted water, until al dente. Drain and transfer to the pan; toss with the sauce. Shake the pan and cook for 2 minutes. Remove from heat and serve with grated pecorino.

Linguine with tuna & peas

Difficulty **easy**
Preparation time **30 minutes**
Calories **470**

Ingredients *for 4 servings*

Linguine *12 oz*
Tuna in water *4 oz*
Fresh green peas *7 oz*
Zucchini *1/4 lb*
Onion *1*
Garlic *1 clove*
Parsley *1 bunch*
Extra virgin olive oil *5 tablespoons*
Salt *&* **pepper** *to taste*

● Rinse, dry and slice the zucchini. Peel and chop the onion. Peel the garlic clove. Rinse, dry and finely chop parsley. Drain the tuna and mash with a fork.

● In a large saucepan, heat 2 tablespoons of extra virgin olive oil. Cook the chopped onion until just transparent. Add peas. Season with salt and fresh ground pepper. Add 1/4 cup of water and cook for about 10 minutes, stirring from time to time.

● During this time, in a pan, heat the remaining extra virgin olive oil, with the garlic clove. After a few minutes, remove the garlic. Add the zucchini slices and cook for 2 to 3 minutes. Season with a pinch of salt and fresh ground pepper. Continue cooking for 5 to 6 minutes, on low heat.

● Add the peas to the zucchini. Mix in the mash tuna and cook for a few minutes. Sprinkle with the chopped parsley. Cook the linguine in abundant salted water, until al dente. Drain well and transfer to the sauce mixture. Add 6 to 7 tablespoons of the pasta cooking water to the sauce. Toss well and serve immediately.

Spaghetti with herring

Difficulty **easy**
Preparation time **30 minutes**
Calories **400**

Ingredients *for 4 servings*

Spaghetti *12 oz*
Smoked herring filet *7 oz*
Tomatoes *14 oz*
Garlic *2 cloves*
Chili pepper *1 small*
Extra virgin olive oil *2 tablespoons*
Salt *to taste*

● Blanch the tomatoes in boiling water. Drain, peel and press gently to remove all seeds. Cut in small pieces.

● Peel garlic cloves and remove green sprout. Chop the garlic and smoked herring together. In a large pan, heat the extra virgin olive oil. Add the garlic and herring. Cook on very low heat for a few minutes. Add the chopped tomatoes, the chili pepper and cook on medium heat, stirring from time to time.

● During this time, cook the spaghetti in abundant salted water, until al dente. Drain well and transfer the spaghetti to the pan with the sauce. Sauté together for a few minutes. Transfer to a warm serving dish and serve very hot.

Difficulty **average**
Preparation time **1 hour**
+ raising time
Calories **445**

Ingredients *for 4 servings*

Spaghetti *13 oz*

Shellfish *2 1/4 lbs (mussels, clams, sea snails, razor shells, etc.)*

Parsley *1 bunch*

Garlic *4-5 cloves*

Extra virgin olive oil *6 tablespoons*

Salt *&* **pepper** *to taste*

Spaghetti alla marinara

● Brush the mussels and rinse several times under running water. Rinse all the shellfish and soak them in cold salted water. Rinse, dry and chop parsley. Peel the garlic; rinse and dry.

● Drain the shellfish. In a large pan, heat one tablespoon of extra virgin olive oil. Add a good pinch of chopped parsley, one garlic clove and the shellfish. Shaking the pan, cook on high heat until all shells are open. Drain and remove all meat from the shells. Discard any that did not open and keep a few shells whole for decoration. Filter the cooking liquid and set aside.

● In another pan, heat the remaining extra virgin olive oil. Add one or two slightly crushed garlic cloves and cook on low heat for one minute. Remove the garlic and add all the shellfish meat and the filtered liquid. Season with fresh ground pepper and cook for a few minutes.

● During this time, cook the spaghetti in abundant salted water until al dente. Drain and transfer to the pan with the shellfish. Toss well and sprinkle with the remaining chopped parsley. Add the shells to decorate and serve immediately.

Tripoline alla casalese

Difficulty **easy**
Preparation time **40 minutes**
Calories **550**

Ingredients *for 4 servings*

Tripoline *12 oz*

Artichokes *4*

Mushrooms *5 oz*

Tomatoes *3/4 lb, ripe and firm*

Shallot *1*

Lemons *1*

Provola cheese *4 oz*

Parsley *a few leaves*

Extra virgin olive oil *5 tablespoons*

Salt *&* **pepper** *to taste*

● Remove stems from the artichokes; cut off the outside leaves and the needles. Slice in half and remove all chokes from the center. Cut in small slices and place in a large bowl, covered with cold water and the juice of a lemon. Clean the mushrooms with a humid cloth, dry them and cut-off any dirty parts of the stems; slice them. Peel the shallot; rinse, dry and chop finely. Rinse the parsley; dry and finely chop.

● Blanch the tomatoes in boiling water. Drain and press lightly to remove seeds. Chop tomatoes. Remove the peel from the Provola cheese and chop cheese. In a pan, heat 3 tablespoons of extra virgin olive oil. Add the shallot and cook until just transparent. Add

drained artichokes and cook for 3 to 4 minutes on medium-high heat, stirring often. Add the chopped tomatoes. Season with a pinch of salt and pepper. Cook on medium heat, for 7 to 8 minutes, stirring with a wooden spoon.

● During this time, in another pan, heat the remaining extra virgin olive oil. Add the mushrooms and sauté for 3 to 4 minutes on medium-high heat. Season with salt and fresh ground pepper. Transfer to the tomato and artichokes mixture. Sprinkle with chopped parsley. Cook the tripoline in abundant salted water until al dente. Drain and place in a large serving bowl with the prepared sauce and chopped Provola. Toss well and serve.

Spicy spaghetti

Difficulty **easy**
Preparation time **20 minutes**
Calories **750**

Ingredients *for 4 servings*

Spaghetti *12 oz*

Hot Italian-style sausage *1/2 lb*

Tomato sauce *6 oz*

Smoked Provola cheese *7 oz*

Garlic *1 clove*

Sage *a few leaves*

Extra virgin olive oil *3 tablespoons*

Salt *to taste*

● Rinse and dry the sage. Peel the garlic, crush lightly and place in a pan with the extra virgin olive oil on low heat. When the garlic starts to brown lightly, remove it immediately. Add the tomato sauce and cook for 5 minutes, stirring often.

● Dice the smoked Provola cheese and set aside. Slice the sausage and

add to the tomato sauce. Cook for another 10 minutes. If necessary, season with salt.

● During this time, cook the spaghetti in abundant salted water until al dente. Drain and transfer to pan with sauce. Add Provola and toss well. Serve immediately.

Perciatelli with mussels

Difficulty **average**
Preparation time **45 minutes**
Calories **530**

Ingredients *for 4 servings*

Perciatelli *12 oz*

Mussels *1 lb*

Tomatoes *1 lb, ripe and firm*

Day-old Italian-style bread *60 g*

Garlic *2 cloves*

Parsley *a few leaves*

Eggs *1*

Grated pecorino *1/2 cup*

Extra virgin olive oil *to taste*

Salt *&* **pepper** *to taste*

● Brush the mussels well; rinse under running water and open with an oyster knife to obtain mussels on half shells. Discard empty shells. Blanch the tomatoes in boiling water; drain, peel and press gently to remove seeds; dice. Rinse parsley; dry carefully and chop finely. Peel garlic, remove the green sprout; chop one clove and crush the other one with the back of a knife.

● In a bowl, place the bread and soak in water. Press it to remove the water and tear it in small pieces. Mix together the bread, the crushed garlic, chopped parsley, grated pecorino and egg. Season with a pinch of salt and pepper; mix well until all ingredients are blended.

● In each mussel shell, place a bit of the bread preparation and press gently. Place the mussels on a cookie sheet. Drizzle with a little extra virgin olive oil and bake in a preheated oven at 450°F for 5 minutes. In a saucepan, heat 4 tablespoons of olive oil with the remaining garlic clove for a minute. Remove the garlic and add the tomatoes. Season with salt and pepper; cook for 10 minutes, on medium heat. Transfer the mussels to the tomato sauce and cook on low heat, for 2 minutes.

● Cook the perciatelli in abundant salted water until al dente. Drain and transfer to a large serving bowl. Remove mussels from the sauce. Toss sauce with the pasta; add mussels and serve immediately.

Spaghetti with basil sauce

Difficulty **easy**
Preparation time **20 minutes**
Calories **630**

Ingredients *for 4 servings*

Spaghetti *14 oz*

Basil *8 oz*

Walnuts *12*

Grated pecorino *3 tablespoons*

Extra virgin olive oil *8 tablespoons*

Salt *to taste*

● Rinse the basil; dry well on paper towels. In the bowl of a food processor, mix the basil with the walnuts until the texture is very fine. Set aside 2 walnuts and a few basil leaves for decoration.

● Place the mixture in a bowl, add the grated pecorino and whisk in the extra virgin olive oil, very slowly; mix until the sauce is very creamy.

● During this time, cook the spaghetti in abundant salted water until just al dente. Drain and place the spaghetti in a serving dish. Pour the sauce and toss well. Decorate with the walnuts and basil. Serve at once.

Difficulty **average**
Preparation time **40 minutes**
Calories **460**

Ingredients *for 4 servings*

Spaghettini *11 oz*

Small shrimp *14 oz*

Garlic *2 cloves*

Onion *1*

Parsley *1 small bunch*

Breadcrumbs *2 tablespoons*

Dry white wine *1/4 cup*

Nutmeg *1/4 teaspoon*

Extra virgin olive oil *6 tablespoons*

Salt *&* **pepper** *to taste*

Spaghettini with shrimp

● Peel garlic and onion; rinse, dry and chop them finely. Rinse, dry and chop the parsley. Peel the shrimp; devein, rinse, dry and chop them. In a large pan, heat the oil. Add the onion and garlic. Cook until the onion is just transparent and add the shrimp.

● Cook for a few minutes, stirring with a wooden spoon. Add the white wine and let evaporate, on high heat. Add the freshly grated nutmeg; season with salt and pepper. Cook for 5 minutes. Reduce heat. Add chopped parsley and mix well. Remove from heat and cover to keep warm.

● During this time, cook the spaghettini in abundant salted water until al dente. Toast the breadcrumbs in a non-stick pan. Drain the pasta and transfer to a serving dish. Pour the sauce over and toss well. Sprinkle with the breadcrumbs and fresh ground pepper. Serve very hot.

Spaghetti with mussels

Difficulty **easy**
Preparation time **30 minutes**
Calories **450**

Ingredients *for 4 servings*

Spaghetti *12 oz*

Mussels *2 1/4 lbs*

Tomato sauce *4 tablespoons*

Saffron *1/2 teaspoon*

Extra virgin olive oil *4 tablespoons*

Salt *to taste*

● Brush the mussels well. Remove any filaments and rinse under running water. Transfer to a large pan with 2 tablespoons of extra virgin olive oil and the tomato sauce. On high heat, shake the pan until mussels have opened. Remove from heat; discard any unopened mussels. Keep a few mussels whole for decoration and remove all others from their shells. Filter the cooking liquid and set aside.

● Cook the spaghetti in abundant salted water until al dente. During this time, dissolve the saffron in the filtered liquid. Whisk in the remaining extra virgin olive oil. When well blended, add the mussels and mix delicately.

● Drain the spaghetti and transfer to a serving dish with the prepared sauce. Toss well and decorate with the mussels in the shell. Serve immediately.

Fettucini with seafood

Difficulty **average**
Preparation time **50 minutes**
Calories **550**

Ingredients *for 4 servings*

Fettucini *12 oz*

Baby octopus *1/2 lb*

Crab meat *1/4 lb*

Mussels *1 lb*

Tomatoes *10 oz, ripe and firm*

Garlic *1 clove*

Shallot *1*

Parsley *1 small bunch*

Dry white wine *3 tablespoons*

Extra virgin olive oil *6 tablespoons*

Salt *&* **pepper** *to taste*

● Clean the octopus; rinse and dry well; slice in large pieces. Brush and rinse the mussels under running water; drain well. Blanch the tomatoes in boiling water; drain, peel and press gently to remove all seeds; dice. Peel the garlic clove and crush it lightly using the back of the blade of a large knife. Peel the shallot and chop finely. Rinse and dry parsley; chop finely.

● Drain the crab meat and break it out with a fork; set aside. In a pan, place the garlic, half the chopped parsley, white wine, 1 tablespoon of extra virgin olive oil and mussels. Cook on high heat, shaking the pan often until all mussels are open. Remove from heat. Remove all mussels from their shells and set aside in a bowl. Discard any closed mussels. Filter the cooking liquid and set aside.

● In a saucepan, heat the remaining extra virgin olive oil. Add the shallot and cook until just transparent. Add the chopped octopus and let them dry. Add mussels and crab meat. Stirring, let cook for a few minutes. Add the chopped tomatoes with half the cooking liquid. Season with salt and pepper; cook on high heat, for a few minutes. Sprinkle with the remaining parsley. Cook the paglia e fieno pasta in abundant salted water until al dente. Drain and place in a large shallow bowl. Pour the sauce over and toss well. Serve.

Difficulty **average**
Preparation time **40 minutes**
Calories **510**

Ingredients *for 4 servings*

Spaghetti *12 oz*

Fresh sardines *3/4 lb*

Tomatoes *1 lb, ripe and firm*

Parsley *1 small bunch*

Basil *1 small bunch*

Black olives *2 oz*

Garlic *1 clove*

Chili pepper *1 small*

Extra virgin olive oil *4 tablespoons*

Salt *&* **pepper** *to taste*

Ligurian-style spaghetti with sardines

● Clean the sardines; remove head and debone. Remove the filets, rinse under running water and dry on paper towels. Slice in small pieces.

● Blanch the tomatoes in boiling water; drain, peel and press gently to remove seeds, then chop. Peel the garlic, remove the sprout and, with the back of a blade, crush it lightly. Rinse and dry parsley; chop half of it finely. Rinse and dry the basil; chop half of it finely. Pit the olives if necessary.

● In a large pan, on low heat, place the oil, garlic, chili pepper, parsley and basil. When the garlic starts turning gold, remove it. Add sardines and sauté for 2 minutes. Stir in the chopped tomatoes. Season with salt and fresh ground pepper. Cook on high heat for 5 minutes. Add the black olives and cook for another 2 minutes. Sprinkle with the chopped basil and parsley.

● Cook the spaghetti in abundant salted water until al dente. Drain well and transfer to a large shallow serving bowl. Pour the sardine and tomato sauce; toss well. Serve immediately.

Difficulty **easy**
Preparation time **30 minutes**
Calories **430**

Ingredients *for 4 servings*

Spaghetti *12 oz*

Boston lettuce *4 heads*

Chili pepper *1*

Extra virgin olive oil *5 tablespoons*

Salt *to taste*

Spaghetti with lettuce

● Leaving the heads whole, clean the lettuce and discard any brown or withered leaves. In a large saucepan, boil a large amount of water; add salt and lettuce heads.

● Cook just for a minute; drain well and press very gently to eliminate all the water. Slice in long strips. Cook the spaghetti in abundant salted water until al dente, mixing from time to time with a long fork.

● In a pan, heat the oil with the crushed garlic clove and the chopped chili pepper. When the garlic starts to brown, remove immediately and add the lettuce strips. Stir delicately for a few minutes. Pour the sauce into a large serving bowl. Drain the spaghetti and transfer to the serving bowl. Toss well and serve immediately.

Spaghettini alla bottarga

Difficulty **easy**
Preparation time **20 minutes**
Calories **540**

Ingredients *for 4 servings*

Spaghettini *14 oz*
Bottarga *4 oz*
Sage *a few leaves*
Extra virgin olive oil *5 tablespoons*
Salt *to taste*

● Rinse and dry the sage leaves. In a large pan, heat the oil. Add sage leaves and let them turn golden. Grate the bottarga directly into the pan, keeping just a little for later. Warm it up on low heat.

● During this time, cook the spaghetti-ni in abundant salted water. Drain very well and transfer the spaghettini to the pan. Sauté the spaghettini and toss carefully, so they take all the flavors from the warm bottarga. Serve very hot in individual bowls, grating the remaining bottarga over each plate.

Difficulty **easy**
Preparation time **30 minutes**
Calories **450**

Spaghetti with garlic & anchovy sauce

Ingredients *for 4 servings*

Spaghetti *12 oz*
Tomatoes *1 lb, ripe and firm*
Garlic *1 clove*
Anchovy paste *1 1/2 teaspoons*
Parsley *1 bunch*
Extra virgin olive oil *6 tablespoons*
Salt *&* **pepper** *to taste*

● Blanch the tomatoes in boiling water; drain, peel, press gently to remove seeds and chop. Peel the garlic; remove the green sprout and, with the blade of a knife, crush lightly. Rinse and dry the parsley; chop finely.

● In a pan, heat 4 tablespoons of extra virgin olive oil with the crushed garlic clove on low heat. When the garlic just turns golden, remove it and add anchovy paste. Remove from heat and stir until the paste is completely dissolved. Add the chopped tomatoes and season with a pinch of salt. Cook the sauce, on medium heat, for about 10 minutes, stirring from time to time.

● During this time, cook the spaghetti in abundant salted water until al dente. Drain well. Transfer to a serving bowl. Pour the tomato and anchovy sauce over; toss well. Sprinkle with chopped parsley and serve.

Difficulty **easy**
Preparation time **30 minutes**
Calories **500**

Ingredients *for 4 servings*

Egg tagliatelle *12 oz*

Zucchini flowers *10*

Onion *1, small*

Parsley *3 sprigs*

Rosemary *1 small sprig*

Sage *4 leaves*

Grated parmigiano *4 tablespoons*

Vegetable broth *3 tablespoons*

Extra virgin olive oil *4 tablespoons*

Salt *&* **pepper** *to taste*

Andrea's note : Rosemary and sage can be replaced by 1/2 teaspoon of good quality saffron. This makes a colorful and very aromatic summer dish. Zucchini flowers can be difficult to find. Ask any farm growers; they have them but rarely think about selling them.

Tagliatelle with zucchini flowers

● Peel the onion and slice it very thinly. Remove the pistils from the zucchini flowers; clean the flowers very delicately with a humid cloth. Cut them in long strips. Rinse, dry and chop finely the parsley, rosemary and sage.

● In a large pan, heat the extra virgin olive oil. Add the sliced onion and cook on low heat until just transparent. Add the zucchini flowers and continue cooking on low heat for 7 to 8 minutes. After 5 minutes, add the vegetable bouillon and chopped herbs.

● During this time, cook the tagliatelle in abundant salted water until al dente. Drain well and transfer to the pan with zucchini flower sauce. Sauté for a few minutes. Sprinkle with grated parmigiano. Season with fresh ground pepper. Serve at once.

Spaghettoni with tomato sauce & eggplant

Difficulty **easy**
Preparation time **40 minutes + raising time**
Calories **430**

Ingredients *for 4 servings*

Spaghettoni *12 oz*
Tomatoes *12 oz*
Eggplants *2*
Basil *6 leaves*
Garlic *1 large clove*
Grated pecorino *4 tablespoons*
Extra virgin olive oil *6 tablespoons*
Salt *&* **pepper** *to taste*

● Rinse and dry the eggplants; slice thinly. Place the sliced eggplants in a colander; sprinkle with salt and set aside for 1 hour to draw out the juices. Rinse, dry and peel the tomatoes. Peel the garlic clove, remove the green sprout and slice thinly. Rinse, dry and tear the basil leaves.

● In a large saucepan, heat 3 tablespoons of extra virgin olive oil. Add garlic and cook for a minute. Add tomatoes (whole) and cook on high heat. Break the tomatoes with a spoon and stir often. Season with salt and pepper and add the shredded basil leaves.

● Rinse the eggplant; drain well and dry on paper towels. Brush the eggplant slices with extra virgin olive oil and season with salt. Bake in a preheated oven at 375°F. Cook the spaghettoni in abundant salted water until al dente. Drain well and transfer to the tomato sauce. Let cook together for one minute, on medium heat, tossing well. Transfer the spaghettoni in a serving bowl; add the baked eggplant. Sprinkle wit the grated pecorino and serve.

Maccheroncelli with sardines

Difficulty **average**
Preparation time **1 hour**
Calories **560**

Ingredients *for 4 servings*

Long maccheroncelli *12 oz*
Fresh sardines *1 lb*
Wild fennel *1 lb*
Raisins *2 oz*
Pine nuts *2 oz*
Onion *1*
Saffron *1/4 teaspoon*
Extra virgin olive oil *5 tablespoons*
Salt *to taste*

● Prepare the fennel. Rinse well and remove the hard bottom parts. Cook in 4 cups of salted boiling water until just tender. Drain, keeping the cooking liquid aside. Chop the fennel. Clean the sardines; debone, remove heads, and butterfly. Rinse and dry delicately on paper towels.

● Soak the raisins in a bowl of warm water. Peel the onion and slice thinly. In a large pan, heat the extra virgin olive oil; add onion and cook until transparent. Add sardines and cook on low heat, stirring often with a wood-en spoon to crush the sardines. Add the fennel, the pine nuts, drained raisins, saffron, a pinch of salt and a few tablespoons of the fennel cooking water. Cook for about 10 minutes.

● In a large pot, bring to boil the remaining fennel cooking water with 5 cups of water. Cook the maccheroncelli, in this water, until al dente. Drain and transfer to a large serving bowl. Pour the sardine sauce over and toss well. Place the serving bowl on the open door of a preheated oven for 8 minutes before serving.

Garden-style spaghetti

Difficulty **easy**
Preparation time **30 minutes**
Calories **430**

Ingredients *for 4 servings*

Spaghetti *12 oz*

Garlic *1 clove*

Leek *1*

Scallion *1*

Celery *1 branch*

Marjoram *4 sprigs*

Basil *8 leaves*

Parsley *10 leaves*

Rosemary *1 small sprig*

Sage *4 leaves*

Tomato paste *1 tablespoon*

Extra virgin olive oil *6 tablespoons*

Salt *to taste*

● Peel the garlic and remove the green sprout; chop finely. Rinse and dry the celery, leek and scallions; slice thinly. Rinse, dry and chop the marjoram, basil and parsley. Rinse and dry rosemary and sage leaves.

● In a pan, heat 4 tablespoons of extra virgin olive oil. Add the garlic, leek, celery and scallions. Cook until the scallion is transparent. Add sage and rosemary. Pour in 5 tablespoons of water and cook for another 5 minutes.

● Remove sage and rosemary. Add tomato paste and 1/2 cup of warm water. Cook the sauce for 5 minutes. Add the remaining extra virgin olive oil and chopped herbs. Cook for another 5 minutes.

● During this time, cook the spaghetti in abundant salted water until al dente. Drain and transfer to the pan with the herb sauce. Sauté for a few minutes. Transfer to a serving plate and serve immediately.

Tagliatelle with tuna & herbs

Difficulty **easy**
Preparation time **30 minutes**
Calories **520**

Ingredients *for 4 servings*

Tagliatelle *14 oz*

Ventresca tuna in oil *6 oz*

Tomatoes *3/4 lb, ripe and firm*

Onion *1 small*

Garlic *1 clove*

Parsley *1 small bunch*

Wild fennel *a few sprigs*

Extra virgin olive oil *4 tablespoons*

Salt *& pepper to taste*

Andrea's note : Ventresca tuna can be hard to find. It can be replaced by very good quality white tuna.

● Drain the ventresca from its oil; mash it and set aside. Peel the onion and the garlic; chop them finely. Rinse and dry parsley and fennel; chop finely. Blanch the tomatoes in boiling water. Drain, peel and press lightly to remove seeds; chop coarsely.

● In a pan, heat the oil and cook the onion and garlic until onion is transparent. Add to chopped tomatoes. Season with salt and fresh ground pepper.

Cook the sauce on medium heat, for 8 to 10 minutes, stirring often. Add the mashed ventresca and cook for 3 minutes. Stir in the chopped parsley and fennel.

● Cook the tagliatelle in abundant salted water until al dente. Drain and transfer to a warm serving bowl. Pour the prepared sauce over and toss well. Serve immediately.

Difficulty **easy**
Preparation time **40 minutes**
Calories **540**

Ingredients *for 4 servings*

Fresh egg tagliatelle *12 oz*

Peeled tomatoes *12 oz*

Capers *1 teaspoon*

Eggplant *1 small*

Pitted green olives *10 oz*

Oregano *1 teaspoon*

Garlic *1 clove*

Dry white wine *1/4 cup*

Grated pecorino *4 tablespoons*

Extra virgin olive oil *4 tablespoons*

Salt *&* **white pepper** *to taste*

Sardinian tagliatelle

● Rinse and dry the eggplant; chop finely. Peel the garlic and remove the green sprout. Rinse the capers under running water. Chop the green olives coarsely.

● In a large pan, heat the extra virgin olive oil; add garlic and chopped eggplant. Cook for 5 minutes, stirring from time to time. Add the dry white wine and let evaporate completely. Add capers, chopped olives and a good pinch of salt. Mix well and let cook on medium heat for 10 minutes. Add the peeled tomatoes and oregano. Stirring often, cook for 15 minutes. Remove the garlic clove.

● During this time, cook the tagliatelle in abundant salted water until al dente. Drain well and transfer to the pan into the sauce. Sauté the pasta a few minutes and transfer to a large shallow serving bowl. Add the grated pecorino and plenty of fresh ground white pepper. Toss and serve.

Tagliatelle with chicken sauce

Difficulty **easy**
Preparation time **40 minutes**
Calories **510**

Ingredients *for 4 servings*

Tagliatelle *14 oz*
Chicken breast *1/2 lb*
Tomatoes *1/2 lb, ripe and firm*
Celery *1 stalk*
Carrots *1 large*
Onion *1 large*
Basil *1 small bunch*
Dry white wine *1/4 cup*
Extra virgin olive oil *5 tablespoons*
Salt & **pepper** *to taste*

● Rinse the chicken breasts and dry carefully on paper towels. Dice the chicken. Blanch the tomatoes in boiling water; drain, peel and press gently to remove seeds; chop coarsely. Rinse, dry and chop the celery. Peel the onion and chop finely. Peel the carrot and chop. Rinse, dry and tear basil in small pieces.

● In a pan, heat the extra virgin olive oil. Add onion, chopped carrot and celery. Cook until onion is just transparent. Add diced chicken and cook over medium heat until slightly golden. Add the dry white wine and let evaporate on high heat. Add tomatoes. Season with a pinch of salt and fresh ground pepper. Continue cooking, stirring, for 15 minutes. Sprinkle with basil leaves.

● Cook the tagliatelle in abundant salted water until al dente. Drain well and transfer to a warm serving dish. Pour the sauce over and toss water. Serve extremely hot.

Mediterranean linguine

Difficulty **easy**
Preparation time **40 minutes**
Calories **380**

Ingredients *for 4 servings*

Linguine *12 oz*
Canned tomatoes *10 oz*
Red bell peppers *1/2*
Eggplant *1 large slice*
Zucchini *1 medium-size*
Carrots *1 large*
Onion *1*
Chili pepper *1*
Extra virgin olive oil *3 tablespoons*
Salt *to taste*

● Peel and dry the vegetables. Slice the sweet pepper in julienne; dice the eggplant. Coarsely grate the carrot. Slice the zucchini in julienne and thinly slice the onion.

● In a pan, heat the extra virgin olive oil. Add hot chili pepper and all prepared vegetables. Cook on low heat, for about 10 minutes, stirring often. Add the chopped tomatoes and cook for 10 minutes, stirring well. Season with salt and remove hot chili pepper. Taste again for salt and remove from heat.

● During this time, cook the linguine in abundant salted water until al dente. Drain carefully and transfer to a large shallow bowl. Add prepared sauce and toss well. Serve immediately.

Pasta alla chitarra with nettles

Difficulty **average**
Preparation time **1 hour**
+ raising time
Calories **490**

Ingredients *for 4 servings*

Unbleached flour *14 oz*

Eggs *4*

Nettles *12 oz*

Tomatoes *12 oz*

Onion *1 small*

Chili pepper *1*

Extra virgin olive oil *2 tablespoons*

Salt *to taste*

Andrea's note : A "chitarra" is a rectangle of wood filled with metallic strings – like a guitar. The pasta dough is placed on top and, with a rolling pin, it is rolled through the strings to cut it – the same principle as an egg-slicer.

● Sift the flour in a large bowl and make a well in the center. Add the eggs and a pinch of salt. Work the ingredients together to form a smooth elastic dough. Cover dough with a kitchen towel and set aside in a cool place for 15 minutes.

● Roll out dough, with a rolling pin, to 3/4-inch thick. Cut a large rectangle; place it on a "chitarra" and press it with a rolling pin to cut the pasta. (If you do not have this tool, slice the dough like for tagliatelle.)

● Peel and slice the onion. Rinse, dry and coarsely chop the nettles. In a pan, heat the extra virgin olive oil. Add onions and cook until just transparent. Add the chopped tomatoes and coarsely chopped hot chili pepper. Season with salt and cook for 10 minutes. Add nettles and 1/2 cup of water. Cook for 5 minutes.

● Cook the pasta in abundant salted water until al dente. Drain well and transfer to the pan into the sauce. Toss well one minute so the pasta takes the taste of the sauce. Serve immediately.

Spaghetti with fresh tomatoes

Difficulty **average**
Preparation time **20 minutes**
Calories **410**

Ingredients *for 4 servings*

Spaghetti *12 oz*

Cherry tomatoes *12 oz*

Garlic *1 clove*

Basil *8 leaves*

Extra virgin olive oil *5 tablespoons*

Salt *to taste*

● Rinse the cherry tomatoes and dry on a kitchen towel. Cut each tomato in quarters. Peel the garlic; remove the green sprout if needed; slice finely. Clean the basil leaves with a humid towel. Cook the spaghetti in abundant salted water until al dente.

● In a pan, heat 2 tablespoons of extra virgin olive oil with garlic clove. When the garlic starts to brown, remove it. Add tomatoes and a pinch of salt; stir with a wooden spoon. (The cherry tomatoes should cook very quickly, otherwise the dish would lose its fresh taste.)

● Remove from the heat; add the broken basil leaves, and remaining extra virgin olive oil. Drain the spaghetti and transfer to a large shallow serving bowl. Pour the prepared tomato sauce over the pasta and toss delicately. Serve very hot.

Pasta panzanella

Difficulty **easy**
Preparation time **40 minutes**
Calories **390**

Ingredients *for 4 servings*

Fusilli *12 oz*

Small vine-ripened tomatoes *4, firm and ripe*

Large tomatoes *2*

Celery *1 heart*

Cucumber *1*

Red onions *1*

Basil *10 leaves*

Arugula *1 bunch*

Capers *2 tablespoons*

Extra virgin olive oil *6-8 tablespoons*

Salt *&* **pepper** *to taste*

● Cook pasta in abundant salted water until al dente. Drain well and mix with one tablespoon of extra virgin olive oil. Place on a large plate or on a work surface to cool completely.

● Peel the cucumber, dice and place in a colander. Season with salt and set aside. Rinse, dry and dice the celery. Peel and slice the onion. Dice the small tomatoes. Rinse, dry and tear the basil and arugula. In a food processor, or through a food mill, mix the large juicy tomatoes.

● Rinse and dry diced cucumber. Rinse and dry capers. Place all ingredients in a large salad bowl. Add 3 tablespoons of extra virgin olive oil. Mix the ingredients with a fork. Season with salt and fresh ground pepper. Toss again to mix well. Cover the bowl and set aside in a cool place (do not refrigerate) for at least 30 minutes before serving.

1 *Spread the cooked fusilli on a flat surface and let cool.*

2 *Chop the celery; dice the salad tomatoes; slice the onion; and cut the basil.*

3 *Add the rest of the vegetables, transfer to a bowl, and add the pasta.*

Sardinian gnocchetti with fish sauce

Difficulty **average**
Preparation time **40 minutes**
Calories **450**

Ingredients *for 4 servings*

Sardinian gnocchetti *12 oz*

Shark *1/4 lb, in 1 slice*

Tomatoes *14 oz, firm and ripe*

Onions *1*

Garlic *1 clove*

Basil *a few leaves*

Parsley *1 small bunch*

Extra virgin olive oil *4 tablespoons*

Salt *&* **pepper** *to taste*

Andrea's note : If you can't find them, "Sardinian gnocchetti" can be replaced by lumache, conchiglie or orecchiette – types of pasta that are easier to find in food shops.

● Blanch the tomatoes in boiling water. Drain, peel and press gently to remove all seeds; chop coarsely. Peel the onion; chop finely. Peel the garlic and, with the blade of a knife, crush it lightly. Rinse, dry and dice the slice of shark.

● In a large pan, heat the extra virgin olive oil. Add the onion, shredded basil leaf and garlic clove. Cook until onion is just transparent. Remove garlic clove. Add diced shark and mix well with a wooden spoon. Cook for a few minutes. Add tomatoes and season with salt and fresh ground pepper. Cook for another 10 minutes.

● During this time, cook the gnocchetti in abundant salted water until al dente. Drain well and place in a serving bowl. Pour the prepared sauce over the pasta and toss well. Taste for salt and season generously with fresh ground pepper. Sprinkle with the chopped parsley and toss again. Serve immediately.

Gramigna with peppers & pesto

Difficulty **average**
Preparation time **30 minutes**
Calories **660**

Ingredients *for 4 servings*

Gramigna *12 oz*
Red bell peppers *1 large*
Basil leaves *1 small bunch*
Garlic *1 clove*
Pine nuts *2 oz*
Walnuts *5*
Grated grana cheese *3 tablespoons*
Grated pecorino *2 tablespoons*
Extra virgin olive oil *10 tablespoons*
Salt *&* **pepper** *to taste*

● Roast the sweet red pepper on an open flame; peel carefully, cut in two and remove seeds and white threads. Wipe with paper towels to remove any peel; slice and dice.

● Rinse the basil leaves and place on a kitchen towel to dry. In a food processor, place the garlic, pine nuts, walnuts and mix briefly. Add the basil leaves, a pinch of salt and mix until the preparation is very fine.

● Transfer the basil mixture into a large bowl. Stir in the grana and pecorino. Slowly stir in the extra virgin olive oil until all absorbed and the sauce is smooth. Mix in the diced red pepper.

● During this time, cook the gramigna in abundant salted water until al dente. Drain well. Dilute the prepared pesto sauce with 3 or 4 tablespoons of pasta cooking water. Add pasta to the sauce and toss well. Transfer to a warm serving plate and serve immediately.

Fusilli with fresh tuna

Difficulty **easy**
Preparation time **30 minutes**
Calories **510**

Ingredients *for 4 servings*

Fusilli *12 oz*
Fresh tuna *12 oz*
Tomatoes *1/2 lb, firm and ripe*
Shallots *1*
Capers *2 teaspoons*
Parsley *1 small bunch*
Basil *1 small bunch*
Extra virgin olive oil *4 tablespoons*
Salt *&* **pepper** *to taste*

● Peel the shallot and chop finely. Blanch the tomatoes in boiling water; drain, peel and press gently to remove all seeds; chop coarsely.

● Rinse the tuna; dry delicately with a kitchen towel and dice carefully. Rinse, dry and chop the basil and parsley. Rinse capers under running water; drain well and set aside.

● In a pan, heat the extra virgin olive oil and cook shallot until tender. Add the diced tuna, and cook until golden on all sides. Add chopped tomatoes and capers. Season with a pinch of salt and fresh ground pepper. Cook on low-medium heat for 10 minutes. Sprinkle with the chopped basil and parsley.

● During this time, cook the fusilli in abundant salted water until al dente. Drain the pasta and transfer to a large serving bowl. Pour the prepared sauce over and toss well. Serve immediately.

Maccheroncini with scampi & fresh beans

Difficulty **average**
Preparation time **40 minutes**
Calories **630**

Ingredients *for 4 servings*

Maccheroncini *12 oz*

Scampi *8-12*

Fresh shelled beans *6 oz*

Tomatoes *1/2 lb, firm and ripe*

Onions *1 small*

Parsley *1 small bunch*

Basil *1 small bunch*

Extra virgin olive oil *5 tablespoons*

Salt *&* **pepper** *to taste*

● Peel the scampi; devein, rinse and dry carefully. Blanch the beans in boiling water. Drain and remove the light skin; set aside. Blanch the tomatoes in boiling water; drain, peel and press gently to remove seeds; chop coarsely.

● Peel and finely chop the onion. Rinse, dry and chop the parsley and basil. In a saucepan, heat 3 tablespoons of extra virgin olive oil and cook the onion until just transparent. Add the beans and stir gently for about one minute. Add 1/2 cup of hot water and cook, from time to time, for 10 minutes or until the beans are tender.

● Add the chopped tomatoes. Season with a pinch of salt and fresh ground pepper. Sprinkle with the chopped parsley and basil. In a pan, heat the remaining extra virgin olive oil. Add the scampi and sauté for 2 to 3 minutes. Season with salt and fresh ground pepper. During this time, cook the maccheroncini in abundant salted water, until al dente. Drain and transfer to a serving plate. Add the prepared sauce and toss well. Top with the cooked scampi. Serve immediately.

Sardinian gnocchetti with peppers

Difficulty **easy**
Preparation time **30 minutes**
Calories **390**

Ingredients *for 4 servings*

Sardinian gnocchetti *12 oz*

Yellow bell peppers *1*

Red bell peppers *1*

Tomato *3 large*

Onions *1 small*

Parsley *a few leaves*

Extra virgin olive oil *4 tablespoons*

Salt *to taste*

● Rinse and dry the yellow and red peppers. Cut and remove all seeds and white parts. Slice thinly. Peel the onion and chop coarsely. Rinse, dry and finely chop the parsley.

● In a pan, heat the extra virgin olive oil and cook the onion until just transparent. Add the sliced peppers. Season with a pinch of salt and cook for 8 to 10 minutes, stirring often with a wooden spoon. Add the finely chopped tomatoes and cook for another 10 minutes, mixing often. Taste for salt and add the chopped parsley.

● Cook the Sardinian gnocchetti in abundant salted water until al dente. Drain well and transfer to the pan with the prepared sauce. Toss well and set aside for a minute or two. Transfer to a serving dish and serve immediately.

Difficulty **easy**
Preparation time **30 minutes**
Calories **460**

Ingredients *for 4 servings*

Rigatoni *12 oz*

Tomatoes *12 oz, firm and ripe*

Garlic *1 clove*

Oregano *a good pinch*

Basil *1 small bunch*

Parsley *a few sprigs*

Grated grana cheese *to taste*

Extra virgin olive oil *6 tablespoons*

Salt *& pepper to taste*

Rigatoni with baked tomatoes

● Rinse the parsley and basil; dry carefully on paper towels. Chop half of the herbs together and the other half with the garlic clove. Rinse and dry the tomatoes; cut in thick slices of 1/2 inch and remove seeds.

● Brush a large cookie sheet carefully with 2 tablespoons of olive oil. Place the tomato slices on the sheet, so they touch each other. Season with salt and generous fresh ground pepper. Sprinkle the tomatoes with chopped basil, parsley and garlic. Drizzle with the remaining olive oil. Bake in a preheated oven at 435°F for about 15 minutes. Lower the heat for 350°F and continue baking for 10 minutes.

● Cook the rigatoni in abundant salted water until al dente. Make sure you stir the pasta often during cooking period. Drain the pasta very well. Transfer to a large shallow bowl with the baked tomatoes. Sprinkle with oregano and remaining chopped basil and parsley.

● Toss very carefully for the pasta to retain all the flavors. Serve in warm individual bowls. Serve with grated grana or parmigiano.

Difficulty **easy**
Preparation time **30 minutes**
Calories **420**

Ingredients *for 4 servings*

Casereccia *12 oz*

Green beans *12 oz*

Anchovies *2*

Garlic *1 clove*

White wine vinegar *1 tablespoon*

Extra virgin olive oil *5 tablespoons*

Salt *to taste*

Casereccia with green beans & anchovies

● Rinse the green beans in abundant cold water; drain well and slice in small pieces, after removing any strings. Cook the beans in abundant salted water for about 7 minutes. Drain and set aside. Keep 6 tablespoons of cooking water.

● Peel the garlic and crush it lightly. Rinse the anchovies under running water; debone and cut in small pieces. In a pan, heat the extra virgin olive oil and garlic. When the garlic starts to brown, Add the anchovies and mash with a fork until completely melted.

● Add the white wine vinegar and let evaporate on high heat. Add the green beans and 6 tablespoons of cooking water. Cook on medium heat for about 10 minutes, stirring often. Remove the garlic clove. During this time, cook the casereccia in abundant salted water until al dente. Drain and transfer to a large bowl. Add the prepared sauce and toss well. Serve hot.

Short pasta with cucumbers

Difficulty **easy**
Preparation time **30 minutes**
Calories **450**

Ingredients *for 4 servings*

Short pasta *12 oz*

Peeled tomatoes *14 oz*

Cucumbers *12 oz*

Onions *2*

Basil *a few leaves*

Garlic *1 clove*

Extra virgin olive oil *6 tablespoons*

Salt *&* **pepper** *to taste*

● Peel, rinse, dry and chop the onion. Peel and chop the garlic clove. In a pan, heat 4 tablespoons of extra virgin olive oil and cook the garlic and onion on low heat. Dice the tomatoes and add to the onions and garlic, stirring often. Rinse and dry the basil leaves; add to the sauce. Season with salt and fresh ground pepper. Mix well and cook the sauce, on low heat until it has thickened.

● Peel the cucumbers; slice in half lengthwise. Remove all seeds and chop in 1/4-inch cubes. Cook the cu-cumbers in boiling salted water for 5 minutes. Drain well and transfer to a pan with the remaining extra virgin olive oil. Taste for salt and season with fresh ground pepper. Cook for a few minutes then set aside.

● Cook the mezze maniche rigate in abundant salted water until al dente. Drain the pasta very well and transfer to a large serving dish. Add the hot tomato sauce and the cucumbers with its oil. Mix all ingredients very well and serve immediately.

Difficulty **easy**
Preparation time **45 minutes**
Calories **420**

Ingredients *for 4 servings*

Penne lisce *12 oz*
Yellow squash *12 oz*
Red radicchio *1 head*
Shallots *1*
Parsley *a few leaves*
Extra virgin olive oil *5 tablespoons*
Salt *&* **pepper** *to taste*

Penne with squash & radicchio

● Peel the squash; remove all seeds and filaments; rinse and dry well on paper towels, then slice in strips. Blanch the squash strips in boiling water for one minute; drain and set aside.

● Clean the red radicchio. Discard the exterior leaves, rinse and dry it carefully. Slice the radicchio in long strips. Peel the shallot and chop. Rinse, dry and finely chop the parsley.

● In a pan, heat the extra virgin olive oil. Cook the shallot until just tender.

Add the squash and sauté for a few minutes. Add 1/4 cup of water. Season with salt and fresh ground pepper. Cover the pan and cook for 5 minutes, stirring often. Add the radicchio strips and half the chopped parsley. Continue cooking for about 7 minutes.

● During this time, cook the penne in abundant salted water until al dente. Drain well and transfer to a large shallow serving bowl. Add the squash sauce and mix well. Sprinkle with the remaining chopped parsley and serve.

Difficulty **easy**
Preparation time **30 minutes**
Calories **480**

Ingredients *for 4 servings*

Wheel pasta *13 oz*
Broccoli *12 oz*
Cauliflower *12 oz*
Tomatoes *2, firm and ripe*
Anchovy filets in oil *2*
Small black olives *2 oz*
Onions *1*
Garlic *1 clove*
Oregano *a pinch*
Extra virgin olive oil *4 tablespoons*
Salt *&* **pepper** *to taste*

Wheel pasta with broccoli & cauliflower

● Blanch the tomatoes in boiling water; drain, peel and press lightly to remove all seeds, then chop coarsely. Rinse and dry the broccoli and cauliflower; separate in flowerets and set aside in a bowl.

● Peel the garlic and remove the green sprout, if necessary, then chop finely. Peel the onion and slice thinly. Chop the anchovy filets. Pit the olives and chop finely. In a large pan, heat the extra virgin olive oil. Cook the onion and the garlic, until onion is just transparent. Remove from heat and add the

chopped anchovies; mash with a fork.

● Add the chopped tomatoes. Season with salt and fresh ground pepper. Cook on medium heat for 5 minutes. Add the olives, a pinch of oregano and cook for one more minute, stirring with a wooden spoon.

● During this time, cook the pasta in abundant salted water until al dente. Add the broccoli and cauliflower to the pasta. Drain the pasta and vegetables well. Transfer to a bowl with the prepared sauce. Toss and serve.

Difficulty **easy**
Preparation time **40 minutes**
+ resting time
Calories **490**

Apulia-style short pasta

Ingredients *for 4 servings*

Short pasta *12 oz*
Tomatoes *1 lb, firm and ripe*
Red bell peppers *1*
Eggplants *1*
Pitted black olives *3 oz*
Shallots *2*
Capers *1 teaspoon*
Anchovy filets in oil *2*
Basil *1 small bunch*
Extra virgin olive oil *5 tablespoons*
Salt *&* **pepper** *to taste*

● Rinse, dry and chop the eggplant in 1/4-inch cubes; place in a colander, sprinkle with coarse salt and set aside over a bowl for 30 minutes. Blanch the tomatoes in boiling water; drain, peel and press gently to remove all seeds; chop coarsely.

● Rinse and dry the eggplant. In a pan, heat 2 tablespoons of extra virgin olive oil. Add the eggplant and sauté until lightly golden. Remove from heat and drain the eggplant. Set aside.

● In a saucepan, cook the shallot in the remaining extra virgin olive oil, until softened. Add the anchovy filets and mash until dissolved. Add tomatoes. Season with salt and pepper. Cook on medium heat for 10 minutes.

● Add the eggplant, the sweet pepper, the olives and capers; cook for another 5 minutes. Cook the pasta in abundant salted water until al dente. Drain and add to the prepared sauce. Toss and serve sprinkled with the shredded basil.

Difficulty **easy**
Preparation time **40 minutes**
Calories **400**

Farfalle with artichokes, zucchini & leeks

Ingredients *for 4 servings*

Farfalle *12 oz*
Artichokes *2*
Zucchini *8 oz*
Leeks *1*
Tomatoes *1/4 lb, firm and ripe*
Lemons *the juice of 1*
Garlic *1 clove*
Extra virgin olive oil *4 tablespoons*
Salt *&* **pepper** *to taste*

● Prepare the artichokes. Remove the stems, cut off the ends and any hard outside leaves. Slice in half, lengthwise and remove all chokes. Cut in thin slices and set aside in a bowl of cold water with the lemon juice. Cut the end of the leek; remove the first exterior leaves and cut off the dark green ends. Rinse well, dry and slice in thick pieces. Rinse, dry and julienne the zucchini. Peel the garlic and crush it lightly. Blanch the tomatoes in boiling water; drain, peel and press lightly to remove all seeds. chop coarsely.

● In a pan, heat the extra virgin olive oil and cook the leeks until softened. Add the garlic. Add the drained artichokes and cook for 5 minutes, stirring often. Add the zucchini and cook 2 minutes. Add the chopped tomatoes. Season with salt and fresh ground pepper. Cook for about 10 minutes, on low heat. During this time, cook the farfalle in abundant salted water until al dente. Drain and transfer to a serving bowl. Add the prepared sauce and toss well. Serve immediately.

Difficulty **average**
Preparation time **40 minutes**
+ resting time
Calories **480**

Ingredients *for 4 servings*

Orecchiette *13 oz*

Broccoli *1 3/4 lbs*

Little neck clams *1 lb*

Anchovy filets in oil *3*

Garlic *2 cloves*

Dry white wine *1/2 cup*

Extra virgin olive oil *5 tablespoons*

Salt *&* **pepper** *to taste*

Orecchiette, garden & sea

● Soak the clams in cold water for one hour. During this time, prepare the broccoli. Remove the stems and the hard leaves; detach the flowerets with the tender leaves; rinse under running water, drain and set aside. Peel the garlic clove and remove the green sprout if necessary; crush lightly.

● Drain the clams and place in a large pan with the white wine, one tablespoon of extra virgin olive oil and one garlic clove. Place on high heat and cook, shaking the pan often, until the clams are opened. Remove from heat; detach the clams from their shells and set aside in a bowl. Discard any clams that have not opened. Filter the cooking liquid and set aside.

● Cook the orecchiette in abundant salted water until al dente. Five minutes before the end of cooking time, add the broccoli to the pasta and cook together.

● In a pan, heat the remaining oil and garlic clove, until the garlic starts to brown. Remove the garlic. Add the chopped anchovy filets, the clams and their strained liquid. Let the sauce reduce on high heat. Drain the orecchiette and vegetables. Transfer to a large serving bowl and add the sauce. Toss well. Season with a pinch of pepper; mix and serve.

Fusilli with caper & oregano sauce

Difficulty **easy**
Preparation time **30 minutes**
Calories **430**

Ingredients *for 4 servings*

Fusilli *12 oz*

Tomatoes *1 lb, firm and ripe*

Onions *1*

Capers *1 tablespoon*

Garlic *1 clove*

Fresh oregano *1 sprig*

Bay leaves *1 leaf*

Extra virgin olive oil *4 tablespoons*

Salt *&* **pepper** *to taste*

● Peel the onion and garlic; rinse, dry and chop finely. Blanch the tomatoes in boiling water; drain, peel and squeeze gently to remove all seeds, then chop coarsely. Rinse the capers, drain and dry well.

● In a pan, heat the extra virgin olive oil. Cook the onion and garlic with bay leaf, until onion is just transparent. Add the tomatoes. Season with salt and fresh ground pepper. Cook for 12 to 15 minutes, on medium heat. Add the capers and the fresh oregano. Remove bay leaf and cook for a few minutes.

● During this time, cook the fusilli in abundant salted water until al dente. Drain well and transfer to a large shallow bowl. Add the sauce and toss well. Serve immediately.

Penne with herb sauce

Difficulty **easy**
Preparation time **40 minutes**
Calories **380**

Ingredients *for 4 servings*

Penne rigate *12 oz*

Tomatoes *1 lb, firm and ripe*

Green chili peppers *3*

Onions *1*

Green olives *3 oz*

Capers *2 oz*

Herbs *a few sprigs of each (thyme, parsley, marjoram)*

Red hot chili peppers *1 small piece*

Extra virgin olive oil *4 tablespoons*

Salt *&* **pepper** *to taste*

● Blanch the tomatoes in boiling water; drain, peel and squeeze gently to remove all seeds, then chop coarsely. Clean the green chili peppers; remove seeds and white parts; rinse, dry and chop. Pit the olives, slice very thinly and set aside.

● Peel the onion; rinse, dry and chop finely. Rinse and dry the thyme, parsley and marjoram, then chop finely. In a large pan, heat the extra virgin olive oil. Cook the chopped onion until just transparent. Add the red hot pepper and the green chili pepper. Sauté for 3 minutes.

● Add the chopped tomatoes. Season with salt and pepper if needed. Continue cooking for 15 to 20 minutes, stirring often. Add the sliced olives, capers, parsley, thyme and marjoram. Cook for another 3 minutes. During this time, cook the penne rigate in abundant salted water until al dente. Drain the pasta and transfer to the sauce. Toss well. Serve in warm pasta bowls.

Fusilli with squid & spinach

Difficulty **average**
Preparation time **40 minutes**
Calories **460**

Ingredients *for 4 servings*

Fusilli *12 oz*
Squid *1/4 lb*
Spinach *12 oz*
Tomatoes *12 oz, firm and ripe*
Shallots *1*
Extra virgin olive oil *4 tablespoons*
Salt *&* **pepper** *to taste*

● Clean the squid. Remove the cartilage, exterior skin, insides, eyes and mouth; rinse well, dry then cut in long strips. Rinse the spinach three times in cold water; drain well and cut in long strips.

● Blanch the tomatoes in boiling water; drain, peel and press gently to remove all seeds then chop coarsely. Peel the shallot and chop finely.

● In a pan, heat the extra virgin olive oil. Add the shallot and cook until just tender. Add the squid strips and cook until they render all their water, stirring all the time. Drain and set aside.

● In the same pan, add the spinach and sauté for 2 minutes. Drain and set aside. To the pan, add the tomatoes. Season with a pinch of salt and pepper; cook for 5 or 6 minutes. Return the squid strips and the spinach to the sauce. Cook, stirring, for another 2 minutes.

● Cook the fusilli in abundant salted water until al dente. Drain well and transfer to the pan with the prepared

Gnocchetti with shrimp & white beans

Difficulty **average**
Preparation time **1 hour 30 minutes + soaking time**
Calories **480**

Ingredients *for 4 servings*

Gnocchetti *12 oz*
Dry white beans *6 oz*
Small shrimp *1/4 lb*
Celery *1 stalk*
Onions *1*
Bay leaves *1*
Garlic *1 clove*
Parsley *1 small bunch*
Extra virgin olive oil *4 tablespoons*
Salt *&* **pepper** *to taste*

● Soak the white beans in plenty of cold water for 12 hours, then drain. Peel the onion, rinse, dry and chop. Rinse, dry and chop celery. Peel the garlic.

● In a large saucepan, place the white beans, half of the chopped onion, the celery, the bay leaf and the garlic. Cover with cold water. Slowly bring to boil and cook for about one hour. Season with salt. If needed, add more boiling water during the cooking.

● In a pan, heat the extra virgin olive oil and cook the remaining onion until just transparent. Drain the white beans and add to the pan. Sauté for a minute. Mix well.

● During this time, peel the shrimp; devein, rinse and dry carefully on paper towels. Add to the white beans. Season with salt and fresh ground pepper. Continue cooking for 2 to 3 minutes. Add the chopped parsley and toss.

● Cook the gnocchetti in abundant salted water until al dente. Drain well and transfer to a serving bowl. Add the sauce and toss. Serve immediately.

Difficulty **easy**
Preparation time **35 minutes**
Calories **480**

Ingredients *for 4 servings*

Spiral pasta *12 oz*

Grouper *1 filet of 10 oz*

Cherry tomatoes *1/4 lb*

Pine nuts *2 teaspoons*

Onions *1*

Garlic *2 cloves*

Basil *a few leaves*

Red hot chili peppers
1 small piece

Extra virgin olive oil *4 tablespoons*

Salt *&* **pepper** *to taste*

Spiral pasta with grouper

● Peel the onion; rinse and dry. Peel the garlic cloves and remove the green sprout if needed. Finely chop garlic with the onion. Rinse, dry and tear the basil leaves. Rinse and dry the cherry tomatoes. Rinse and dry the fish; cut in cubes.

● In a pan, heat the extra virgin olive oil. Cook the onion and garlic until onion is just transparent. Add the cherry tomatoes, a few basil leaves and the piece of chili pepper. Season with salt and generous fresh ground pepper.

● Cook the sauce, on high heat, for about 10 minutes, stirring often with a wooden spoon. When the sauce has reduced, add the pieces of fish, pine nuts, and the remaining basil. Cover and cook for 10 minutes, on low heat.

● During this time, cook the eliche in abundant salted water until al dente. Drain very well and transfer to a large serving bowl. Add the sauce and mix very well. Serve immediately.

Difficulty **average**
Preparation time **40 minutes**
Calories **470**

Ingredients *for 4 servings*

Maccheroncini *1/2 lb*

Asparagus *12 oz*

Mullet *8*

Extra virgin olive oil *4 tablespoons*

Salt *&* **pepper** *to taste*

Maccheroncini with asparagus & mullet

● Prepare the asparagus. Cut off the white hard stems; peel with a potato peeler, rinse, dry and steam asparagus for about 6 minutes. Drain well. Cut the heads and slice stems in strips.

● Prepare the mullet. Remove the filets and debone; rinse and dry carefully on paper towels. Cut in strips. In a non-stick pan, heat the extra virgin olive oil and add the mullet strips.

Sauté for 2 minutes. Season with salt and generous fresh ground pepper. Mix well. Add the asparagus and re-heat.

● During this time, cook the maccheroncini in abundant salted water until al dente. Drain well and in a large bowl mix with the prepared fish and asparagus. Transfer to a warm serving dish and serve very hot.

1 *Cook the asparagus in a steamer.*

2 *Cut off the asparagus heads and slice the stems.*

3 *In a non-stick pan, cook the mullet strips and add the asparagus.*

Penne with zucchini

Difficulty **easy**
Preparation time **30 minutes**
Calories **390**

Ingredients *for 4 servings*

Penne *12 oz*

Zucchini *12 oz*

Tomatoes *3, firm and ripe*

Onions *1*

Basil *1 small bunch*

Garlic *1 clove*

Extra virgin olive oil *4 tablespoons*

Salt *&* **pepper** *to taste*

● Rinse and dry the zucchini very well, then dice. Blanch the tomatoes in boiling water for 1 minute. Drain, peel and press gently to remove all seeds, then dice.

● Peel, rinse and dry the onion and garlic; chop both finely. In a non-stick pan, heat the oil and cook on medium heat the garlic and onion until just tender.

● Add the zucchini, a few shredded leaves of basil, a pinch of salt and fresh ground pepper. Cook for 7 to 8 minutes, stirring often with a wooden spoon. Add the diced tomatoes and cook on high heat for a few minutes

● During this time, cook the penne in abundant salted water until al dente. Drain and place in a bowl. Mix with the prepared vegetables. Transfer to warm individual serving bowls and sprinkle with chopped basil leaves. Serve immediately.

1 *Rinse, dry and dice the zucchini.*

2 *Cook the zucchini with the cooked onions; add basil leaves and stir often.*

3 *Add the prepared vegetables to the cooked penne and mix well.*

Difficulty **easy**
Preparation time **40 minutes + resting time**
Calories **490**

Ingredients *for 4 servings*

Short penne *12 oz*

Eggplants *1 large*

Tomatoes *3, firm and ripe*

Mozzarella *1*

Garlic *1 clove*

Basil *10 leaves*

Extra virgin olive oil *4 tablespoons*

Salt *&* **pepper** *to taste*

Short penne with eggplant

● Peel the eggplant and dice finely. Place on a cookie sheet, slightly inclined and season with salt. Set aside for half an hour. Rinse the eggplant and dry on paper towels.

● Blanch the tomatoes in boiling water; drain, peel and press gently to remove seeds, then chop finely. Peel the garlic and remove the green sprout, if needed. Dice the mozzarella.

● In a pan, heat the extra virgin olive oil. Add the garlic clove and cook on low heat until it starts to brown. Remove the garlic. Add the diced eggplant and cook for about 10 minutes, or until they have rendered most of their liquid and are golden. Add the diced tomatoes, chopped basil leaves and a generous pinch of salt. Cover and continue cooking on low heat, so the sauce does not reduce too much.

● Cook the short penne in abundant salted water until al dente. Drain well and transfer to a warm serving dish. Add the prepared sauce, the diced mozzarella and generous fresh ground pepper. Toss well and serve.

Difficulty **easy**
Preparation time **40 minutes**
Calories **540**

Ingredients *for 4 servings*

Short pasta *14 oz*

Tomatoes *3/4 lb*

Zucchini *1/2 lb*

Green beans *1/2 lb*

Mozzarella *1*

Chopped basil *1 bunch*

Extra virgin olive oil *5 tablespoons*

Salt *&* **pepper** *to taste*

Classic pasta salad

● Blanch the tomatoes in boiling water; drain, peel and press gently to remove seeds; dice and place in a large bowl; season with salt. Rinse and dry the zucchini and the green beans; slice in bite-size pieces. Dice the mozzarella and set aside.

● Cook the pasta in abundant salted water until al dente. A few minutes after beginning, add the zucchini and the green beans to the pasta. Stir often.

Remove from the heat and drain vegetables and pasta together. Transfer all to a large dish to cool completely.

● Drain the tomatoes and discard the juices that may have gathered in the bowl. Add the diced mozzarella and the other ingredients, now cold. Drizzle with extra virgin olive oil; add the shredded basil and generous fresh ground pepper. Mix well and serve.

Difficulty **easy**
Preparation time **30 minutes**
Calories **420**

Ingredients *for 4 servings*

Short pasta *12 oz*

Arugula *6 oz*

Celery *1 stalk*

Onions *1*

Extra virgin olive oil *5 tablespoons*

Salt *&* **pepper** *to taste*

Short pasta with arugula & celery

● Rinse and dry the celery; slice thinly and blanch the tomatoes in boiling water; drain, peel and press gently to remove seeds, then in salted boiling water for one minute. Drain and set aside. Peel the onion, rinse, dry and chop finely. Rinse the arugula in cold water, several times; drain and cut in strips.

● In a pan, heat the extra virgin olive oil. Add the slices of celery and cook for 2 minutes, stirring with a wooden spoon. Add 4 tablespoons of water. Season with salt and fresh ground pepper. Cover and cook on medium heat for about 10 minutes.

● During this time, cook the anelloni in abundant salted water until al dente. Two minutes before the end of cooking time, add the arugula strips. Drain the pasta and the arugula. Transfer to a large bowl, add the sauce and toss well. Serve very hot.

Conchiglie with zucchini

Difficulty **easy**
Preparation time **30 minutes**
Calories **380**

Ingredients *for 4 servings*

Conchiglie *12 oz*
Zucchini *1/2 lb*
Tomato paste *1 tablespoon*
Garlic *1 clove*
Parsley *a few leaves*
Extra virgin olive oil *4 tablespoons*
Salt *to taste*

● Rinse, dry and finely chop the parsley. Rinse and dry the zucchini; cut in 4 pieces, lengthwise, then slice thinly. Peel the garlic and remove the green sprout, if needed; chop finely.

● In a pan, heat 2 tablespoons of extra virgin olive oil with garlic. Add zucchini. Mix and season with salt. Dissolve the tomato paste in 1/4 cup of warm water; add to the zucchini and cook for 10 minutes, stirring from time to time with a wooden spoon.

● During this time, cook the conchiglie in abundant salted water until al dente. Drain well and transfer to the pan with the sauce. Sauté for a few minutes. Sprinkle with the chopped parsley leaves. Pour into a warm serving dish. Serve very hot.

Short penne with artichokes

Difficulty **easy**
Preparation time **30 minutes**
Calories **420**

Ingredients *for 4 servings*

Short penne *12 oz*
Artichokes *3*
Anchovies *2*
Lemons *1*
Capers *1 teaspoon*
Garlic *1 clove*
Parsley *1 small bunch*
Dry white wine *1/2 cup*
Extra virgin olive oil *5 tablespoons*
Salt *&* **pepper** *to taste*

● Prepare the artichokes. Remove the stems, the hard leaves and prickly ends of leaves. Slice in half and remove the chokes. Cut in thin slices and place in a bowl, covered with cold water and the juice of the lemon. Rinse the anchovies under running water, debone and cut in small pieces.

● Peel the garlic and remove the green sprout if necessary; chop finely. In a pan, heat the extra virgin olive oil with the garlic. Drain and dry the artichokes on a kitchen towel. Add to the pan and cook on high heat for a minute, stirring. Remove the garlic.

● Season with salt and pepper. Add the white wine and let reduce. Cover and continue cooking for a further 15 minutes, stirring from time to time. After 8 minutes, add the chopped anchovies and capers.

● Cook the short penne in abundant salted water until al dente. Drain and add to the artichoke sauce. Toss; add the chopped parsley and toss again. Serve very hot.

Orecchiette with eggplant

Difficulty **easy**
Preparation time **30 minutes**
Calories **400**

Ingredients *for 4 servings*

Orecchiette *12 oz*

Round eggplants *1*

Tomatoes *2*

Garlic *1 clove*

Dried oregano *1 teaspoon*

Cumin seeds *1/2 teaspoon*

Parsley *a few sprigs*

Extra virgin olive oil *4 tablespoons*

Salt *to taste*

● Rinse, dry and finely chop the parsley. Rinse, dry and cut the eggplant in 1/2-inch cubes. Peel the garlic, remove its green sprout if necessary and chop. Blanch the tomatoes in boiling water; drain, peel and press gently to remove seeds, then cut in small pieces.

● In a pan, heat the extra virgin olive oil. Add cumin seeds and garlic. Cook until garlic is golden; remove garlic and add eggplant. Season with a little salt. Mix well and cook for 10 minutes. Add tomatoes and cook for another 10 minutes. Add parsley, oregano and taste for salt.

● Cook the orecchiette in abundant salted water until al dente. Drain and transfer to a large serving plate. Add the prepared sauce and mix well.

Fusilli with herbs

Difficulty **easy**
Preparation time **30 minutes**
Calories **420**

Ingredients *for 4 servings*

Fusilli *12 oz*

Shallots *1*

Tarragon *2 sprigs*

Basil *1 small bunch*

Marjoram *2 sprigs*

Thyme *1 sprig*

Sage *1 leaf*

Bay leaves *1*

Tomatoes *1 lb, firm and ripe*

Extra virgin olive oil *5 tablespoons*

Salt *& pepper to taste*

● Blanch the tomatoes in boiling water; drain, peel and press gently to remove seeds, then chop coarsely. Rinse the tarragon, basil, marjoram and thyme; delicately dry them on paper towel then chop coarsely. Peel and finely chop the shallot.

● In a pan, heat 2 tablespoons of extra virgin olive oil. Add chopped shallot and half the chopped basil, all tarragon, thyme, sage, bay leaf and half the marjoram. Cook until the shallot is just transparent. Add the chopped tomatoes. Season with salt and cook on low heat for 10 to 12 minutes, stirring often with a wooden spoon.

● Add the remaining basil, marjoram and extra virgin olive oil; remove the bay leaf. During this time, cook the fusilli in abundant salted water until al dente. Drain and transfer to a warm serving bowl. Add the prepared sauce and toss well. Serve immediately.

Risotto with pears & almonds

Difficulty **easy**
Preparation time **40 minutes**
Calories **570**

Ingredients *for 4 servings*

Carnaroli or Arborio rice *12 oz*

Pears *1 lb, ripe and juicy*

Walnuts *4 oz*

Onions *1 slice*

Lemons *1*

Dry white wine *1/2 cup*

Vegetable broth *4 cups*

Extra virgin olive oil *3 tablespoons*

White pepper *to taste*

● Rinse and dry the lemon carefully. Press the lemon and keep the peel aside. Peel the pears and quarter; core and slice thinly. Place in a bowl and mix with the lemon juice. Set aside. Coarsely chop the walnuts, keeping a few whole for decoration. Heat the vegetable broth.

● In a saucepan, heat the extra virgin olive oil. Add the piece of onion and cook until transparent. Remove the onion; add the rice and sauté for a minute. Add the white wine and let evaporate completely on high heat, stirring all the time with a wooden spoon. Add the hot vegetable broth, one cup at a time. Stir all the time. When the broth is absorbed, add more broth.

● When the rice is cooked al dente, add the sliced pears (drained from the lemon juice). Add half of the lemon rind, grated. Mix well; remove from the heat. Add the chopped walnuts; season with fresh ground pepper. Serve in warm individual bowl, decorated with a few whole walnuts.

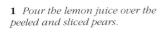
1 *Pour the lemon juice over the peeled and sliced pears.*

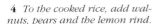
4 *To the cooked rice, add walnuts, pears and the lemon rind.*

3 *Chop the walnuts coarsely.*

2 *Sauté the rice in a pan, stirring with a wooden spoon.*

Risotto with peas & basil

Difficulty **easy**
Preparation time **40 minutes**
Calories **440**

Ingredients *for 4 servings*

Carnaroli or Arborio rice *12 oz*

Fresh peas *10 oz*

Basil *1 bunch*

Shallots *1*

Onions *1 small*

Dry white wine *1/2 cup*

Vegetable broth *5 cups*

Extra virgin olive oil *4 tablespoons*

Salt *&* **pepper** *to taste*

● Peel the onion and shallot; chop them separately. Rinse, dry and tear the basil. In a pan, heat 2 tablespoons of extra virgin olive oil. Add the onion and cook until transparent. Add the rice and toast it for one or two minutes, stirring with a wooden spoon. Add the white wine and let evaporate completely on high heat. Mix well.

● Add the vegetable broth, 1/2 cup at a time. Stirring with a wooden spoon, cook for 15 minutes. During this time, in a pan, heat the remaining extra virgin olive oil. Add the shallot and cook until tender; add the peas and sauté for a few minutes. Season with salt and fresh ground pepper. Stir in 1/2 cup of water and cook for 8 minutes.

● Drain half the peas and press through a food mill; add to the whole peas. Pour this mixture over the rice, mix well and cook for 3 minutes, stirring. Remove from heat. (The rice should be al dente.) Add the basil. Cover and set aside for 2 minutes. Serve in warm individual bowls.

Risotto with zucchini flowers

Difficulty **easy**
Preparation time **40 minutes**
Calories **350**

Ingredients *for 4 servings*

Carnaroli or Arborio rice *12 oz*

Zucchini flowers *1/2 lb*

Onions *1 small*

Chopped parsley *1 tablespoon*

Saffron *1/2 teaspoon*

Dry white wine *1/2 cup*

Vegetable broth *5 cups*

Extra virgin olive oil *2 tablespoons*

● Remove stems and pistils from zucchini flowers. Clean them delicately with a humid towel; cut in long strips. Peel and finely chop the onion. In a saucepan, heat 2 tablespoons of extra virgin olive oil. Add the onion and cook until just tender. Add the zucchini flower strips and cook on low heat, stirring for a minute.

● Add the rice and let it dry for a minute. Add the white wine and let evaporate completely on high heat, stirring all the time. Add the saffron, dissolved in 1/2 cup of broth, and mix well. Add the broth, 1/2 cup at a time, stirring until completely absorbed. Cook for 12 minutes. Add the chopped parsley and continue cooking 5 to 6 minutes. Remove from heat, cover and set aside for 2 minutes. Serve in warm individual bowls.

Brown rice with vegetables

Difficulty **easy**
Preparation time **1 hour + resting time**
Calories **370**

Ingredients *for 4 servings*

Brown rice *12 oz*

Zucchini *1*

Carrots *1*

Red bell peppers *1*

Onions *1*

Herbs *1 small bunch (parsley, basil, chervil)*

Vegetable broth *5 cups*

Dry white wine *1/2 cup*

Extra virgin olive oil *2 tablespoons*

● Place the rice in a large bowl; cover with cold water and set aside for 3 hours. During this time, peel the onion and chop finely. Rinse and dry the zucchini. Remove seeds and white parts from red pepper. Peel the carrot. Rinse, dry and chop the herbs. Dice the vegetables.

● In a large saucepan, heat 2 table-spoons of extra virgin olive oil. Add chopped onion and cook until just transparent. Add pepper, carrot and zucchini. Stirring with a wooden spoon, cook for a few minutes. Drain the rice and add to the vegetables. Cook for a few minutes. Add the white wine and let evaporate on high heat, mixing all the time.

● Add the vegetable broth, 1/2 cup at a time. Continue cooking on low heat, for about 40 minutes. Add the chopped herbs and mix well. Remove from heat. The rice should be al dente. Cover and set aside for 2 minutes. Serve immediately.

Risotto with red radicchio

Difficulty **easy**
Preparation time **40 minutes**
Calories **390**

Ingredients *for 4 servings*

Carnaroli or Arborio rice *12 oz*

Red radicchio *2 heads*

Onions *1 small*

Vegetable broth *5 cups*

Dry white wine *1/2 cup*

Extra virgin olive oil *4 tablespoons*

● Prepare the radicchio. Remove the exterior leaves, rinse, dry and cut in long strips. Peel and finely chop the onion. In a pan, heat the extra virgin olive oil and cook onion until just transparent. Add half the radicchio strips and cook for one minute.

● Add the rice and toast for a minute. Add the white wine and let evaporate completely, stirring with a wooden spoon. Add the broth, 1/2 cup at a time. Continue cooking for 15 to 18 minutes, stirring all the time. Six minutes before the end of cooking time, add the remaining radicchio strips and mix well. Remove the risotto from the heat. Cover for a few minutes. Transfer to a serving dish and serve hot.

Difficulty **easy**
Preparation time **40 minutes**
Calories **440**

Ingredients *for 4 servings*

Carnaroli or Arborio rice *12 oz*

Small fennel bulb *8 oz*

Onions *1*

Vegetable broth *5 cups*

Grated parmigiano *1/2 cup*

Extra virgin olive oil *2 tablespoons*

Salt *to taste*

Andrea's note: To get the best of any risotto, serve it very hot and as soon as it is ready.

Risotto with fennel

● Remove the outside leaves of the fennel bulbs; cut the extremities and keep the heart. Rinse under running water and cut in thin strips. Peel the onion and finely slice. Heat the vegetable broth in a saucepan. In another saucepan, heat the extra virgin olive oil. Add the onion and cook on low heat for 2 minutes. Add the strips of fennel. Season with salt and set aside for 10 minutes.

● Add the rice and mix well; cook on low heat for 2 minutes. Add the boiling hot broth and continue cooking on medium heat. Add the broth, 1/2 cup at a time, stirring with a wooden spoon until all absorbed. Cook until the rice is al dente. Add the grated parmigiano and mix cheese. Transfer to a serving dish and serve immediately.

Risotto with anchovies & pine nuts

Difficulty **average**
Preparation time **40 minutes**
Calories **430**

Ingredients *for 4 servings*

Carnaroli or arborio rice *12 oz*

Fresh anchovies *12 oz*

Roasted pine nuts *2 tablespoons*

Chopped tomatoes *6 oz*

Chopped parsley *2 tablespoons*

Chopped onions *1 small*

Dry white wine *1/2 cup*

Fish broth *4-5 cups*

Extra virgin olive oil *3 tablespoons*

● Clean the anchovies. Remove the heads and interiors; cut in filets and rinse under running water; cut in small pieces. In a pan, heat the extra virgin olive oil and cook half the chopped onion until transparent for a few minutes, stirring delicately with a wooden spoon. Drain and set aside.

● In the same pan, add the remaining onion and cook briefly. Add chopped tomatoes and cook for 2 minutes. Add the rice and cook, stirring for 2 minutes. Add the dry white wine and let evaporate on high heat, stirring all the time. Add the fish broth, 1/2 cup at a time and cook for 15 to 18 minutes, stirring.

● A few minutes before the rice is al dente, add the pieces of anchovy and toasted pine nuts. Remove from the heat and sprinkle with chopped parsley. Mix well. Cover for one minute. Serve in warm individual bowls.

Risotto with artichokes

Difficulty **easy**
Preparation time **40 minutes**
Calories **360**

Ingredients *for 4 servings*

Carnaroli or Arborio rice *12 oz*

Artichokes *2*

Anchovy paste *1/2 teaspoon*

Garlic *1 clove*

Lemons *the juice of 1/2*

Parsley *1 small bunch*

Dry white wine *1/2 cup*

Vegetable broth *5 cups*

Extra virgin olive oil *2 tablespoons*

● Peel the garlic. Rinse and dry parsley; chop parsley and garlic together. Remove exterior hard leaves from the artichokes; cut off stems and remove chokes from the center. Slice in strips and place in a bowl of cold water with the lemon juice. Bring the vegetable broth to boil.

● In a saucepan, heat the extra virgin olive oil. Add the garlic clove and drained artichokes. Cook for 2 minutes. Add the rice and stir a few minutes. Add the white wine and let evaporate on high heat. Add vegetable broth, 1/2 cup at a time, adding the next one after the prior one is absorbed. Cook 15-18 minutes, stirring.

● Remove from the heat when the rice is al dente. Add the anchovy paste, the garlic and the parsley. Mix well and cover for a few minutes. Serve very hot in individual bowls.

Risotto with herbs & scampi

Difficulty **easy**
Preparation time **40 minutes**
Calories **450**

Ingredients *for 4 servings*

Carnaroli or Arborio rice *12 oz*

Scampi *16, cleaned*

Onions *1 small*

Chopped herbs *1 teaspoon of each (parsley, chervil, tarragon, chives)*

Fish broth *5 cups*

Dry white wine *5 tablespoons*

Extra virgin olive oil *4 tablespoons*

Salt *&* **pepper** *to taste*

● Peel the onion and chop finely. In a saucepan, heat 2 tablespoons of extra virgin olive oil and cook the chopped onion until just transparent.

● Add the rice and cook for a minute. Add the dry white wine and let evaporate, stirring with a wooden spoon. Add the boiling fish broth, 1/2 cup at a time, until the rice is al dente and almost all broth has been absorbed. The dish should result a little soupy.

Sprinkle with the chopped herbs.

● In a non-stick pan, heat the remaining olive oil. Add the scampi. Season with salt and fresh ground pepper. Cook for 2 minutes. Serve the rice in warm individual bowls with the scampi on top.

Risotto with tomatoes

Difficulty **easy**
Preparation time **40 minutes**
Calories **310**

Ingredients *for 4 servings*

Carnaroli or Arborio rice *10 oz*

Tomatoes *1/4 lb, firm and ripe*

Onions *1*

Dry white wine *1/4 cup*

Vegetable broth *4-5 cups*

Extra virgin olive oil *2 tablespoons*

● Blanch the tomatoes in boiling water; drain, peel and press gently to remove seeds, then chop coarsely. Peel the onion; rinse, dry and chop finely. In a large non-stick saucepan, heat the extra virgin olive oil and the onion. Cook until just transparent. Add half the chopped tomatoes. Stir with a wooden spoon from time to time.

● Add the rice and cook for 2 minutes, on high heat. Add the white wine and let it evaporate, stirring. Add the vegetable broth, 1/2 cup at a time. Cook for about 15 minutes or until the rice is al dente. Five minutes before the end of cooking time, add the remaining tomatoes and mix. Remove from heat; transfer to a warm serving dish and serve immediately.

Risotto with saffron & shrimp

Difficulty **average**
Preparation time **45 minutes**
Calories **470**

Ingredients *for 4 servings*

Carnaroli or Arborio rice *14 oz*

Shrimp *1 lb*

Shallots *2*

Saffron *1/2 teaspoon*

Dry white wine *1/2 cup*

Fish broth *5 cups*

Extra virgin olive oil *2 tablespoons*

Salt *to taste*

● Peel and devein the shrimp; cook in salted boiling water for 5 minutes. Drain and set aside between 2 plates, to keep warm. Peel the shallots and chop finely.

● In a large saucepan, heat the extra virgin olive oil. Add the chopped shallots and cook until just transparent. Add the rice and cook for a few minutes. Add the white wine and let evaporate completely, stirring all the time with a wooden spoon.

● Dissolve the saffron in the fish broth. Add the broth to the rice, 1/2 cup at a time, stirring. Cook for 10 minutes, then add the shrimp and continue to cook for another 8 minutes. Remove from heat and cover for 2 minutes. Transfer to a serving dish and serve immediately.

Risotto with lentils

Difficulty **easy**
Preparation time **1 hour**
+ resting time
Calories **460**

Ingredients *for 4 servings*

Carnaroli or arborio rice *12 oz*

Lentils *5 oz*

Celery *1 stalk*

Onions *1*

Garlic *1 clove*

Parsley *1 small bunch*

Bay leaves *1*

Chicken or vegetable broth *5 cups*

Extra virgin olive oil *4 tablespoons*

Salt *to taste*

● Soak the lentils in cold water for 12 hours. Peel the garlic. Peel the onion and slice thinly. Rinse and dry the celery. Rinse the parsley. Drain the lentils; place them in a saucepan. Cover with 8 cups of water; add the bay leaf, half a garlic clove and half the chopped onion.

● Slowly bring to boil and cook on medium heat for 30 minutes. Add more boiling water if needed. Season with salt when the lentils are cooked. During this time, finely chop the remaining garlic with the parsley and celery.

● In a large saucepan, heat the extra virgin olive oil and cook the remaining chopped onion until transparent. Add the chopped herbs, garlic and rice. Drain the lentils and add to the rice. Pour in the broth, 1/2 cup at a time, letting it be absorbed before adding more. When the rice is al dente, transfer to a serving dish and serve immediately.

Risotto with broad beans

Difficulty **easy**
Preparation time **40 minutes**
Calories **390**

Ingredients *for 4 servings*

Carnaroli or Arborio rice *12 oz*
Fresh broad beans *1 1/4 lbs*
Leeks *2*
Shallots *1 small*
Parsley *1 small bunch*
Thyme *3 sprigs*
Dry white wine *1/4 cup*
Vegetable broth *4-5 cups*
Extra virgin olive oil *3 tablespoons*

● Peel the beans and cook in abundant salted water. Drain and remove the thin skin. Prepare the leeks. Remove the ends and darker green leaves; rinse, dry and slice them. Peel the shallot and chop finely. Rinse the thyme and the parsley; dry on paper towels and chop finely.

● In a large saucepan, heat the extra virgin olive oil. Add the onion and leeks; cook until just tender. Add the broad beans and let stand for a minute. Add the rice and cook for 2 minutes. Pour in the white wine and let evaporate on high heat, mixing continuously. Add the boiling broth, 1/2 cup at a time. Cook, stirring all the time, until the rice is soft but still al dente. Remove from heat. Sprinkle with the chopped parsley and thyme. Serve immediately.

Risotto with zucchini

Difficulty **easy**
Preparation time **30 minutes**
Calories **400**

Ingredients *for 4 servings*

Carnaroli or Arborio rice *12 oz*
Zucchini *12 oz*
Shallots *1*
Onions *1 small*
Dry white wine *1/4 cup*
Vegetable broth *5 cups*
Extra virgin olive oil *4 tablespoons*
Salt *&* **pepper** *to taste*

● Rinse, dry and dice the zucchini. Peel the onion and shallot; chop separately. In a large saucepan, heat the extra virgin olive oil and cook chopped onion until just transparent. Add the carnaroli rice and cook for a minute, stirring with a wooden spoon. Add the white wine and let evaporate on high heat.

● Add the vegetable broth, 1/2 cup at a time and continue cooking on medium heat, for 15 to 18 minutes, stirring often. During this time, heat the remaining extra virgin olive oil in a pan, with the remaining chopped onion and chopped shallot. Cook until just transparent. Add the diced zucchini and sauté for a few minutes. Season with a good pinch of salt and fresh ground pepper to taste. Continue cooking on medium heat. A few minutes before the rice is cooked, add the zucchini. Mix well and remove from heat when the rice is still al dente. Cover and set aside for 2 minutes. Serve very hot.

Risotto with scallops & peppers

Difficulty **average**
Preparation time **40 minutes**
Calories **500**

Ingredients *for 4 servings*

Carnaroli or Arborio rice *12 oz*

Scallops *16 large*

Red bell peppers *1*

Shallots *2 large*

Parsley *1 small bunch*

Dry white wine *1/2 cup*

Fish or vegetable broth *5 cups*

Extra virgin olive oil *4 tablespoons*

Salt *&* **pepper** *to taste*

● Peel the shallot; rinse, dry and finely chop. Rinse, dry and finely chop parsley. Cut the pepper. Remove seeds and all white parts; then dice. In a large saucepan, heat 2 tablespoons of extra virgin olive oil and cook shallot until just transparent. Add the diced pepper and cook for a few minutes.

● Add the rice and stir for a minute. Pour in the white wine and let it evaporate on high heat, stirring all the time. Add the broth, 1/2 cup at a time. Continue cooking for 15 to 18 minutes, stirring very often.

● During this time, rinse the scallops under running water and dry on paper towels. Divide the scallops in two, horizontally. In a non-stick pan, heat the remaining extra virgin olive oil and cook the scallops for a minute. Season with salt and fresh ground pepper. A few minutes before the rice is cooked, add the scallops and mix delicately. Remove from heat when rice is al dente and general texture is slightly soupy. Mix in the chopped parsley and serve.

Risotto with squid ink

Difficulty **average**
Preparation time **45 minutes**
Calories **420**

Ingredients *for 4 servings*

Arborio rice *10 oz*

Squid *4 small*

Chopped shallots *1 tablespoon*

Dry white wine *1/4 cup*

Fish broth *4-5 cups*

Extra virgin olive oil *4 tablespoons*

Salt *&* **pepper** *to taste*

● Remove the tentacles from the squid pouch; empty them and keep small ink pouches. Clean squid. Remove mouth and eyes; rinse and dry well. In a pan, heat 2 tablespoons of extra virgin olive oil and cook squid with tentacles. Add shallots and cook for 3 minutes. Season with salt and pepper. Add dry white wine; cover and cook on medium heat until squid is dry.

● Remove squid from the pan and set aside, keeping it warm. Add squid ink to the cooking juices. Season with salt and a pinch of pepper.

● In a saucepan, heat the remaining extra virgin olive oil. Add rice and cook for 2 minutes. Add the boiling fish broth, 1/2 cup at a time, until all broth is absorbed and the rice is al dente. Remove from heat and mix in the cooking juices from the squid. Transfer risotto to individual warm bowls; place one squid in the center of each bowl. Serve immediately.

Drunken rice

Difficulty **average**
Preparation time **1 hour**
Calories **450**

Ingredients *for 4 servings*

Carnaroli or Arborio rice *11 oz*

Calamari *2 1/4 lbs*

Peeled tomatoes *4 oz*

Sweet peas *6 oz*

Celery *2 stalks*

Onions *3*

Garlic *2 cloves*

Chopped parsley *2 tablespoons*

Dry white wine *2 cups*

Extra virgin olive oil *2 tablespoons*

Salt *&* **pepper** *to taste*

● Clean the calamari. Remove mouth and eyes; keep part of their ink. Rinse well and dry on paper towel. Peel the onion and garlic clove. Rinse and dry the celery. Chop all vegetables together. In a large pot, heat the oil and cook the chopped vegetables until onion is transparent.

● Add calamari to vegetables and cook on moderate heat until they are dry. Add the ink and parsley; season with salt and pepper. Add peeled tomatoes and half dry white wine. Cook on low heat for 30 minutes.

● When the calamari are almost done, add the rice. Mix and pour in the remaining white wine. The rice should be almost covered. Bring to boil; taste for salt and transfer the pot to a preheated oven at 375°F for 20 minutes. Remove from oven and transfer to a warm serving dish. Serve immediately.

Risotto with carrots

Difficulty **easy**
Preparation time **40 minutes**
Calories **320**

Ingredients *for 4 servings*

Carnaroli or Arborio rice *10 oz*

Carrots *12 oz*

Onions *1 small*

Vegetable broth *4 cups*

Nutmeg *1/4 teaspoon*

Extra virgin olive oil *2 tablespoons*

● Peel the carrots with a potato peeler; rinse, dry and chop finely. Peel the onion, rinse, dry and chop finely. In a saucepan, heat the extra virgin olive oil and add onion. Cook until onion is just transparent. Add chopped carrots and cook for 5 minutes, stirring with a wooden spoon. Season with fresh ground nutmeg.

● Add carnaroli rice and cook for 2 minutes, stirring. Add dry white wine and let evaporate on high heat, stirring so the rice does not attach. Add vegetable broth, 1/2 cup at a time, stirring often. Cook until the rice is al dente. Remove from heat when risotto is still soupy. Cover and set aside for 2 minutes. Serve immediately.

Difficulty **average**
Preparation time **50 minutes**
Calories **380**

Ingredients *for 4 servings*

Carnaroli or Arborio rice *10 oz*

Mushrooms *9 oz*

Baby squid *9 oz*

Spinach *9 oz*

Shallots *2, chopped finely*

Chopped parsley *2 tablespoons*

Fish broth *4 cups*

Dry white wine *1/2 cup*

Extra virgin olive oil *4 tablespoons*

Salt *&* **pepper** *to taste*

Risotto with squid, mushrooms & spinach

● Delicately brush the mushrooms; rinse, dry and slice. Clean the baby squid. Remove the exterior skin, interiors and bone. Rinse under running water, dry and cut in strips. Rinse and dry spinach; cut in thin strips.

● In a saucepan, heat 2 tablespoons of extra virgin olive oil. Add 1/2 chopped shallots and cook until just transparent. Add rice and stir for 1 minute. Pour the white wine and let evaporate on high heat, stirring continuously. Slowly add the boiling fish broth, 1/2 cup at a time. Cook stirring often, for 15 to 18 minutes.

● In a pan, heat the remaining extra virgin olive oil with remaining chopped shallots and parsley. Add mushrooms and cook for a few minutes. Add sliced squid and cook shortly. Add spinach. Season with salt and fresh ground pepper. Continue cooking on medium heat for 5 minutes. Five minutes before the rice is cooked, add mixture to rice and mix well. Transfer to a serving plate.

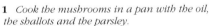

2 *Add the sliced baby shrimp and cook briefly.*

1 *Cook the mushrooms in a pan with the oil, the shallots and the parsley.*

4 *Five minutes before the rice is done, add the prepared mixture.*

3 *Add the cleaned spinach sliced in strips.*

Risotto with squash & spinach

Difficulty **easy**
Preparation time **40 minutes**
Calories **370**

Ingredients *for 4 servings*

Carnaroli or Arborio rice *12 oz*
Squash *12 oz*
Spinach *10 oz*
Onions *1 small*
Dry white wine *1/2 cup*
Vegetable broth *5 cups*
Extra virgin olive oil *2 tablespoons*

● Rinse the spinach several times in cold water; drain and slice thinly. Peel the squash and remove the seeds; rinse, dry and dice. Peel onion, rinse, dry and chop finely.

● In a saucepan, heat the olive oil. Add chopped onion and cook until transparent. Add the diced squash and cook briefly, stirring with a wooden spoon. Add 1/2 cup of vegetable broth and cook for 3 minutes. Add rice and half the spinach; cook for 2 minutes. Add the dry white wine and let evaporate on high heat, stirring.

● Add broth, 1/2 cup at a time. Cook on medium heat for about 15 minutes, stirring often. Add the remaining strips of spinach. Mix well and cook for another 3 minutes. Remove from heat when the rice is al dente and mixture is a little soupy. Set aside for 2 minutes and serve in warm bowls.

Rice with anchovy filets

Difficulty **easy**
Preparation time **30 minutes**
Calories **350**

Ingredients *for 4 servings*

Rice *12 oz*
Anchovy filets in oil *5*
Garlic *1 clove*
Parsley *1 small bunch*
Extra virgin olive oil *3 tablespoons*
Salt *to taste*

● Chop the anchovies finely. Peel garlic and remove green sprout if necessary. Rinse, dry and finely chop parsley. Cook the rice in abundant salted water until al dente.

● In a large pan, heat the extra virgin olive oil and garlic clove. When the garlic starts to turn brown, remove it immediately. Remove pan from heat and add chopped anchovy filets. Mash them with a wooden spoon until completely dissolved.

● Drain the rice well and transfer to the pan with anchovy oil. Add 2 tablespoons of the rice cooking liquid and mix well. Sprinkle with the chopped parsley and serve.

Risotto with parsley

Difficulty **easy**
Preparation time **40 minutes**
Calories **390**

Ingredients *for 4 servings*

Carnaroli or Arborio rice *12 oz*

Parsley *1 bunch*

Garlic *3 cloves*

Zucchini *1 small*

Vegetable broth *5 cups*

Extra virgin olive oil *4 tablespoons*

Salt *to taste*

● Peel the garlic cloves; remove green sprout if necessary; finely chop. Rinse, dry and dice zucchini. In a saucepan, heat the oil and add the chopped garlic and diced zucchini. Season with a little salt and cook on low heat for about 5 minutes.

● Add rice and cook for a few minutes, mixing well with a wooden spoon. Add broth, 1/2 cup at a time and cook for 15-18 minutes, stirring often. During this time, rinse, dry and finely chop the parsley. Remove the rice from the heat. Add chopped parsley and mix well. Taste for salt. Let stand for 2 minutes and serve in individual bowls.

Lemon risotto

Difficulty **easy**
Preparation time **35 minutes**
Calories **340**

Ingredients *for 4 servings*

Carnaroli or Arborio rice *12 oz*

Lemons *1 large*

Onions *1 small*

Saffron *1/2 teaspoon*

Chives *1 small bunch*

Vegetable broth *5 cups*

Extra virgin olive oil *2 tablespoons*

Pepper *to taste*

● Peel the onion and chop finely. Rinse, dry and chop the chives. Rinse and dry the lemon; grate the peel and press the juice; set aside.

● In a large saucepan, heat the oil and cook the onion until transparent. Add the rice and cook for a few minutes. Add the lemon juice and the boiling broth, 1/2 cup at a time. Cook on medium heat for 15-18 minutes, stirring often.

● After 7 minutes of cooking, add saffron, dissolved in half a cup of broth and mix well. Add chopped chives and grated lemon peel. When rice is al dente, remove from heat and cover for 2 minutes before serving in individual bowls.

Rice crown with vegetables

Difficulty **average**
Preparation time **1 hour**
Calories **580**

Ingredients *for 4 servings*

Arborio rice *7 oz*

Carrots *1*

Celery *1 stalk*

Onions *1*

Grated cheese *3 oz*

Vegetable broth *as needed*

Extra virgin olive oil *3 tablespoons*

To garnish

Zucchini *2*

Artichokes *2*

Asparagus tips *1/2 lb*

Frozen peas *1/2 lb*

Thyme *2 sprigs*

Lemon juice *4 tablespoons*

Vegetable broth *2 cups*

Butter *1 teaspoon*

Extra virgin olive oil *3 tablespoons*

Salt *&* **pepper** *to taste*

● Prepare the garnish. Remove stems and hard leaves from artichokes; with a good knife, turn them and cut in half; remove chokes and cut in thin slices. Place in a large bowl with cold water and lemon juice. Rinse and dry the zucchinis well, then dice. Rinse, dry and slice asparagus tips in half.

● In a pan, heat the extra virgin olive oil. Drain artichokes well and add to pan. Add all prepared vegetables and frozen peas. Mix well and cook for a few minutes. Add vegetable broth, thyme and a pinch of salt. Cook on low heat for about 15 minutes, adding more broth if necessary. Turn off the heat; season with fresh ground pepper and keep warm.

● Rinse and dry the celery. Peel onion and carrot. Finely chop celery, carrot and onion together. In a large saucepan, heat 3 tablespoons of extra virgin olive oil. Cook the vegetables for a few minutes; add rice and mix well. Add vegetable broth, 1/2 cup at a time, mixing often with a wooden spoon.

● When the rice is cooked al dente, mix in the grated cheese and cover saucepan. Set aside for 2 minutes. Transfer the rice to a round tubular mold, previously buttered. Bake in a preheated oven at 400°F for about 10 minutes. Remove from oven and turn the mold onto a large serving dish. Place the prepared vegetables in the center of the crown and serve immediately.

Difficulty **easy**
Preparation time **40 minutes**
Calories **320**

Ingredients *for 4 servings*

Green beans *2 1/4 lbs*

Onions *1*

Tomato sauce *3 tablespoons*

Basil *8 leaves*

Mint *a few leaves*

Garlic *1 clove*

Day-old Italian-style bread *8 slices*

Grated parmigiano *4 tablespoons*

Extra virgin olive oil *4 tablespoons*

Salt *& pepper to taste*

Green bean soup

● Cut the ends of the green beans; rinse and carefully dry; cut in bite-size pieces. Peel garlic and remove green sprout if necessary. Peel onion, rinse, dry and slice thinly. Rinse basil leaves and dry on paper towels.

● In a saucepan, heat the extra virgin olive oil with the garlic clove and chopped onion. Cook until onion is transparent. Add the tomato sauce, the green beans, basil leaves, mint, a pinch of salt and fresh ground pepper. Add 1 cup of hot water. Cover saucepan and cook for about 20 minutes.

● In a preheated oven at 400°F, toast bread slices until golden. Remove from oven and place in 4 individual soup bowls. Pour the prepared soup over the toasted bread and sprinkle with grated parmigiano. Serve immediately.

Cream of beet soup

Difficulty **easy**
Preparation time **1 hour**
Calories **210**

Ingredients *for 4 servings*

Fresh beets *2 large*

Shallots *2 large*

Dry white wine *1/4 cup*

Vegetable broth *4 cups*

White wine vinegar *to taste*

Sour cream *1/2 cup*

Extra virgin olive oil *2 tablespoons*

Salt *&* **pepper** *to taste*

● Peel and finely chop shallots. In a saucepan, heat 2 tablespoons of extra virgin olive oil and cook shallots until transparent. Add white wine and let evaporate for a few minutes on low heat. Add vegetable broth and bring to boil on medium heat. Cook until broth has reduced to 2 1/4 cups.

● During this time, peel the beets, cut in pieces and cook for 20 minutes in half cold water and half white wine vinegar. Drain beets well and mix in a food processor. Add the sour cream to the reduced broth and mix well with a wooden spoon. Cook on very low heat. Add puréed beets and heat until just the first boil. Remove from heat at once. Season with salt and pepper. Transfer to a warm soup tureen and serve immediately.

2

2 *Peel the beets.*

1 *Peel and rinse the scallions and chop finely with a half-moon.*

1

3

4

4 *Add to the broth the sour cream and the puréed beets.*

3 *Dice the beets, cook them and purée in a food processor.*

Leek soup

Difficulty **easy**
Preparation time **30 minutes**
Calories **210**

Ingredients *for 4 servings*

Short pasta *4 oz*
Leeks *3*
Spinach *12 oz*
Basil *1 small bunch*
Parsley *1 small bunch*
Garlic *1 clove*
Extra virgin olive oil *3 tablespoons*
Salt *&* **pepper** *to taste*

● Prepare the leeks. Cut off the roots and dark green leaves. Rinse well and slice. Rinse spinach in cold water three times; drain and dry, then cut in thin strips. Peel the garlic, remove the green sprout if necessary and then rinse.

● In a saucepan, place garlic and sliced leeks; cover with 4 cups of water. Bring to boil. Season with salt and cook for 10 minutes. Add spinach and cook for another 5 minutes. Add pasta and cook until al dente. Rinse parsley and basil; chop and add to soup; mix well. Drizzle with extra virgin olive oil and season with fresh ground pepper. Serve immediately.

Fennel & pasta soup

Difficulty **easy**
Preparation time **40 minutes**
Calories **210**

Ingredients *for 4 servings*

Short pasta *4 oz*
Fennel bulbs *2*
Garlic *1 clove*
Parsley *a few sprigs*
Yogurt *3 tablespoons*
Fennel seeds *a pinch*
Extra virgin olive oil *4 tablespoons*
Salt *&* **black pepper** *to taste*

● Remove the first leaves and the hard stems from the fennel. Keep the feathery leaves aside. Slice the fennel in thin strips and rinse well. In a large saucepan, place fennel, peeled garlic, fennel seeds, chopped parsley, 3 tablespoons of extra virgin olive oil and a pinch of salt. Cover with cold water. Slowly bring to boil. Cover and cook on medium heat for 15 minutes. Remove garlic clove.

● During this time, cook pasta in abundant salted water until al dente. Drain well and add to fennel broth. Remove from heat, stir in yogurt and set aside for a minute. Sprinkle with fresh ground black pepper and chopped feathery fennel leaves. Drizzle with remaining extra virgin olive oil and serve hot.

Bean & pasta soup

Difficulty **easy**
Preparation time **1 hour 10 minutes**
Calories **310**

Ingredients *for 4 servings*

Short pasta *4 oz*

Borlotti beans *6 oz*

Lean pancetta *3 oz, in 1 slice*

Tomato paste *1 teaspoon*

Onions *1*

Celery *1 stalk*

Garlic *1 clove*

Bay leaves *1*

Parsley *a few sprigs*

Extra virgin olive oil *4 tablespoons*

Salt *&* **pepper** *to taste*

● Peel the onion and slice thinly. Peel garlic and chop. Rinse, dry and slice celery stalk. Rinse, dry and chop parsley. Rinse borlotti beans and place in a large saucepan with bay leaf, sliced onion, celery and half the parsley. Cover with cold water. Bring to a boil on low heat and cook for about 1 hour. After 30 minutes of cooking time, stir in the tomato paste, dissolved in 1/4 cups of water. Season with salt and continue cooking.

● During this time, in a pan, heat remaining extra virgin olive oil. Add garlic, a bit of parsley and chopped lean pancetta. Cook for a few minutes. Transfer to bean soup and cook for another 5 minutes. Cook pasta in abundant salted water until al dente. Drain well and add to bean soup. Season with fresh ground pepper and remaining parsley. Serve very hot in warm bowls, accompanied by extra virgin olive oil, to add to the soup.

Pasta & wild herb soup

Difficulty **easy**
Preparation time **1 hour**
Calories **190**

Ingredients *for 4 servings*

Small star pasta *4 oz*

A mix of wild herbs *1/2 lb, (hops, dandelions, etc.)*

Fresh peas *6 oz*

Asparagus *12 oz*

Potatoes *2*

Onions *1 large*

Salt *&* **pepper** *to taste*

● Rinse wild herbs in cold water and drain well. Peel asparagus; remove tough part of stems, rinse and chop. Keep 2 asparagus whole. Peel, rinse and dice potatoes. Peel the onion, rinse and chop.

● Place the prepared vegetables in a saucepan; add the sweet peas and 8 cups of water. Season with salt and bring to a rolling boil. Cover and cook on medium heat for about 45 minutes. Remove from heat. Transfer one cup of liquid to a bowl; pass the rest in a food mill (or processor) and return to saucepan.

● Add reserved broth. Slice reserved asparagus and add to soup. Bring to a boil; add pasta; when al dente, season with pepper and drizzle with extra virgin olive oil. Serve at once.

Radicchio & pasta soup

Difficulty **easy**
Preparation time **20 minutes**
Calories **270**

Ingredients *for 4 servings*

Tagliolini "nests" *4*
Red radicchio *1 head*
Vegetable broth *5 cups*
Grated parmigiano *4 tablespoons*
Extra virgin olive oil *to taste*
Salt *&* **pepper** *to taste*

● Remove any wilted leaves from the radicchio. Rinse under running water and slice in long strips. Bring vegetable broth to boil in a large saucepan. Add radicchio strips and cook on medium heat for 10 minutes.

● Add tagliolini nests and cook until al dente. Taste for salt and add a pinch of fresh ground pepper. Transfer to warm individual serving bowls and sprinkle with grated parmigiano. Serve drizzled with extra virgin olive oil.

Broad bean soup

Difficulty **easy**
Preparation time **1 hour 30 minutes + soaking time**
Calories **410**

Ingredients *for 4 servings*

Spaghetti *6 oz*
Dry broad beans *1/2 lb*
Onions *1 small*
Potatoes *1*
Tomatoes *2, firm and ripe*
Dill *a few sprigs*
Bay leaves *1*
Extra virgin olive oil *4 tablespoons*
Salt *&* **pepper** *to taste*

● Soak the broad beans in a large bowl of cold water for 24 hours. Peel onion and slice thinly. Drain broad beans. Place in a large saucepan with bay leaf and sliced onion; cover with cold water. Bring to boil; cover and cook on low heat for about 1 hour. Season with salt at the end of cooking period.

● During this time, blanch the tomatoes in boiling water; drain, peel and squeeze gently to remove seeds, then chop. Rinse dill, drain and chop in small pieces. Peel potato, rinse and dice. Fifteen minutes before the beans are cooked, add the diced potato.

● Remove one cup of beans and set aside. Pass the rest in a food mill (or processor) and return to saucepan. Stir in the reserved beans and if necessary, a little hot water to have a smooth soup. Bring back to boil, stirring all the time.

● During this time, cook the spaghetti in abundant salted water until al dente. Drain and add to the soup. Add dill and chopped tomatoes; cook, stirring for a few minutes. Remove from heat and drizzle with extra virgin olive oil. Season with fresh ground pepper and serve immediately.

Fennel & baccalà soup

Difficulty **easy**
Preparation time **40 minutes**
Calories **300**

Ingredients *for 4 servings*

Small bow tie pasta *4 oz*

Soaked dried salted cod (baccalà) *12 oz*

Fennel bulbs *2*

Pine nuts *1 tablespoon*

Parsley *1 small bunch*

Garlic *1 clove*

Extra virgin olive oil *4 tablespoons*

Salt *&* **pepper** *to taste*

● Remove stems and exterior leaves from the fennel. Keep feathery leaves. Slice lengthwise and rinse. Rinse and chop parsley. Peel garlic. Place fennel, garlic and chopped parsley in a saucepan. Add 3 tablespoons of extra virgin olive oil and cover with cold water. Slowly bring to a boil. Season with a pinch of salt; cover and continue cooking for about 20 minutes. Remove garlic clove.

● During this time, toast the pine nuts in a non-stick pan and set aside. Remove peel and debone from dried salted cod. Rinse well and cut in bite-size pieces. In a non-stick pan, heat remaining extra virgin olive oil. Add dry salted cod and sauté for 3 minutes. Transfer to the fennel broth and cook for another 5 minutes.

● Cook the pasta in abundant salted water until al dente. Drain well and add to fennel soup. Season with a pinch of fresh ground pepper and stir in the reserved fennel leaves. Serve hot.

Cold cream of asparagus & rice soup

Difficulty **easy**
Preparation time **40 minutes + refrigeration time**
Calories **150**

Ingredients *for 4 servings*

Balilla or baldo rice *3 oz*

Asparagus *1 1/2 lbs*

Chopped onions *1 small*

Lemon juice *2 tablespoons*

1% milk *1 cup*

Nutmeg *a good pinch*

Extra virgin olive oil *2 tablespoons*

Salt *&* **pepper** *to taste*

● Cut off and discard the hard parts of asparagus stems; peel the asparagus. Rinse, cut off tips and set aside. Slice remaining stems. In a saucepan, bring 3 cups of water to boil. Add a good pinch of salt and cook the asparagus tips for 5 minutes; drain well and set aside. Add the sliced stems to the water and simmer.

● During this time, heat the extra virgin olive oil in a large pan. Add rice and sauté for a few minutes. Pour in the water with the asparagus pieces. Season with pepper and nutmeg. Simmer for about 15 minutes. Remove from heat and blend the preparation in a food processor. Add lemon juice and mix again. Pour mixture in a soup tureen.

● Cool completely and place in refrigerator for at least 2 hours. Before serving, stir in the milk. Transfer the cream in individual bowls. Decorate with asparagus tips and serve.

Angel hair pasta with curly endive salad

Difficulty **easy**
Preparation time **40 minutes**
Calories **230**

Ingredients *for 4 servings*

Angel hair pasta *4 oz*
Curly endive salad *1/2 lb*
Carrots *2*
Onions *1*
Celery *1 stalk*
Parsley *1 small bunch*
Extra virgin olive oil *4 tablespoons*
Salt *&* **pepper** *to taste*

● Remove exterior leaves from endive; rinse in cold water; drain and chop. Peel the carrots; rinse and slice in julienne. Peel the onion, rinse and finely slice. Rinse the celery and slice in julienne. Rinse and dry the parsley, then finely chop.

● In a large saucepan, heat 2 tablespoons of extra virgin olive oil. Cook the onion until just transparent. Add the carrots and celery and cook for a minute. Add 5 cups of water. Season with salt. Cover and cook on medium heat, for about 15 minutes. Add the curly endive and cook for 5 minutes.

● During this time, cook the angel hair in abundant salted water until al dente. Drain and add to the endive soup. Drizzle with the remaining extra virgin olive oil. Sprinkle with the parsley and a pinch of fresh ground pepper. Serve very hot.

Velouté of cauliflower & tagliatelle

Difficulty **easy**
Preparation time **40 minutes**
Calories **210**

Ingredients *for 4 servings*

Tagliatelle *4 oz*
Cauliflower *1 1/4 lbs*
Spinach *1/2 lb*
Spring onions *2*
Potatoes *1*
Vegetable broth *6 cups*
Salt *to taste*

● Divide the cauliflower in flowerets and rinse carefully. Cut roots of the spring onions; rinse and chop coarsely. Peel the potato, rinse and dice. Rinse the spinach in cold water three times; drain and cut in strips.

● In a large pot, place the cauliflower, the potato, the spinach, the chopped spring onions and the vegetable broth. Slowly bring to boil and cook on medium heat for 20 minutes, stirring often. Remove a scoop of cauliflower flowerets and set aside. Pass the rest of the soup through a food mill (or processor). Return soup to pot and slowly bring to boil.

● During this time, break the tagliatelle in pieces and cook in abundant salted water until al dente. Drain and add to soup. Add reserved cauliflower flowerets and cook on medium heat for 2 minutes. Transfer the velouté to a small warm tureen and serve immediately.

Difficulty **easy**
Preparation time **40 minutes**
Calories **350**

Ingredients *for 4 servings*

Short pasta *6 oz*

Fresh broad beans *6 oz, shelled and peeled*

Lean pancetta *2 oz*

Chopped onions *2 tablespoons*

Vegetable broth *5 cups*

Extra virgin olive oil *4 tablespoons*

Salt *&* **pepper** *to taste*

Pasta & broad beans in broth

● In a saucepan, heat 2 tablespoons of extra virgin olive oil. Add sliced pancetta and onion. Cook until just transparent. Add broad beans and cook on high heat for a minute. Pour in one cup of vegetable broth. Cover and cook, on medium heat for about 20 minutes.

● Cook the short pasta in abundant salted water until al dente. Drain well and add to the broad beans. Add the remaining vegetable broth. Season with generous fresh ground pepper. Bring to boil and cook for a few minutes. Transfer the soup into a warm soup tureen. Drizzle with extra virgin olive oil and bring to the table.

Difficulty **easy**
Preparation time **1 hour 20 minutes**
+ soaking time
Calories **430**

Ingredients *for 4 servings*

Short pasta *4 oz*

Barley *4 oz*

Dried black-eyed beans *4 oz*

Tomatoes *2, firm and ripe*

Potatoes *2*

Celery *1 stalk*

Onions *1 small*

Sage *1 leaf*

Rosemary *1 sprig*

Bay leaves *1*

Garlic *1 clove*

Pancetta *2 oz*

Extra virgin olive oil *2 tablespoons*

Salt *&* **pepper** *to taste*

Barley & black-eyed bean soup

● Place the barley and black eye beans in separate bowls; cover both with cold water and soak for 12 hours. Peel the potatoes, rinse and dice. Place the black-eyed beans, the potatoes and the bay leaf in a saucepan; add 8 cups of water. Bring to boil and cook for about 70 minutes, on medium heat. In another saucepan, place barley with 4 cups of water; season with salt. Bring to boil and cook for 1 hour on moderate heat.

● During this time, finely dice the pancetta with peeled garlic and small onion. Rinse celery stalk, rosemary and sage; chop together finely. Blanch the tomatoes in boiling water; drain, peel and squeeze gently to remove seeds, then chop coarsely.

● In a pan, heat the extra virgin olive oil. Add pancetta, garlic and onion mixture; cook for a few minutes. Add chopped celery, sage, rosemary and tomatoes. Cook for 5 minutes on medium heat. Transfer the preparation to the black eye beans. Season with salt and cook until beans are tender.

● During this time, cook the short pasta in abundant salted water until al dente, then drain. Drain half the bean mixture and pass through a food mill (or processor); return to saucepan. Drain barley and add to saucepan with beans. Add pasta and season with fresh ground pepper. Stir well and bring soup to boil. Transfer to a warm tureen and serve immediately.

Difficulty **easy**
Preparation time **1 hour 40 minutes**
+ soaking time
Calories **300**

Ingredients *for 4 servings*

Bulgur *9 oz*

Celery *1 stalk*

Onions *1*

Garlic *1 clove*

Bay leaves *1*

Extra virgin olive oil *4 tablespoons*

Salt *&* **pepper** *to taste*

Bulgur & celery soup

● Rinse the bulgur; place in a bowl and cover with cold water; set aside for about 12 hours. Peel garlic clove and onion; rinse. Slice onion thinly and crush garlic clove. Rinse celery stalk and slice thinly.

● Drain bulgur. Rinse and transfer to a saucepan. Cover with cold water. Add sliced onion, crushed garlic, sliced celery and bay leaf.

● Slowly bring to boil. Reduce heat to low and cook for 1 hour 30 minutes. Ten minutes before the end of cooking time, season with salt. When ready to serve, pour into warm bowls and drizzle with fresh extra virgin olive oil. Season with generous fresh ground pepper and serve with thick slices of toasted bread.

Vermicelli & green bean soup

Difficulty **easy**
Preparation time **45 minutes**
Calories **250**

Ingredients *for 4 servings*

Vermicelli *4 oz*

Green beans *1/2 lb*

Tomatoes *2, firm and ripe*

Squash *6 oz*

Onions *1*

Salted anchovies *1*

Dried mushrooms *1/2 oz*

Pine nuts *1 teaspoon*

Extra virgin olive oil *4 tablespoons*

Salt *to taste*

● Soak the dried mushrooms in a bowl of warm water. Rinse the green beans and chop coarsely. Blanch the tomatoes in boiling water; drain, peel and squeeze gently to remove seeds, then finely chop.

● Remove and discard all seeds from squash; rinse and finely chop. Rinse the anchovy under cold running water to remove any salt; debone and chop. Peel the onion, rinse and chop. Finely chop pine nuts and set aside.

● Drain and squeeze the mushrooms. In a saucepan, place chopped squash, mushrooms, half the chopped onions and the tomatoes. Add 4 cups of water and bring to boil. Reduce heat to medium and cook for about 20 minutes.

● During this time, in a pan, heat the extra virgin olive oil. Add the remaining onion and cook until just transparent. Add the anchovy and the chopped pine nuts. Cook for a few minutes, stirring. Cook pasta in abundant salted water until al dente. Drain and transfer to prepared broth. Also add onion-anchovy-pine-nut mixture and cook for a few minutes. Drizzle with extra virgin olive oil and serve.

Quadrucci in fish broth

Difficulty **average**
Preparation time **1 hour**
Calories **180**

Ingredients *for 4 servings*

Quadrucci (square) pasta *4 oz*

Hake *1, about 12 oz*

Tomatoes *1*

Celery *1 stalk*

Carrots *1*

Leeks *2*

Parsley *1 small bunch*

Salt *to taste*

● Rinse the celery stalk. Peel the carrot. Remove green parts from the leek; slice the white part in four, lengthwise. Rinse all vegetables and chop. Place vegetables in a saucepan with 6 cups of water. Bring to boil; season with salt and cook for 30 minutes. After 15 minutes of cooking time, add the parsley, keeping a few leaves aside.

● During this time, scale the fish, emp-ty it and rinse carefully. Cook in the prepared broth for 15 minutes on very low heat without covering the pan. Drain the fish, peel and flake. Skim the broth carefully. Blanch the tomatoes in boiling water; drain, peel and squeeze gently to remove seeds, then chop fine-ly. Add to broth. Cook pasta in the broth for 10 minutes. Gently stir in the flaked fish. Chop the remaining parsley and add to soup. Serve very hot.

Lentil soup

Difficulty **easy**
Preparation time **1 hour**
+ soaking time
Calories **270**

Ingredients *for 4 servings*

Lentils *7 oz*

Tomatoes *6 oz, firm and ripe*

Celery *1 stalk*

Carrots *1*

Onions *1*

Garlic *2 cloves*

Bay leaves *2*

Extra virgin olive oil *4 tablespoons*

Salt *&* **pepper** *to taste*

● Place the lentils in a bowl; cover with cold water and set aside for at least 2 hours. Drain and rinse well. Transfer lentils to a saucepan and cover with water. Add bay leaf and a pinch of salt. Cook for 30 minutes, adding more water, if necessary, so the lentils are always covered.

● During this time, peel and rinse the onion, the carrot and the celery stalk. Peel the garlic and remove the green sprout if necessary. Chop all together very finely. In a pan, heat the extra virgin olive oil and cook the chopped mixture of vegetables until the onion is transparent. Add the chopped tomatoes; season with salt and fresh ground pepper. Cover the pan and cook on medium heat for about 15 minutes.

● When the lentils are cooked, add the tomato-vegetable preparation. Mix well with a wooden spoon and bring the soup to boil for a few minutes. Taste for salt. Season again with generous fresh ground pepper. Transfer the soup to a warm tureen and serve immediately.

Cereal & vegetable soup

Difficulty **easy**
Preparation time **3 hours 15 minutes**
+ soaking time
Calories **380**

Ingredients *for 4 servings*

Dried chickpeas *2 oz*

Dried borlotti beans *2 oz*

Lentils *2 oz*

Bulgur *2 oz*

Barley *2 oz*

Farro *2 oz*

Corn *2 oz*

Carrots *1*

Celery *1 stalk*

Garlic *2 cloves*

Bay leaves *2*

Extra virgin olive oil *4 tablespoons*

Salt *&* **pepper** *to taste*

● Soak the cereals and the beans separately for 12 hours in cold water. Peel the carrot, remove the ends, rinse and dry. Rinse the celery stalk, dry and slice. Peel the garlic, rinse and remove the green sprout if necessary.

● After soaking, drain the cereals and the beans; rinse them under cold running water. In a saucepan, place the chickpeas. In another large saucepan, place the borlotti beans, barley, farro, corn, bulgur and lentils. To each saucepan, add half a carrot, half the celery, one bay leaf and one garlic clove. Cover with water and slowly bring both to boil.

● Cook the chickpeas on medium heat for about 3 hours. Cook the other preparation for about 1 hour or until just tender. At the end of cooking time, season with salt.

● When cooked, add the chickpeas to the other cereal and beans; cook for another 10 to 15 minutes. Drizzle the soup with extra virgin olive oil. Season with fresh ground pepper and serve very hot in the saucepan.

Difficulty **average**
Preparation time **1 hour 30 minutes**
Calories **470**

Ingredients *for 4 servings*

Unbleached flour *7 oz*

Eggs *2*

Fresh beans *1/2 lb*

Tomatoes *10 oz, firm and ripe*

Potatoes *2*

Celery *2 stalks*

Carrots *1*

Onions *1*

Garlic *1 clove*

Basil *a few leaves*

Parsley *1 small bunch*

Grated parmigiano *5 tablespoons*

Extra virgin olive oil *2 tablespoons*

Salt *to taste*

*Andrea's note: 'Maltagliati' means
'badly cut.' This pasta designates any
homemade pasta that does not have a
uniform shape. It also serves for any
quick simple made pasta. This recipe
is more than a soup: it is more like a
pasta-bean stew.*

Maltagliati soup

● In a large mixing bowl, place flour and make a well in the middle; add eggs and a pinch of salt. Work into the flour until you have a smooth dough. Roll out dough into a thin sheet. Cut dough into irregular diamond shape pieces; set aside to dry.

● Peel the garlic; rinse and dry the parsley; chop together. Chop the celery and onion. In a saucepan, heat the extra virgin olive oil. Add the basil leaves, celery and onion; cook on low heat for 3 minutes. Rinse, dry and slice the carrot; add to saucepan. Add beans. Chop tomatoes and add to preparation.

● Add 5 cups of water. Season with salt. Cover saucepan and cook on low heat for 50 minutes. The soup will be quite dense. Add the pieces of pasta and cook until tender. Transfer soup to a warm soup tureen. Serve very hot with much grated parmigiano cheese sprinkled over each plate.

Malfattini & vegetable soup

Difficulty **easy**
Preparation time **45 minutes**
Calories **210**

Ingredients *for 4 servings*

Malfattini pasta *4 oz*
Spinach *6 oz*
Zucchini *2*
Fresh peas *3 oz*
Celery *1 stalk*
Carrots *1*
Onions *1*
Extra virgin olive oil *2 tablespoons*
Salt *to taste*

● Remove the filaments from the celery. Peel the onion and the carrot. Rinse and dry onion, zucchini, celery and carrot; chop finely. Rinse spinach several times in cold water; drain and slice in long thin strips.

● In a large saucepan, place the celery, carrot, zucchini and onion. Add peas and 7 cups of water. Bring to boil. Season with salt and continue cooking on medium heat for about 30 minutes.

● Add spinach strips to the soup. Add malfattini pasta and continue cooking for 3 or 4 minutes. Transfer the soup to a warm tureen and serve drizzled with extra virgin olive oil.

Difficulty **easy**
Preparation time **30 minutes**
Calories **170**

Crab soup

Ingredients *for 4 servings*

Linguini *4 oz*
Crab meat *4 oz*
Zucchini *1/2 lb*
Tomatoes *1, ripe and firm*
Garlic *1 clove*
Marjoram *1 small bunch*
Fish broth *4 cups*

● Rinse and dry the zucchini; discard both ends. Dice zucchini. Peel garlic and rinse. Rinse marjoram and set aside. Blanch the tomatoes in boiling water; drain, peel and squeeze gently to remove seeds.

● Drain crab meat in a colander. Remove all cartilage and shred the crab meat. In a saucepan, bring the fish broth to boil with the garlic clove and half the marjoram. Add the diced zucchini and cook for 5 minutes.

● Break the linguini in small pieces; add to the broth and cook for 5 minutes. Add the remaining marjoram and the shredded crab meat. Cook for 3 minutes. Transfer to a soup tureen and serve the soup very hot.

Pasta soup with marjoram

Difficulty **easy**
Preparation time **20 minutes**
Calories **220**

Ingredients *for 4 servings*

Short pasta *4 oz*
Marjoram *2 sprigs*
Garlic *2 cloves*
Vegetable broth *5 cups*
Eggs *2*
Nutmeg *to taste*
Extra virgin olive oil *2 tablespoons*

● Rinse the marjoram; dry on paper towels. Peel garlic and remove green sprout if necessary; crush lightly. Pour broth in a saucepan; add garlic cloves and bring to boil. Let boil for 2 minutes.

● Add pasta to broth and cook until al dente. During this time, whisk the eggs in a small bowl; add marjoram and a pinch of nutmeg; mix well.

● When the pasta is just cooked, add extra virgin olive oil. Pour the beaten eggs into the soup, whisking rapidly until eggs are dispersed and almost cooked in the hot broth. Remove the saucepan from the heat immediately. Quickly pour the soup in a soup tureen or in warm individual bowls, and serve very hot.

Onion soup

Difficulty **easy**
Preparation time **45 minutes**
Calories **190**

Ingredients *for 4 servings*

Onions *1 lb*
Unbleached flour *1 tablespoon*
Dry white wine *1/2 cup*
Day-old Italian-style bread *4 slices, toasted*
Extra virgin olive oil *4 tablespoons*
Salt *&* **pepper** *to taste*

● Peel the onions; rinse, dry and slice very thinly. In a large saucepan, gently heat the oil. Add onions and sauté for a few minutes, just until onions are transparent. Sprinkle the flour on the onions and cook for a few minutes, stirring. Pour in the white wine and let evaporate on high heat.

● Add 5 cups of water. Bring to boil; lower heat to medium and cook for 30 minutes, mixing often with a wooden spoon. Season with salt and pepper. When the soup is ready, transfer to a warm soup tureen. Serve with large slices of toasted country-style bread.

Nettle soup

Difficulty **easy**
Preparation time **30 minutes**
Calories **260**

Ingredients *for 4 servings*

Nettle tips *1 1/4 lbs*

Tomato sauce *10 oz*

Onions *1*

Lean pancetta *2 oz*

Vegetable broth *4 cups*

Italian-style bread *4 thick slices*

Powdered red hot chili pepper *to taste*

Extra virgin olive oil *3 tablespoons*

Salt *to taste*

● Clean the nettles; rinse and delicately dry. In a saucepan, heat 2 tablespoons of extra virgin olive oil. Add nettles and sauté for a few minutes. Add tomato sauce, season with salt and cook for 15 minutes. Heat the broth and add to the tomato-nettle preparation. Keep on low heat.

● Peel the onion, rinse and dice. Place onion in a pan with remaining extra virgin olive oil and diced pancetta. Cook on medium heat until the onion is golden. Transfer to the nettle soup.

● Toast the slices of bread in a preheated oven at 400°F. Remove from oven and place each slice in a warm bowl. Pour the soup over the bread. Sprinkle with a pinch of red hot chili pepper and serve.

Farro soup

Difficulty **easy**
Preparation time **2 hours**
+ soaking time
Calories **290**

Ingredients *for 4 servings*

Farro *4 oz*

Dried cannellini beans *4 oz*

Potatoes *1*

Carrots *1*

Onions *1*

Celery *1 stalk*

Garlic *1 clove*

Bay leaves *1 leaf*

Parsley *1 small bunch*

Basil *2 leaves*

Sage *2 leaves*

Extra virgin olive oil *4 tablespoons*

Salt *& peppercorns* *to taste*

● Rinse the farro and beans separately. Place farro and beans in separate bowls; cover with cold water and set aside to soak for 24 hours. Drain the beans and place in a saucepan. Peel and rinse the potato, carrot, onion and celery; dice and place in saucepan. Peel the garlic; remove green sprout if necessary; chop finely. Rinse, dry and chop parsley; mix with the garlic; add to saucepan with bay leaf and sage. Pour in 9 cups of water.

● Bring the preparation to boil; lower the heat to medium, cover the saucepan and cook for about 1 hour. Season with salt. Drain the beans and vegetables; pass through a vegetable mill or in a mixer. Return the purée into the saucepan with remaining broth. Add 2 tablespoons of extra virgin olive oil and drained farro. Cook on medium heat for 30 minutes, stirring often with a wooden spoon.

● Remove from the heat. Serve in warm bowls; drizzle with remaining extra virgin olive oil. Sprinkle with a pinch of peppercorns and crumbled basil leaves. Can be served hot or warm.

Difficulty **easy**
Preparation time **40 minutes**
Calories **140**

Ingredients *for 4 servings*

Small artichokes *12*

Onions *11 oz*

Carrots *11 oz*

Marjoram *a few sprigs*

Thyme *1 small bunch*

Lemons *the juice of 1*

Unbleached flour *1 tablespoon*

Vegetable broth *4 cups*

Dry white wine *1/2 cup*

Extra virgin olive oil *2 tablespoons*

Salt *to taste*

Artichoke soup

● Clean the artichokes; remove hard leaves, cut off stems and tips; rinse them and slice lengthwise. Place in a bowl, cover with water and the lemon juice, to prevent them from turning black. Peel the carrot, rinse and slice. Peel and dice the onion.

● In a large saucepan, heat the extra virgin olive oil. Add the carrot, onion and drained artichokes. Sauté for a few minutes. Pour in the white wine and the boiling vegetable broth. Rinse and chop the thyme and marjoram; add to soup. Cover and cook on low heat for 30 minutes.

● If the soup seems too thin, you can add one teaspoon of flour, dissolved in 1/4 cup of cold water. When the soup is ready, transfer to a warm soup tureen or serve directly from the saucepan.

Difficulty **easy**
Preparation time **40 minutes**
Calories **220**

Ingredients *for 4 servings*

Angel hair pasta *4 oz*

Tomatoes *14 oz, firm and ripe*

Onions *1*

Carrots *1*

Parsley *a few sprigs*

Celery *1 stalk*

Bay leaves *1*

Sage *1 leaf*

Basil *1 small bunch*

Extra virgin olive oil *4 tablespoons*

Salt *to taste*

Angel hair pasta in tomato sauce

● Blanch the tomatoes in boiling water; drain, peel and squeeze gently to remove seeds, then chop coarsely. Rinse and dry the basil and parsley. Peel carrot, onion and celery; rinse; dice carrot and celery; slice half the onion and chop the other half.

● In a saucepan, pour 5 cups of water. Add carrot, celery, parsley, bay leaf, sage, sliced onion and half the basil. Bring to boil. Season with a good pinch of salt; cook for 15 to 20 minutes.

● During this time, in a large saucepan, heat 2 tablespoons of extra virgin olive oil; add chopped onion and cook until transparent. Add chopped tomatoes and cook for 3 minutes. Add the prepared vegetables and their broth. Cook for another 10 minutes. Pass the preparation through a vegetable mill and return mixture to saucepan.

● Cook the angel hair pasta in abundant salted water until al dente; drain and add to tomato mixture. Cook for a minute; add the remaining basil leaves. Serve the mixture drizzled with remaining extra virgin olive oil.

Difficulty **easy**
Preparation time **1 hour 45 minutes + soaking time**
Calories **260**

Ingredients *for 4 servings*

Ditalini pasta *2 oz*

Bulgur *5 oz*

Savoy cabbage *1/2 lb*

Potatoes *1/2 lb*

Vegetable broth *7 cups*

Salt *to taste*

Bulgur soup with ditalini pasta

● Soak the bulgur in cold water for 12 hours. Drain well; rinse under running water and drain again. Rinse the cabbage leaves in cold water; slice in long strips. Dip cabbage strips in salted boiling water for 1 minute, then drain. Peel potatoes, rinse and dice.

● In a saucepan, place the bulgur, the cabbage and the diced potatoes. Add the boiling vegetable broth. Cover and cook on medium heat for an hour and 30 minutes, stirring often. Add more boiling water if necessary. Add pasta to broth and cook until al dente. Transfer the preparation in a soup tureen and serve immediately.

Shell pasta with lentils & broccoli

Difficulty **easy**
Preparation time **1 hour 15 minutes + soaking time**
Calories **360**

Ingredients *for 4 servings*

Small shell pasta *5 oz*

Lentils *4 oz*

Cauliflower *7 oz*

Broccoli *7 oz*

Tomatoes *3, firm and ripe*

Carrots *1*

Potatoes *1*

Leeks *1*

Bay leaves *1*

Extra virgin olive oil *4 tablespoons*

Salt *&* **pepper** *to taste*

● Place the lentils in a large bowl, cover with cold water and set aside for 12 hours. Peel the carrot, rinse and slice. Peel, rinse and dice the potato. Remove the outside leaves from the leek; cut off the hard green parts; rinse carefully and slice.

● Blanch the tomatoes in boiling water; drain, peel and squeeze gently to remove seeds, then chop coarsely. Drain lentils and transfer to a saucepan. Cover with abundant cold water, add bay leaf and slowly bring to boil on low heat. Cook for about 35 minutes.

● To the lentils, add diced potato, sliced carrot and leek. Season with salt and cook for another 10 minutes. During this time, prepare the cauliflower and broccoli. Cut and discard stems; detach flowerets and rinse in abundant cold water. Add both to the lentil preparation. Add the chopped tomatoes and cook for 5 minutes.

● During this time, cook the pasta in abundant salted water until al dente. Drain and add to lentils. Set aside for a minute. Drizzle with extra virgin olive oil; sprinkle with fresh ground pepper. Can be served hot or warm.

Rice & parsley soup

Difficulty **easy**
Preparation time **20 minutes**
Calories **270**

Ingredients *for 4 servings*

Arborio rice *5 oz*

Parsley *1 small bunch*

Vegetable broth *5 cups*

Grated grana cheese *4 tablespoons*

Extra virgin olive oil *2 tablespoons*

● Rinse the parsley, dry delicately on a kitchen towel and chop finely. Pour broth in a saucepan and bring to boil. Add rice and cook for 15 minutes, stirring from time to time, with a wooden spoon.

● Remove the saucepan from the heat. Add the extra virgin olive oil and chopped parsley. Mix well. Pour the prepared soup in warm individual bowls. Drizzle each with one tablespoon of grated grana; mix and serve immediately.

Fish

Difficulty **average**
Preparation time **40 minutes**
Calories **265**

Ingredients *for 4 servings*

Hake *4, about 1/2 lb each*

Parsley *1 small bunch*

Sage *2 leaves*

Rosemary *1 sprig*

Basil *10 leaves*

Chervil *a few leaves*

Garlic *2 cloves*

Breadcrumbs *1 tablespoon*

Dry white wine *1/4 cup*

Extra virgin olive oil *5 tablespoons*

Salt *&* **pepper** *to taste*

Hake with herbs

● Clean the fish and rinse well under running water; dry on paper towels. Season the interior with salt and pepper. Place the fish on a large cookie sheet brushed with 2 tablespoons of extra virgin olive oil. Preheat the oven to 400°F.

● Rinse and dry parsley, sage, basil, rosemary and chervil. Peel garlic and chop with all prepared herbs. Mix in a bowl with breadcrumbs. Use this mixture to cover the fish. Season with salt and pepper. Drizzle with 3 tablespoons of extra virgin olive oil and white wine.

● Transfer the cookie sheet to the preheated oven and cook for 20 minutes. Baste often with the cooking juices. Remove from oven and serve immediately.

Apulia-style sole

Difficulty **easy**
Preparation time **30 minutes**
Calories **285**

Ingredients *for 4 servings*

Sole filets *8*
Tomatoes *11 oz, firm and ripe*
Onions *1*
Pitted black olives *2 oz*
Parsley *1 small bunch*
Garlic *1 clove*
Dry white wine *1/4 cup*
Extra virgin olive oil *4 tablespoons*
Salt *&* **pepper** *to taste*

● Rinse the sole filets delicately. Pat dry with paper towels. Transfer fish to a plate and season with salt and pepper on both sides. Set aside.

● Blanch the tomatoes in boiling water; drain, peel and squeeze gently to remove seeds, then chop coarsely. Rinse and dry parsley, then chop finely. Peel garlic and onion. Chop garlic and slice onion thinly.

● Brush a cookie sheet with 2 tablespoons of extra virgin olive oil. Place the sliced onion on the prepared sheet. Top with chopped tomatoes, garlic, olives and half the chopped parsley. Season with salt and pepper. Cover with filets. Drizzle with remaining extra virgin olive oil, white wine and sprinkle with the remaining parsley.

● Plate the preparation in a preheated oven at 400°F. Cook for 8 to 10 minutes, basting often with its own juices. Remove from the oven; transfer to a warm serving plate. Should be eaten very hot.

Anchovies with fennel

Difficulty **easy**
Preparation time **30 minutes**
Calories **200**

Ingredients *for 4 servings*

Anchovies *12, large*
Fennel seeds *1 tablespoon*
Garlic *3 cloves*
Dry white wine *1/4 cup*
Extra virgin olive oil *4 tablespoons*
Salt *&* **pepper** *to taste*

● Rinse the anchovies. Cut them open and remove insides; rinse well. Remove heads and debone; flatten lightly.

● Peel and chop the garlic. In a large pan, heat the oil and the chopped garlic; cook until the garlic starts to brown. Place the open anchovies in the pan, in one layer. Season with salt and generous pepper. Sprinkle with fennel seeds.

● Cook the anchovies for 3 to 4 minutes. Add the white wine and cook for less than a minute. With a spatula, delicately turn the anchovies. Cook for a few more minutes. Transfer the anchovies and their juices to a serving dish. To be eaten immediately.

Grouper with tomato

Difficulty **average**
Preparation time **40 minutes**
Calories **285**

Ingredients *for 4 servings*

Grouper *1, about 1 1/2 lbs*
Tomatoes *14 oz, firm and ripe*
Yellow bell pepper *1*
Basil *1 small bunch*
Shallots *2*
Extra virgin olive oil *6 tablespoons*
Salt *&* **pepper** *to taste*

● Clean the fish; remove head and insides; scale the fish; cut in small slices, rinse and dry. Season with a pinch of salt and pepper. Blanch the tomatoes in boiling water; drain, peel and squeeze gently to remove seeds, then chop coarsely. Peel the shallots; rinse, dry and finely chop. Rinse, dry and tear the basil in small pieces. Rinse bell pepper; cut open and remove all white parts and seeds; dry well and dice.

● In a non-stick pan, heat 2 tablespoons of extra virgin olive oil. Add the fish slices and brown both sides. Drain the fish and set aside. In a saucepan, heat 3 tablespoons of extra virgin olive oil; add chopped shallots and cook until just transparent. Add the tomatoes, half the basil leaves and a pinch of salt and pepper. Cook this sauce for 10 minutes on moderate heat, stirring often.

● During this time, heat the remaining extra virgin olive oil in the non-stick pan. Add bell pepper and sauté a few minutes. Season with salt and drain. Add the peppers to the tomato sauce. Transfer the fish slices to the sauce and cook for 10 minutes on low heat. Sprinkle with remaining basil leaves. Delicately transfer the preparation on a warm serving dish and serve very hot.

Turbot with peppers & onions

Difficulty **easy**
Preparation time **40 minutes**
Calories **235**

Ingredients *for 4 servings*

Turbot filets *4, about 1 lb each*
Bell peppers *2*
Onions *1*
Garlic *1 clove*
Thyme *a few sprigs*
Extra virgin olive oil *5 tablespoons*
Salt *&* **pepper** *to taste*

● Clean the peppers. Cut open and remove white parts and seeds. Rinse, dry and slice thinly. Peel onion; slice thinly. Peel garlic and gently crush.

● In a large saucepan, heat 3 tablespoons of extra virgin olive oil. Add onion and garlic. Cook until onion is just transparent. Add peppers and cook for 15 minutes, on medium heat, stirring often. Remove garlic and transfer mixture to a baking dish. Place the fish filets over the peppers; brush them with the remaining extra virgin olive oil and season with a pinch of salt and pepper.

● Place the dish in a preheated oven at 400°F. Bake for about 8 minutes. Remove from oven. Divide the filets lengthwise. Serve the fish in warm individual plates with a few spoonful of peppers.

Swordfish with basil

Difficulty **average**
Preparation time **45 minutes**
Calories **240**

Ingredients *for 4 servings*

Swordfish *4 slices*
Tomatoes *1/2 lb, firm and ripe*
Basil *2 bunches*
Parsley *1 small bunch*
Pitted green olives *2 oz*
Breadcrumbs *1 tablespoon*
Extra virgin olive oil *4 tablespoons*
Salt *&* **pepper** *to taste*

● Brush 2 large sheets of wax paper with a little water. Place slices of fish between paper and beat lightly to flatten the fish. Trim a little around the fish, so all pieces are of equal size. Keep the trimmings aside. Rinse the basil and parsley; dry well and chop together. Place in a bowl and mix with chopped fish trimmings and chopped olives. Add breadcrumbs and enough oil to make a thin paste. Blanch the tomatoes in boiling water; drain, peel and squeeze gently to remove seeds, then chop coarsely.

● Place dollops of the mixture over the slices of fish and roll them up. Close the rolls with toothpicks. In a non-stick pan, heat 3 tablespoons of extra virgin olive oil. Add fish rolls and cook on high heat; turn the rolls often until golden on all sides. Season with salt and fresh ground pepper.

● Remove fish rolls from pan. Add chopped tomatoes to the pan and cook for 5 to 6 minutes. Return the fish rolls to the pan and cook for just a few minutes. Serve immediately.

Sea bream with olives

Difficulty **average**
Preparation time **45 minutes**
Calories **235**

Ingredients *for 4 servings*

Sea bream *2, about 1 lb each*
Cherry tomatoes *1/2 lb*
Black olives *2 tablespoons*
Onions *1 small*
Garlic *1 clove*
Parsley *1 small bunch*
Dry white wine *3 tablespoons*
Extra virgin olive oil *5 tablespoons*
Salt *&* **pepper** *to taste*

● Scale the fish, clean the insides and rinse carefully. Peel the onion and slice. Peel the garlic and chop finely. Rinse the parsley, dry and chop. Pit the olives and slice. Rinse the cherry tomatoes; dry and cut in half.

● In a baking dish, pour 2 tablespoons of extra virgin olive oil. Add sliced onion, tomatoes, chopped garlic, sliced olives and half the chopped parsley. Season the fish, inside and outside, with salt and fresh ground pepper. Place in the oven dish. Pour the white wine in the dish. Drizzle the fish with the remaining extra virgin olive oil. Sprinkle with the remaining chopped parsley.

● Place the dish in a preheated oven at 400°F. Bake for about 20 minutes, basting often with the cooking juices. Transfer the fish to a warm serving plate; place the juices and vegetables around the fish. Serve very hot.

Cuttlefish with spinach

Difficulty **average**
Preparation time **1 hour 30 minutes**
Calories **215**

Ingredients *for 4 servings*

Cuttlefish *2 lbs*
Spinach *1 lb*
Dried mushrooms *2 oz*
Milk *1/4 cup*
Onions *1*
Celery *1 stalk*
Parsley *1 small bunch*
Basil *1 bunch*
Extra virgin olive oil *2 tablespoons*
Salt *&* **pepper** *to taste*

● Clean the cuttlefish carefully. Rinse well under running water and cut in thin slices. Rinse the spinach several times in cold water, to remove any dirt. Soak the dried mushrooms in 1/4 cup of milk and 1/4 cup of warm water.

● Peel the onion, rinse and dry the celery. Rinse and dry parsley and basil; chop all together finely. In a large pan, heat extra virgin olive oil. Add chopped mixture and cook on low heat for a few minutes. Drain mushrooms well; chop coarsely and add to the pan. Season with salt and fresh ground pepper. Cook for 15 minutes.

● Add the spinach and cook for 2 minutes. Add sliced cuttlefish and 1/2 cup of hot water. Cover the pan and cook on low heat until cuttlefish is very tender. Transfer to a large serving dish.

Dressed scampi

Difficulty **average**
Preparation time **45 minutes**
Calories **285**

Ingredients *for 4 servings*

Scampi *12*
Zucchini *5*
Prosciutto *6 slices*
Pine nuts *2 tablespoons*
Extra virgin olive oil *4 tablespoons*
Salt *&* **pepper** *to taste*

● Clean the shrimp. Remove heads and peel tails. Cut the prosciutto in half, lengthwise to make 12 long strips. Roll the shrimp in the prosciutto slices. Cut 3 zucchini in half and then in half lengthwise, to get 12 pieces. With a small spoon, empty the zucchini; keep the pulp aside.

● Plunge the zucchini baskets in abundant salted water for 30 seconds, drain and plunge in ice water. Drain again and dry on paper towels. Chop the zucchini pulp. Dice the remaining 2 zucchinis. In a pan, heat 2 tablespoons of extra virgin olive oil. Add the zucchini pulp and the diced zucchini. Sauté for a few minutes. Add pine nuts and season with salt and pepper.

● Fill zucchini baskets with zucchini preparation. Bake in a preheated oven at 400°F for 5 minutes. Brush a cookie sheet with 2 tablespoons of extra virgin olive oil; place the shrimp on the sheet and bake for 5 minutes. Place the shrimp and zucchini baskets on a plate and serve immediately.

Grilled razor shells

Difficulty **easy**
Preparation time **30 minutes + resting time**
Calories **180**

Ingredients *for 4 servings*

Razor shells *2 lbs*
Parsley *1 small bunch*
Garlic *1 clove*
Lemon juice *2 tablespoons*
Extra virgin olive oil *4 tablespoons*
Salt *&* **pepper** *to taste*

● Rinse the razor shells carefully and place in a large bowl, covered with cold water for a few hours. Peel the garlic clove and slice thinly. Rinse, dry and finely chop the parsley.

● In a saucepan, mix the lemon juice with a pinch of salt and fresh ground pepper. Add garlic and a good pinch of chopped parsley. Slowly whisk in the extra virgin olive oil; mix until sauce thickens lightly.

● Drain the razor shells. Place in a large pan, cover and cook on high heat, shaking the pan occasionally, until shells open. Remove from heat. Separate shells from the clams; remove and discard the dark part. Place in a bowl. Discard any shells that did not open.

● Pour the prepared sauce over the razor shells, mix well and set aside for 20 to 30 minutes, stirring a few times. Place a griddle on the fire; when the grill is very hot, place the drained razor shells on the grill, a few at a time. Cook for a few minutes. Serve very hot, sprinkled with chopped parsley.

Trout & chickpea salad

Difficulty **easy**
Preparation time **3 hours 20 minutes + soaking time**
Calories **335**

Ingredients *for 4 servings*

Smoked trout filets *1/2 lb*
Chickpeas *6 oz*
Mixed salad *5 oz (boston lettuce, radicchio)*
Bay leaves *1*
Garlic *1 clove*
Celery *1 stalk*
Lemon juice *3 tablespoons*
Extra virgin olive oil *6 tablespoons*
Salt *&* **pepper** *to taste*

● Place the chickpeas in a bowl; cover with cold water and set aside for 12 hours. Drain, rinse and place in a saucepan. Cover with cold water; add a bay leaf and the unpeeled garlic clove. Slowly bring to boil and cook for about 3 hours. Season with salt, mix and drain well. Set aside to cool.

● During this time, rinse the salad mix; dry on a kitchen towel; tear in small pieces. Peel the celery stalk, rinse and slice. Cut the trout filets in strips. In a bowl, mix the lemon juice with a pinch of salt and fresh ground pepper. Whisk in the extra virgin olive oil slowly until ingredients are well mixed.

● In a large bowl, place the salad mix, the trout filets, the celery and drizzle with half the prepared sauce. Mix well. Pour the remaining sauce on the chickpeas; mix well. Transfer the chickpeas to the salad. Mix delicately and serve.

Mixed grilled fish

Difficulty **average**
Preparation time **40 minutes + marinating time**
Calories **390**

Ingredients *for 4 servings*

Scampi *4 large*
Sea bream *2, about 1 lb each*
Salmon steaks *4*
Garlic *1 clove*
Basil *1 bunch*
Parsley *1 bunch*
Sage *a few leaves*
Rosemary *1 sprig*
Extra virgin olive oil *4 tablespoons*
Salt *& pepper to taste*

● Rinse the parsley; dry and chop finely. Rinse the basil leaves, sage and rosemary; dry and chop coarsely. Scale the sea bream; clean and rinse well. Season the interior of the fish with salt and pepper; fill with a few teaspoons of the herb mixture.

● Clean the scampi. Rinse well and cut lengthwise. Remove and discard the black vein. Rinse the salmon steaks and pat dry with paper towels. Place the sea breams, salmon steaks and scampi in a deep dish.

● In a bowl, mix the extra virgin olive oil with a generous pinch of chopped herbs, sliced garlic and a good pinch of salt and pepper. Whisk the ingredients until well blended. Pour over the fish. Set aside to marinate for 30 minutes, turning the fish a few times.

● Remove the fish from the marinade and drain. Place fish on a hot grill (or on a hot cast-iron pan). Cook the sea breams for about 7 minutes on each side, and the scampi and salmon steaks for 4 to 5 minutes on each side. Sprinkle the mixed grilled fish with remaining chopped herbs. Serve with a fresh mixed salad.

Buridda of mixed fish with tomato

Difficulty **easy**
Preparation time **40 minutes**
Calories **285**

Ingredients *for 4 servings*

Sliced fish *2 lbs (shark, bream)*
Tomatoes *12 oz, firm and ripe*
Lemons *1*
Bay leaves *1*
Garlic *1 clove*
Dry white wine *1/4 cup*
White wine vinegar *1/4 cup*
Extra virgin olive oil *4 tablespoons*
Salt *& pepper to taste*

● Rinse the slices of fish under running water; dry on paper towels. In a large saucepan, pour 4 cups of water; add the white wine vinegar, dry white wine, bay leaf and lemon, sliced thinly. Bring to boil and keep boiling for 15 minutes. Season with salt. Add slices of fish; lower the heat and cook for 5 minutes. Drain the fish and place on a serving dish.

● During this time, blanch the tomatoes in boiling water; drain, peel and squeeze gently to remove seeds, then chop coarsely. Peel the garlic and chop. In a pan, heat the extra virgin olive oil. Add the garlic and cook for a minute. Add chopped tomatoes, a pinch of salt and fresh ground pepper. Cook for about 20 minutes, on medium heat, mixing often.

● Pour the tomato sauce on the fish and set aside to marinate for a few minutes. Serve the buridda warm or cold, garnished with lemon slices or parsley.

Difficulty **easy**
Preparation time **2 hours**
Calories **385**

Ingredients *for 4 servings*

Soaked dried cod *1 1/2 lbs*

Yellow bell peppers *3*

Tomato sauce *14 oz*

Quince *2*

Celery *1 stalk*

Onions *1*

Garlic *1 clove*

Parsley *1 bunch*

Raisins *2 tablespoons*

Chili powder *a pinch*

Extra virgin olive oil *6 tablespoons*

Salt *to taste*

Dried cod with peppers

● Peel the onion. Rinse and dry the celery and parsley. Chop onion, celery and parsley together. Place the mixture in a saucepan with the olive oil, the peeled garlic, the chili powder and the flaked dried cod. Set aside for 10 minutes. Add the tomato sauce. Cover the saucepan and cook, on low heat, for one and a half hour, adding a few spoons of hot water if the preparation becomes too dense.

● During this time, soak the raisins in warm water; when soft, drain and squeeze. Rinse the yellow peppers; dry, slice and remove the white parts and the seeds; slice thinly. Peel the quince and slice thinly. Thirty minutes before the end of cooking time, add the sliced peppers, the raisins and the quince. Season with salt. Mix well. Cover and keep cooking. Serve very hot.

Mixed seafood au gratin

Difficulty **easy**
Preparation time **30 minutes**
+ resting time
Calories **310**

Ingredients *for 4 servings*

Seafood *3 lbs (razor shells, mussels, clams, little necks)*
Chopped parsley *3 tablespoons*
Garlic *3 cloves*
Breadcrumbs *3 tablespoons*
Dry white wine *1/2 cup*
Extra virgin olive oil *7 tablespoons*
Salt *& pepper to taste*

● Rinse the razor shells, clams and little necks. Soak them separately, in cold water for a few hours. Brush the mussels and rinse carefully. Drain the razor shells, clams and little necks. In a large pan, place the little necks and mussels; add one tablespoon of extra virgin olive oil, one garlic clove, a pinch of chopped parsley and 1/4 cup of white wine. Cover the pan and cook on high heat, until the shells are open, shaking the pan often.

● In another pan, place the clams and razor shells. Add one tablespoon of olive oil, one garlic clove, a pinch of chopped parsley and the remaining white wine. Cover the pan and cook on high heat. Until the shells are open, shaking the pan often. Remove both pans from the fire. Remove all mollusks from their shells and place in a large bowl. Discard any unopened shells.

● Chop the remaining garlic clove finely. In a small bowl, mix the breadcrumbs, the remaining parsley, the chopped garlic, a pinch of salt and pepper. Slowly add 4 tablespoons of extra virgin olive oil, to obtain a thick paste.

● Brush a large cookie sheet with olive oil. Place the mollusks on the sheet. Cover with the parsley and the breadcrumbs paste. Place in a preheated oven at 400°F for 4 to 5 minutes, until top is slightly brown. Remove from oven and serve immediately.

Scorpion fish with leeks

Difficulty **easy**
Preparation time **30 minutes**
Calories **360**

Ingredients *for 4 servings*

Scorpion fish filets *4, about 6 oz each*
Leeks *4*
Vegetable broth *1/4 cup*
Extra virgin olive oil *6 tablespoons*
Salt *& pepper to taste*

Andrea's note: This recipe can be done with any other fish filets (sole, catfish, etc.)

● Rinse the scorpion fish filets; dry on paper towels and set aside. Prepare the leeks: Remove the roots and the exterior dark green leaves; rinse well and slice. In a pan, heat 4 tablespoons of olive oil. Add the sliced leeks and cook until soften lightly. Season with salt and a pinch of pepper.

● Pour the vegetable broth over the leeks; cover and cook on medium heat, for about 10 minutes, stirring often with a wooden spoon.

● During this time, heat the remaining olive oil in a non-stick pan. Add the fish filets and cook, on high heat, for 2 to 3 minutes, until lightly brown. Season with a pinch of salt and pepper. Cover the pan and continue cooking, on low heat, for 5 minutes. Serve those fish filets very hot, covered with the cooked leeks.

Scampi & zucchini with pesto

Difficulty **easy**
Preparation time **30 minutes**
Calories **220**

Ingredients *for 4 servings*

Scampi *16*
Zucchini *3/4 lb*
Tomatoes *1/2 lb, firm and ripe*
Basil *2 bunches*
Parsley *a few sprigs*
Pine nuts *1 teaspoon*
Garlic *1 clove*
Dry white wine *1/4 cup*
Extra virgin olive oil *6 tablespoons*
Salt *&* **pepper** *to taste*

● Blanch the tomatoes in boiling water; drain, peel and squeeze gently to remove all seeds, then chop coarsely. Place in a strainer and set aside. Rinse the basil and the parsley; drain and dry. Peel the garlic clove.

● In a food mixer, place the garlic and the pine nuts; mix rapidly. Add the basil and the parsley, a good pinch of salt and mix again. Slowly add, through the feeder tube, 5 tablespoons of extra virgin olive oil, while mixing. Pour the preparation in a bowl. Slowly whisk in the remaining extra virgin olive oil; mix until the sauce is light. Add the chopped tomato pesto.

● Peel the scampi; remove the black vein; rinse well and dry delicately on paper towels. Rinse, dry and dice the zucchini. Steam them for 4 to 5 minutes, drain and mix with the prepared pesto sauce.

● In a non-stick pan, heat the extra virgin olive oil. Add the scampi and sauté for 2 minutes, on high heat. Season with salt and a pinch of pepper. Add the white wine and let evaporate. Place the zucchini and the pesto sauce on a serving dish. Place the scampi on top and serve immediately.

Swordfish with lemon & herbs

Difficulty **easy**
Preparation time **20 minutes**
Calories **400**

Ingredients *for 4 servings*

Swordfish *4 slices, about 6 oz each*
Lemons *the juice of 1*
Garlic *1 clove (optional)*
Fresh oregano *1/2 teaspoon*
Parsley *1 small bunch*
Extra virgin olive oil *1/4 cup*
Salt *&* **pepper** *to taste*

● Rinse the swordfish slices carefully, then pat dry. Heat a cast-iron pan until very hot. Brush lightly with a few drops of olive oil. Add the fish and cook for 2-3 minutes. Turn delicately with a spatula and cook the other side for 3 minutes.

● During this time, rinse, dry and finely chop the parsley. Peel the garlic and crush it lightly. In a small saucepan, whisk the extra virgin olive oil while adding, very slowly, 7 tablespoons of hot water, lemon juice, a pinch of salt and fresh ground pepper. Add the crushed garlic, the parsley and the oregano.

● Heat the prepared sauce in a double boiler for about 5 minutes, whisking until well blended. Transfer the few slices to a serving dish, drizzle with the prepared sauce and serve immediately.

Monkfish with vegetables

Difficulty **easy**
Preparation time **30 minutes**
Calories **220**

Ingredients *for 4 servings*

Monkfish *1 1/2 lbs*

Tomatoes *1/4 lb, firm and ripe*

Mushrooms *1/2 lb*

Pitted black olives *2 teaspoons*

Shallots *1*

Garlic *1 clove*

Parsley *1 small bunch*

Basil *1 small bunch*

Dry white wine *1/4 cup*

Extra virgin olive oil *3 tablespoons*

Salt *&* **pepper** *to taste*

● Carefully rinse the monkfish; dry and cut in 4 slices. Season lightly with salt and pepper. Clean the mushrooms; remove the stems and rinse quickly under running water; dry with a kitchen towel; slice in four.

● Blanch the tomatoes in boiling water; drain, peel, press gently to remove all seeds, then slice in strips. Peel the garlic and the shallot; chop finely. Brush a non-stick pan with one teaspoon of extra virgin olive oil. Add the monkfish slices and brown on both sides. Drain and keep warm between two plates.

● In the same pan, add the remaining olive oil; add the chopped garlic and shallot and cook until just softened. Add the fish slices and the white wine; let evaporate on high heat. Add the strips of tomatoes and the mushrooms. Cover the pan and cook, on medium heat, for 5 minutes. Add the black olives and cook for one more minute.

● Drain the slices of fish and transfer to a warm serving dish. On light heat, let the sauce reduce lightly. Rinse, dry and chop the parsley and the basil; stir into the sauce. Pour the prepared sauce over the fish and serve immediately.

1 Brush a non-stick pan with oil and brown the fish on both sides.

2 Add the white wine and let evaporate.

3 Add the tomato strips and the sliced mushrooms.

Difficulty **elaborate**
Preparation time **30 minutes**
Calories **240**

Braided fish with tomatoes

Ingredients *for 4 servings*

Whitefish filets *4, about 6 oz each*

Tomatoes *2, firm and ripe*

Thyme *a few sprigs*

Extra virgin olive oil *4 tablespoons*

Salt *&* **pepper** *to taste*

● Slice each fish filets in 3 pieces, lengthwise, leaving them attached at one end. Delicately braid the pieces together. Blanch the tomatoes in boiling water; drain, peel and squeeze gently to remove all seeds, then dice.

● Brush a baking dish with extra virgin olive oil. Place the fish braids in the dish. Drizzle the fish with 2 tablespoons of extra virgin olive oil. Season with salt and pepper. Transfer to a preheated oven at 400°F and bake for 8 to 10 minutes.

● During this time, heat the remaining oil in a pan. Add the thyme and the tomatoes. Heat through and season with salt and pepper. Transfer the tomatoes to a warm serving dish. Remove the fish from the oven and, with a spatula, carefully place the braids over the tomatoes. Serve immediately, accompanied by steamed vegetables of your choice.

1 *Separate each filet into 3 equally long pieces and form a braid.*

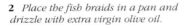
2 *Place the fish braids in a pan and drizzle with extra virgin olive oil.*

3 *In another pan, heat the oil, the thyme and the diced tomatoes.*

Baccalà with vegetables

Difficulty **easy**
Preparation time **45 minutes**
Calories **370**

Ingredients *for 4 servings*

Dried salted cod (baccalà) *1 1/2 lbs*
Tomatoes *10 oz, firm and ripe*
Onions *1*
Shallots *1*
Black olives *2 teaspoons*
Parsley *1 bunch*
Basil *1 bunch*
Capers *2 teaspoons*
Anchovies *2*
Breadcrumbs *2 tablespoons*
Extra virgin olive oil *6 tablespoons*
Salt *&* **pepper** *to taste*

● Blanch the tomatoes in boiling water; drain, peel and squeeze gently to remove all seeds, then chop coarsely. Rinse the anchovies under running water to desalt; remove the bone and slice into filets. Peel the onion and the shallot; rinse, dry and chop finely. Rinse the parsley and basil; dry and chop.

● In a pan, heat 3 tablespoons of olive oil. Add the chopped onion and shallot; cook until transparent. Remove from heat. Add the anchovy filets and mash to dissolve. Return to heat. Add the tomatoes, a handful of chopped basil and parsley, a pinch of salt and pepper. Cook for 10 minutes, on medium heat, stirring often with a wooden spoon.

● During this time, debone the dried salted cod; rinse well; dry and cut in small pieces; pass in the breadcrumbs. In a non-stick pan, heat the remaining extra virgin olive oil. Add the breaded fish and sauté until golden on all sides. Drain and place in the prepared sauce. Add the capers and the olives; cook for another 15 to 20 minutes (add a few tablespoons of hot water, if the preparation becomes too dense). Serve very hot, sprinkled with the remaining parsley and basil.

Sea bream with radicchio

Difficulty **easy**
Preparation time **30 minutes**
Calories **300**

Ingredients *for 4 servings*

Sea bream filets *1 1/3 lbs*
Red radicchio *1/4 lb*
Shallots *1*
Chives *1 bunch*
Unbleached flour *2 tablespoons*
Dry white wine *1/4 cup*
Extra virgin olive oil *5 tablespoons*
Salt *&* **pepper** *to taste*

● Clean the radicchio; remove the external leaves and rinse several times in cold water; drain well and cut lengthwise in thick strips. Peel the shallot; rinse, dry and chop finely. Rinse the chives; dry delicately on a paper towel and chop.

● In a pan, heat 3 tablespoons of extra virgin olive oil. Add the chopped shallot and cook until transparent. Add the radicchio strips and sauté for 2 to 3 minutes, mixing often. Season with salt and fresh ground pepper. Add the white wine and let evaporate on high heat.

● During this time, rinse the sea bream filets carefully, pat dry and roll in the flour. In a non-stick pan, heat the remaining olive oil. Add the fish filets and cook for 8 minutes, turning it delicately so both sides are brown. Season with salt and fresh ground pepper. Transfer the radicchio preparation to a serving dish. Place the sea bream filets on top of the radicchio. Sprinkle with the chopped chives and serve immediately.

Difficulty **easy**
Preparation time **40 minutes**
Calories **350**

Ingredients *for 4 servings*

Whitefish filets *1 1/4 lbs*
Asparagus *1 lb*
Potatoes *10 oz*
Tomatoes *1/2 lb, firm and ripe*
Sugar *a pinch*
Balsamic vinegar *1 teaspoon*
Extra virgin olive oil *5 tablespoons*
Salt *&* **pepper** *to taste*

Whitefish with potatoes & asparagus

● Peel the potatoes, dice, rinse and steam them. Blanch the tomatoes in boiling water; drain, peel and squeeze gently to remove all seeds, then chop coarsely. Rinse the asparagus; remove the hard ends of stems; peel and cut in small pieces, then steam.

● Heat 2 tablespoons of olive oil in a non-stick pan. Cook the white fish filets for 2 to 3 minutes, on high heat, until nicely brown on both sides. Season with a pinch of salt and fresh ground pepper. During this time, in another non-stick pan, heat 1 tablespoon of extra virgin olive oil. Add the tomatoes; season with salt and pepper and a pinch of sugar. Cook until just heated through.

● In a shallow saucepan, heat the remaining extra virgin olive oil. Add the potatoes and the asparagus; sauté briefly. Season with salt and fresh ground pepper. Pour in the balsamic vinegar and sauté for another 2 minutes. Place the white fish filets on a warm serving dish with the potatoes and asparagus. Cover with the warmed up tomatoes and serve immediately.

Difficulty **average**
Preparation time **45 minutes**
Calories **200**

Ingredients *for 4 servings*

Squid *1 1/2 lbs*
Cherry tomatoes *8-10*
Zucchini *2*
Lemon juice *2 tablespoons*
Extra virgin olive oil *5 tablespoons*
Salt *&* **pepper** *to taste*

Grilled squid on skewers

● Empty and clean the squid; remove the external skin, rinse and cut in pieces. Detach the tentacles and set aside. In a bowl, mix the lemon juice with a pinch of salt and pepper. Slowly whisk in the extra virgin olive oil. Mix until the sauce is well blended.

● Place the squid pieces and tentacles in a bowl. Pour in the prepared sauce and mix well. Set aside to marinate for about 15 minutes. During this time, rinse and dry the cherry tomatoes. Rinse the zucchini; dry on paper towels and cut in thick slices.

● On each skewer, place a piece of squid, a slice of zucchini, a squid tentacle and a cherry tomato. Continue with as many skewers as you need. Preheat a large cast-iron grill or pan. Place the prepared skewers on the grill and cook for about 5 minutes, turning them often to brown all sides equally. Transfer to a warm serving dish and serve very hot.

Difficulty **average**
Preparation time **50 minutes**
Calories **315**

Ingredients *for 4 servings*

Fresh anchovies *12*

Spinach *1 1/2 lbs*

Garlic *2 cloves*

Parsley *1 bunch*

Breadcrumbs *2 tablespoons*

Extra virgin olive oil *6 tablespoons*

Salt *&* **pepper** *to taste*

Anchovies filled with spinach

● Rinse the anchovies; butterfly them, leaving the back part attached; remove heads and bones. Peel the garlic cloves; remove the green sprout if necessary and chop finely. Rinse, dry and finely chop the parsley. Pick and rinse the spinach several times in cold water. Blanch the tomatoes in very little salted water for 4 minutes; drain, squeeze to remove excess water and chop coarsely.

● In a pan, heat 4 tablespoons of extra virgin olive oil. Add half of the chopped garlic and cook for 20 seconds. Add the spinach, a pinch of parsley, a pinch of salt and pepper. Cook on low heat, for a few minutes, stirring often. Remove from heat.

● Place 1 teaspoon of the prepared spinach on each anchovy. Roll them up and place very closely on a greased oven dish. Place the remaining spinach on top of the rolled anchovies. Mix the breadcrumbs, the remaining garlic and the parsley; sprinkle over the spinach. Drizzle with the remaining extra virgin olive oil. Bake in a preheated oven at 400°F for 20 minutes. Remove from oven and serve immediately.

Difficulty **easy**
Preparation time **45 minutes**
Calories **300**

Ingredients *for 4 servings*

Curly endive salad *3 lbs*

Fresh anchovies *1 1/2 lbs*

Garlic *2 cloves*

Extra virgin olive oil *5 tablespoons*

Salt *&* **pepper** *to taste*

Timbale of anchovies & curly endive salad

● Rinse the curly endive and tear in small pieces. Clean the anchovies; remove heads and debone. Peel and chop the garlic cloves. Brush a baking dish with extra virgin olive oil. Place a layer of endive on the bottom. Cover with a layer of anchovies. Sprinkle with some chopped garlic. Season with salt and fresh ground pepper. Drizzle with half the extra virgin olive oil.

● Alternate the layers until all ingredients are used. Over the last layer, sprinkle a little salt, pepper and chopped garlic. Drizzle with the remaining extra virgin olive oil. Bake in a preheated oven at 400°F for 20 minutes or until the endive is tender. Serve in the oven dish, as soon as it comes out of the oven.

Sicilian-style tuna

Difficulty **average**
Preparation time **40 minutes + marinating time**
Calories **465**

Ingredients *for 4 servings*

Fresh tuna *1 1/2 lbs in one slice*

Anchovies *4*

Garlic *1 clove*

Lemons *the juice of 1*

Rosemary *1 sprig*

Allspice *a pinch*

Breadcrumbs *3 tablespoons*

Dry white wine *about 3 cups*

Extra virgin olive oil *6 tablespoons*

Salt *&* **pepper** *to taste*

● Rinse the tuna fish and dry well. Place in a bowl and sprinkle with a pinch of allspice, a pinch of salt and generous fresh ground pepper. Pour enough white wine over the tuna to cover it (about 3 cups) and set aside for 2 hours. During this time, rinse and dry the rosemary and chop it finely with the garlic clove. Remove the tuna from its marinade and, with a sharp kitchen knife, make incisions all over the fish. Fill these holes with the rosemary and garlic preparation.

● Brush the tuna with 2 tablespoons of extra virgin olive oil. Heat a cast-iron pan and add the tuna fish. Brown the tuna on every side. Remove the piece of tuna fish and cover with the breadcrumbs. Return to the pan, on medium heat, until thoroughly cooked, basting often with the marinade.

● Rinse and debone the anchovies. When the tuna is almost cooked, place the anchovies and the remaining extra virgin olive oil in a saucepan on medium heat and cook, stirring all the time, until the anchovies are completely dissolved. Place the tuna fish on a warm serving dish. Filter the lemon juice and whisk it into the anchovy oil sauce. Pour that prepared sauce over the tuna and serve at once.

1 *Brown the tuna on all sides, remove and cover with breadcrumbs.*

2 *Just before serving, pour the anchovy sauce over the tuna.*

Difficulty **average**
Preparation time **40 minutes**
Calories **245**

Ingredients *for 4 servings*

Fresh sardines *1 1/4 lbs*

Tomatoes *1 1/4 lbs*

Oregano *3-4 teaspoons*

Extra virgin olive oil *6 tablespoons*

Salt *to taste*

Sardines with tomato

● Blanch the tomatoes in boiling water; drain, peel and squeeze gently to remove all seeds, then chop coarsely. Clean the sardines; remove the heads and debone; rinse and dry well on paper towel.

● Take two sardines at a time; place them face to face. Brush a baking dish with 2 tablespoons of extra virgin olive oil. Place the doubled sardines close to each other. Pour the chopped tomatoes all over. Season with salt and a generous pinch of oregano. Drizzle with extra virgin olive oil and bake in a preheated oven at 400°F for about 20 minutes. Remove from oven. Bring the oven dish to the table. Can be served hot or cool.

Little neck clams with onions

Difficulty **easy**
Preparation time **30 minutes + resting time**
Calories **105**

Ingredients *for 4 servings*

Little neck clams *1 lb*
Onions *2*
Dry sherry *1/4 cup*
Sweep paprika *1 teaspoon*
Extra virgin olive oil *3 tablespoons*
Salt *to taste*

● Place the clams in cold water for a few hours; change the water a few times. Drain the clams and place in a large pan with 1 tablespoon of extra virgin olive oil. Cover the pan and cook on high heat, shaking the pan often, until clams are opened. Remove any unopened clams. Filter the cooking liquid.

● Peel the onions; rinse, dry and cut in thick slices. In a pan, heat the remaining extra virgin olive oil. Add onions and cook for a few minutes. Season with salt and paprika. Add the sherry and cook for another 10 minutes. Add the filtered cooking juices and cook for 10 minutes.

● Add clams, with or without shells (as you wish). Cook for a few minutes and transfer to a warm serving plate. Serve hot with thick slices of toasted country bread rubbed with a garlic clove.

Mullet with tomato sauce

Difficulty **average**
Preparation time **45 minutes + resting time**
Calories **230**

Ingredients *for 4 servings*

Mullet *2, about 1 lb each*
Tomato sauce *1 cup*
White wine vinegar *1/2 cup*
Capers *2 teaspoons*
Garlic *2 cloves*
Mint *a few leaves*
Extra virgin olive oil *2 tablespoon*
Salt *& pepper to taste*

● Scale the fish; clean and rinse well. In an oval saucepan, bring to boil 4 cups of water, the white wine vinegar and a good pinch of salt. Add the mullets and cook on low heat, until the fish eyes are white and protruding. Drain and delicately filet the fish, deboning it carefully. Place the filets on a serving dish and keep warm.

● Place the tomato sauce in a saucepan and cook on medium heat until it thickens. Add the extra virgin olive oil, chopped garlic, mint leaves and capers. Season with salt and fresh ground pepper. Cook for another 5 minutes, on low heat, stirring with a wooden spoon. Remove from heat and pour over the fish. Wait a few minutes before serving.

Swordfish with clams

Difficulty **average**
Preparation time **40 minutes**
+ resting time
Calories **205**

Ingredients *for 4 servings*

Swordfish *1 lb, in 1 slice*
Little neck clams *1 1/4 lbs*
Parsley *1 bunch*
Scallions *2*
Garlic *1 clove*
Dry white wine *1/2 cup*
Extra virgin olive oil *3 tablespoons*
Salt *&* **pepper** *to taste*

● Rinse the clams; cover with water and set aside for a few hours. Peel the garlic and crush it lightly. Rinse parsley, dry and finely chop. Drain the clams; place in a large pan with 1 tablespoon of extra virgin olive oil, garlic, 1/4 cup of white wine and a pinch of parsley. On high heat, let the clams open, shaking the pan often.

● Remove from heat. Detach the clams from shells and place in a bowl. Discard any unopened clams. Filter the cooking juices and set aside. During this time, clean the scallions; remove the roots and external leaves; rinse and finely chop.

● Brush a baking dish with extra virgin olive oil. Add chopped scallions. Rinse swordfish; pat dry and season with salt and pepper. Place fish over scallions. Add remaining white wine. Cover with aluminum paper and bake in a preheated oven at 400°F for 10 to 12 minutes.

● Drain the swordfish and keep warm. Pour the cooking juices into a saucepan. Cook until reduced by half. Add clam cooking juices and clams. Mix in the remaining chopped parsley. Cut the swordfish in 1/4-inch slices; transfer to a serving dish. Cover with prepared clam sauce and serve immediately.

Difficulty **average**
Preparation time **40 minutes**
Calories **180**

Snapper with herbs

Ingredients *for 4 servings*

Snapper *2, about 1 lb each*
Herbs *2 tablespoons (basil, parsley, chives, chervil)*
Tomatoes *1/2 lb, firm and ripe*
Onions *1 small*
Garlic *1 clove*
Dry white wine *1/4 cup*
Extra virgin olive oil *3 tablespoons*
Salt *&* **pepper** *to taste*

● Clean the snapper well; rinse and dry on paper towels; filet them. Blanch the tomatoes in boiling water; drain, peel and squeeze gently to remove seeds, then chop coarsely. Peel the onion and finely chop. Peel the garlic clove; remove the green sprout if necessary; crush lightly. Rinse, dry and chop herbs.

● Pour the extra virgin olive oil in a

baking dish. Add chopped tomatoes, garlic, onion and white wine. Place filets on top; season with salt and pepper. Bake in a preheated oven at 400°F for about 15 minutes. Remove from the oven. Sprinkle the fish filets with chopped herbs. Return to the oven and bake for another 3 minutes. Transfer the filets on serving plates with cooking tomato sauce.

Mussels with lemon

Difficulty **easy**
Preparation time **30 minutes**
Calories **75**

Ingredients *for 4 servings*

Large fresh mussels *2 lbs*
Organic lemons *3*
Romaine lettuce *1 heart*
Pepper *to taste*

● Brush the mussels carefully under running water and rinse. Place in a large bowl; cover with water and the juice of one lemon; set aside for 15 minutes. Drain and open the mussels with a sharp short knife placed between the shells. Detach the mussels, leaving them on the half shells.

● Rinse the Romaine leaves and delicately dry on paper towels. Place around a serving dish. Transfer the mussels on the half shell on the dish. Rinse, dry and quarter the lemons; place on the dish among the mussels. Serve the mussels sprinkled with lemon and seasoned with fresh ground pepper.

Crab with lemon

Difficulty **average**
Preparation time **40 minutes**
Calories **185**

Ingredients *for 4 servings*

Crabs *4*
Parsley *1 bunch*
Lemons *the juice of 1*
Extra virgin olive oil *4 tablespoons*
Salt *to taste*

● Brush the crabs carefully and rinse well. Cook in abundant salted water until al dente for 10 to 12 minutes. Drain the crabs and cool. Open the crabs, separating the lower and upper parts of the shell.

● Remove the crab meat, including that of the legs; chop and set aside in a bowl. Keep the shells. Rinse the parsley, dry and finely chop.

● In a bowl, mix the lemon juice with a pinch of salt. Slowly whisk in the extra virgin olive oil, until the sauce thickens lightly. Mix in the chopped parsley. Pour the prepared sauce over the crab meat and toss well. Transfer to the shells and serve.

Sturgeon with spring onions

Difficulty **easy**
Preparation time **30 minutes**
Calories **230**

Ingredients *for 4 servings*

Sturgeon slices *8, about 4 oz each*
Spring onions *1 lb*
Tomatoes *10 oz, firm and ripe*
Fresh thyme *a few sprigs*
Dry white wine *1/4 cup*
Extra virgin olive oil *4 tablespoons*
Salt *&* **white pepper** *to taste*

● Rinse the sturgeon slices carefully; dry well and season with salt and fresh ground white pepper. Refrigerate for 1 hour. Blanch the tomatoes in boiling water; drain, peel and squeeze gently to remove all seeds, then dice and season with salt and pepper. Transfer to a bowl and refrigerate.

● Clean the onions; remove the ends, roots and outside leaves; rinse, dry and slice. In a pan, heat 2 tablespoons of extra virgin olive oil. Add the sliced onions and thyme. Season with salt and pepper and cook on medium heat, for about 5 minutes, stirring often. Place the sturgeon slices on the cooked onions; add the white wine. Cover the pan and cook on high heat, for 5 minutes, shaking from time to time.

● Add the diced tomatoes and cook on high heat, for 3 minutes. Add the remaining extra virgin olive oil and cook, uncovered, for another 5 minutes. Transfer the preparation to a warm serving dish and serve immediately.

Sea bream carpaccio with olives

Difficulty **average**
Preparation time **30 minutes**
+ resting time
Calories **205**

Ingredients *for 4 servings*

Sea bream *1, about 1 lb*
Pitted black olives *2 tablespoons*
Lemons *the juice of 1/2*
Watercress *1 bunch*
Mustard seeds *1 teaspoon*
Extra virgin olive oil *5 tablespoons*
Salt *&* **white pepper** *to taste*

● Clean and scale the fish; filet, rinse, dry well and place in the coldest part of the refrigerator for a few hours. With a very sharp knife, cut the fish diagonally in very thin slices, removing the skin at the same time. Transfer the slices onto a serving plate. Cover with plastic wrap and refrigerate.

● During this time, rinse, dry and cut the watercress in thin strips. Slice the black olives. In a bowl, mix a pinch of salt and fresh and fresh ground pepper with the lemon juice. Slowly whisk in the extra virgin olive oil, mixing until well blended. Add the mustard seeds and mix well.

● Remove the sliced fish from the refrigerator; cover with watercress and the sliced olives. Drizzle with the prepared sauce and set aside in the refrigerator for at least 15 minutes before serving.

Swordfish & mussels

Difficulty **easy**
Preparation time **40 minutes**
Calories **295**

Ingredients *for 4 servings*

Swordfish slices *1 1/4 lbs*

Mussels *1 lb*

Chopped tomatoes *1/2 lb*

Garlic *1 clove*

Extra virgin olive oil *4 tablespoons*

Salt *& pepper to taste*

● Peel the garlic and chop finely. Peel the swordfish. Brush the mussels under running water; remove any black beard and rinse well.

● In a pan, heat the extra virgin olive oil. Add the garlic and cook for one minute. Add the swordfish slices and cook a few minutes on each side. Remove from pan and keep warm between two plates.

● In the same pan, add the chopped tomatoes and cook for a few minutes.

Add the mussels and cook on medium heat, until they open. Remove the mussels from the sauce. Stir the sauce well to blend in the liquid from the mussels. Add the swordfish to the sauce and cook for 5 minutes. During this time, remove the mussels from their shells, keeping 8 whole ones for decoration.

● When the fish is ready, transfer to a serving dish. Pour the sauce over the fish and the shelled mussels. Decorate with the whole mussels and serve.

Hake with anchovies

Difficulty **average**
Preparation time **40 minutes**
Calories **220**

Ingredients *for 4 servings*

Hake *2, about 1 lb each*

Anchovies *2*

Cherry tomatoes *6*

Garlic *1 clove*

Dry white wine *4 tablespoons*

Extra virgin olive oil *3 tablespoons*

Salt *& pepper to taste*

● Clean the hake; remove the head and debone. Rinse well and dry on paper towels. Rinse the cherry tomatoes and cut in quarter. Peel the garlic. Rinse the anchovies under running water; debone and chop with the garlic.

● Brush a baking dish with 1 tablespoon of extra virgin olive oil. Place the hake in the dish, with the quartered tomatoes, white wine, a pinch of salt and fresh ground pepper. Bake in a preheated oven at 400°F for about 20

minutes, turning the fish after 10 minutes.

● During this time, heat the remaining extra virgin olive oil in a pan. Add the garlic and anchovies mixture. Cook on very low heat, until just heated through, stirring with a wooden spoon. Cook no more than a minute so that the garlic does not brown. Remove the fish from the oven. Pour the prepared garlic and anchovy sauce over the fish and serve immediately.

Mediterranean salad

Difficulty **average**
Preparation time **40 minutes**
Calories **395**

Ingredients *for 4 servings*

Small calamari *1 lb*
Mozzarella *1/2 lb*
Pitted black olives *3 oz*
Large tomatoes *4*
Boston lettuce *2*
White wine vinegar *2 tablespoons*
Extra virgin olive oil *4 tablespoons*
Salt *&* **pepper** *to taste*

● Clean the calamari; remove eyes, beak and cartilage. Rinse well and cook for a few minutes in boiling water. Drain and when cool enough to handle, slice in rings. Rinse, dry and slice tomatoes very thinly. Rinse lettuce; remove any bad outside leaves, dry and cut in thin strips. Dice mozzarella.

● In a bowl, mix the extra virgin olive oil, white wine vinegar, a pinch of salt and fresh ground pepper. Whisk until all ingredients are well blended. In a large salad bowl, place tomatoes, lettuce, olives, diced mozzarella and calamari. Drizzle with prepared sauce and toss well.

Turbot with tomato & kiwi

Difficulty **easy**
Preparation time **40 minutes**
Calories **200**

Ingredients *for 4 servings*

Turbot filets *1 lb*
Kiwis *2*
Tomatoes *1/2 lb, firm and ripe*
Basil *1 small bunch*
Onions *1*
Carrots *1*
Celery *1 stalk*
Parsley *1 branch*
Thyme *2 sprigs*
Bay leaves *1*
Lemon juice *2 tablespoons*
Dry white wine *1/2 cup*
Extra virgin olive oil *5 tablespoons*
Salt *&* **peppercorns** *to taste*

● Rinse and peel the celery. Peel the carrot. Peel the onion. Rinse and slice the vegetables. Place in a saucepan with 4 cups of water, white wine vinegar, parsley, thyme, bay leaf and a pinch of peppercorns.

● Bring to boil; season with salt and cook for 15 minutes. Rinse the fish filets and dry on paper towels. Gently drop the filets in the broth and cook for 3 minutes, on medium heat. Rinse the tomatoes; dry and slice in quarters. Peel the kiwis and slice. Rinse,

dry and cut the basil in strips.

● In a bowl, mix the lemon juice with a pinch of salt and fresh ground pepper. Slowly whisk in the extra virgin olive oil. Mix until all ingredients are well blended.

● In a bowl, place the quartered tomatoes, kiwis and half the prepared sauce. Toss well. Add the turbot and remaining sauce; toss well. Sprinkle with basil and serve.

Hake with fennel & onions

Difficulty **average**
Preparation time **40 minutes**
Calories **260**

Ingredients *for 4 servings*

Hake *8*
Spring onions *2*
Fennel seeds *1 teaspoon*
Dry white wine *4 tablespoons*
Fish or vegetable broth *1/4 cup*
Extra virgin olive oil *4 tablespoons*
Pink peppercorns in brine *1 teaspoon*
Salt *&* **pepper** *to taste*

● In a saucepan, bring the fish or vegetable broth to boil. Clean the hakes; rinse well and dry on paper towels. Rinse the onions; remove roots and hard green leaves; slice thinly.

● In a pan, heat the extra virgin olive oil. Add the sliced onions and cook until transparent. Add the pink peppercorns and fennel seeds; mix well. Add fish and white wine. Cook for a few minutes. Add the boiling broth; cover and cook on low heat, for 15 minutes, turning the fish after 7 or 8 minutes.

● With a spatula, remove the fish from the pan and keep warm between two plates. Reduce the sauce on high heat for a few minutes. During this time, peel and filet the fish. Transfer to a warm serving dish. Season with salt and pour the reduced sauce over the filets. Serve immediately.

Baccalà with walnut sauce

Difficulty **average**
Preparation time **30 minutes**
Calories **555**

Ingredients *for 4 servings*

Dried salted cod (baccalà) *1 1/2 lbs*
Walnuts *1/2 lb*
Parsley *1 bunch*
Extra virgin olive oil *5 tablespoons*
Salt *to taste*

● Skin and debone the fish; rinse and dry well on paper towels. Cut in small pieces. Place the fish in a large saucepan; cover with cold water; bring to boil and cook on medium heat, for 10 minutes. Drain the fish and transfer to a serving dish.

● Rinse parsley and dry on paper towels. In the bowl of a mixer, place parsley, walnuts and a good pinch of salt. Mix well, slowly adding the extra virgin olive oil, until all ingredients are well blended and the sauce is thick. Pour the sauce over the fish and serve immediately.

Roasted lobster

Difficulty **average**
Preparation time **40 minutes**
Calories **180**

Ingredients *for 4 servings*

Lobster *1, pre-cooked*
Parsley *1 bunch*
Lemons *the juice of 1*
Breadcrumbs *2 tablespoons*
Extra virgin olive oil *4 tablespoons*
Salt *to taste*

● Pick, rinse and dry the parsley; chop finely. Rinse the lobster; with kitchen scissors, cut the back shell horizontally. Remove the lobster meat carefully, in one whole piece.

● Brush an oven-dish with little extra virgin olive oil. Add the lobster meat and drizzle with the extra virgin olive oil and the filtered lemon juice. Sprinkle with the chopped parsley and the breadcrumbs. Season with a pinch of salt.

● Bake in a preheated oven at 400°F for about 20 minutes. Remove from oven and slice lobster meat. Arrange on a warm serving dish and serve immediately.

Marinated sea bass

Difficulty **easy**
Preparation time **40 minutes**
+ marinating time
Calories **205**

Ingredients *for 4 servings*

Sea bass *2, about 1 lb each*
Onions *1*
Dill *a few sprigs*
Parsley *1 bunch*
Dry white wine *4 tablespoons*
Extra virgin olive oil *4 tablespoons*
Salt *to taste*

● Clean the sea bass; scale, rinse and dry on paper towels. Peel the onion; rinse and slice thinly. Pick, rinse and dry the parsley carefully; chop very finely.

● In a bowl, mix the extra virgin olive oil, white wine, sliced onion, dill and parsley. Place the fish in a deep dish; pour the marinade over the fish and turn it several times to cover well. Place half the dill and some of the slices of onion into the fish. Set aside to marinate for at least 2 hours.

● When the fish is ready, place 2 tablespoons of the marinade in a baking dish, large enough to hold the fish. Add the fish; season with a pinch of salt. Bake in a preheated oven at 400°F for 20 minutes. Turn the fish at least twice during cooking time. Remove from oven. Filet the fish carefully and serve drizzled with the cooking liquid.

Difficulty **easy**
Preparation time **45 minutes**
Calories **330**

Trastevere-style baccalà

Ingredients *for 4 servings*

Dried salted cod (baccalà) *1 1/2 lbs*

Onions *14 oz, sliced*

Garlic *1 clove*

Salted anchovies *1*

Capers *1 tablespoon*

Raisins *1 tablespoon*

Pine nuts *1 tablespoon*

Chopped parsley *1 tablespoon*

Lemon juice *2 tablespoons*

Unbleached flour *a few tablespoons*

Extra virgin olive oil *5 tablespoons*

Salt *&* **pepper** *to taste*

● Soak the raisins in warm water; set aside. Rinse the anchovy under running water to remove salt; debone. Rinse the capers. Peel the garlic clove and crush lightly. Peel the onion and slice.

● Drain the cod; dry and cut in pieces. Roll the pieces of fish in flour; shake to remove excess flour. In a non-stick pan, heat 2 tablespoons of extra virgin olive oil. Add the pieces of fish and sauté until golden and roasted all over. Drain and keep warm.

● In the same pan, add the remaining extra virgin olive oil and garlic clove; cook for a minute. Remove the garlic; add the onion. Season with salt and pepper. Cover and cook until onion is tender. Add the capers, raisins and pine nuts. Mix well. Remove from heat. Add the anchovy and mash until dissolved.

● Place preparation in a deep oven dish. Cover with the pieces of fish and the cooking juices. Bake in a preheated oven at 425°F for a few minutes. Remove from oven. Sprinkle with the chopped parsley. Drizzle with lemon juice and serve.

Sardine rolls, Palermo-style

Difficulty **average**
Preparation time **1 hour**
Calories **440**

Ingredients *for 4 servings*

Sardines *1 3/4 lbs*
Breadcrumbs *4 oz*
Raisins *2 oz*
Pine nuts *2 oz*
Anchovies *6*
Bay leaves *3*
Parsley *1 oz*
Lemons *the juice of 1*
Sugar *1 tablespoon*
Extra virgin olive oil *3 tablespoons*
Salt *&* **pepper** *to taste*

● Soak the raisins in warm water for 20 minutes. Clean the sardines; scale, remove the heads, debone and butterfly; rinse carefully and dry well on paper towels.

● In a large pan, heat 2 tablespoons of extra virgin olive oil. Add breadcrumbs, keeping 1 tablespoon aside. Mix well and cook on medium heat, until lightly toasted. Remove from heat.

● Pick, rinse, dry and chop parsley. Rinse the anchovies under running water; dry on paper towels; debone and chop coarsely. Chop pine nuts. Drain raisins; squeeze to remove excess water and place in a bowl with anchovies, parsley, pine nuts and toasted breadcrumbs. Season with salt and pepper; mix thoroughly.

● Place the open sardines on a work surface, skin down. Place a little breadcrumb mixture on each sardine; roll the sardines onto themselves and close with a toothpick. Brush a baking dish with extra virgin olive oil. Place filled sardines in dish with bay leaves in between. Sprinkle with remaining breadcrumbs. In a small saucepan, dissolve the sugar in the lemon juice. Pour over the sardines. Bake in a preheated oven at 375°F for 30 minutes. Remove from oven and serve at once.

Escabeche anchovies

Difficulty **average**
Preparation time **30 minutes**
+ marinating time
Calories **255**

Ingredients *for 4 servings*

Anchovies *1 1/4 lbs*
Garlic *2 cloves*
Red hot chili peppers *1*
Mint *a few leaves*
Unbleached flour *2 tablespoons*
White wine vinegar *1/2 cup*
Extra virgin olive oil *to taste*
Salt *to taste*

● Clean the anchovies; remove heads and debone; rinse well and dry carefully, then roll in flour. In a large pan or in a deep-fryer, heat a large quantity of extra virgin olive oil until very hot, but not smoking. Drop the anchovies in the oil, a few at a time. Cook until golden on all sides. Remove anchovies with a slotted spoon. Drain on paper towels and season with salt.

● Peel the garlic and remove green sprout if necessary. Chop chili pepper. In a saucepan, heat white wine vinegar, chili pepper, garlic cloves and mint leaves. Bring to boil. Place anchovies in a ceramic bowl. Pour the prepared marinade on the fish. Cover the bowl and set aside for 24 hours before serving.

Squid & artichokes

Difficulty **average**
Preparation time **1 hour**
Calories **235**

Ingredients *for 4 servings*

Squid *2 1/4 lbs*
Artichokes *8*
Anchovies *2*
Garlic *2 cloves*
Dry white wine *1/2 cup*
Lemons *the juice of 1*
Parsley *1 small bunch*
Extra virgin olive oil *5 tablespoons*
Salt *&* **pepper** *to taste*

● Clean the squid; remove bone, eyes and beak; keep aside with ink pouches; peel and rinse carefully, then slice in thin strips or rings. Remove stems and thick outer leaves from artichokes; cut off tips of leaves; remove chokes; cut in thin slices and soak in cold water, mixed with lemon juice.

● Peel the garlic. Rinse and dry parsley. Rinse, debone and dry anchovies. Chop with garlic and half the parsley. In a saucepan, preferably of copper, mix the extra virgin olive oil and anchovy mixture. When the garlic is just turning gold, add squid and mix well. Sauté for 4 to 5 minutes. Season with salt and pepper. Add dry white wine and let evaporate on high heat. Add 1/4 cup of water; cover saucepan and cook on low heat for about 10 minutes.

● Drain the artichokes, dry and add to squid preparation. Add ink pouches and 1/4 cup of hot water; mix well. Continue cooking for 10 minutes, stirring often. Sprinkle with remaining chopped parsley. Taste for salt. Serve directly in its cooking dish.

Octopus with sun-dried tomatoes

Difficulty **easy**
Preparation time **2 hours
+ marinating time**
Calories **235**

Ingredients *for 4 servings*

Octopus *2 1/4 lbs*
Sun-dried tomatoes *4 oz*
Capers in vinegar *2 oz*
Garlic *1 clove*
Parsley *2 tablespoons*
White wine vinegar *1 cup*
Extra virgin olive oil *4 tablespoons*
Salt *to taste*

● Clean and rinse the octopus carefully; beat it lightly to tenderize it. Place octopus in a saucepan; cover with cold water and a little salt. Bring to boil and cook until tender. Remove from heat and let the octopus cool in its cooking liquid. Drain and cut in large pieces.

● Soak the tomatoes in warm water for 10 minutes. Drain, dry and chop finely with half the capers, garlic and parsley. In a pan, heat the extra virgin olive oil. Add tomato mixture and cook for 3 to 4 minutes, on low heat. Add white wine vinegar and mix well. Season with salt and remove from heat. Place the octopus on a serving dish; pour the prepared tomato sauce over it with remaining capers. Toss gently and set aside for at least 2 hours before serving, tossing often.

Difficulty **average**
Preparation time **2 hours**
Calories **255**

Ingredients *for 4 servings*

Octopus *2 1/4 lbs*

Tomatoes *2, firm and ripe*

Parsley *1 small bunch*

Garlic *2 cloves*

Lemons *the juice of 1*

Red hot chili peppers *1*

Extra virgin olive oil *5 tablespoons*

Salt *to taste*

Octopus in its broth

● Clean the octopus; remove eyes, beak and skin. Beat it for a few minutes to tenderize it; rinse carefully. Peel the garlic. Blanch the tomatoes in boiling water; drain, peel and squeeze gently to remove seeds, then chop coarsely. Rinse, dry and finely chop the parsley.

● In a large saucepan, place the octopus, 2 tablespoons of extra virgin olive oil, 2 garlic cloves, chopped tomatoes, parsley, chili pepper and a pinch of salt.

● Cover the saucepan with aluminum foil firmly closed around edges. Place its cover over the saucepan. Cook the octopus for 2 hours on very lot heat, without ever lifting the cover, to not lose any steam.

● In a bowl, mix the remaining oil with the lemon juice and a pinch of salt. Whisk until sauce is well blended. Remove the octopus from the heat and let cool in the saucepan before removing it. Cut in pieces, transfer to a serving dish and serve with prepared lemon sauce.

Razor shells with tomatoes

Difficulty **easy**
Preparation time **40 minutes**
+ resting time
Calories **185**

Ingredients *for 4 servings*

Razor shells *1 3/4 lbs*

Tomatoes *2*

Parsley *1 small bunch*

Garlic *1 clove*

Pine nuts *1 tablespoon*

Chili powder *1 pinch*

Extra virgin olive oil *4 tablespoons*

Salt *to taste*

● Rinse the razor shells several times; soak in cold water and set aside for 30 minutes. Rinse and dry parsley. Peel garlic and finely chop with parsley. Blanch the tomatoes in boiling water; drain, peel and squeeze gently to remove seeds, then chop finely.

● In a large pan, heat the extra virgin olive oil. Add half the garlic-parsley mixture and cook for a few minutes. Add chopped tomatoes and cook for 15 minutes, stirring often with a wooden spoon.

● Drain the razor shells and add to the hot tomatoes. Mix well and cover the pan. Cook until all shells are open. Add the hot chili powder, pine nuts and remaining garlic-parsley mixture. Mix well, then cook for another 2 minutes. Serve immediately, bringing the pan to the table.

Clams alla napoletana

Difficulty **easy**
Preparation time **30 minutes**
+ resting time
Calories **130**

Ingredients *for 4 servings*

Clams *2 1/4 lbs*

Tomatoes *14 oz*

Garlic *2 cloves*

Parsley *1 small bunch*

Extra virgin olive oil *3 tablespoons*

Salt *& pepper to taste*

● Rinse clams carefully; cover with cold water for at least 1 hour to remove any sand and set aside. Pick and rinse parsley. Peel garlic, removing green sprout if necessary. Chop parsley and garlic together. In a large pan, heat the extra virgin olive oil. Add garlic-parsley mixture. Cook for a few minutes on low heat.

● Blanch the tomatoes in boiling water; drain, peel and squeeze gently to remove seeds, then chop. Add to garlic-parsley mixture. Cook for 3 minutes. Drain the clams and add to pan. Shake pan often. As the clams open, remove them from the pan. Discard any unopened clams. Season sauce with pepper and mix well. Serve clams with tomato sauce.

Shrimp & artichokes

Difficulty **easy**
Preparation time **40 minutes**
Calories **210**

Ingredients *for 4 servings*

Shrimp *1 1/4 lbs*
Artichokes *4*
Spring onions *2*
Parsley *1 small bunch*
Dry white wine *3 tablespoons*
White wine vinegar *5 tablespoons*
Extra virgin olive oil *4 tablespoons*
Salt *to taste*

● Rinse shrimp and remove black vein. Prepare the artichokes: Cut off the stems, remove the tough outer leaves, chop off the tip of the leaves and remove the chokes. Slice the artichokes thinly and place in cold water mixed with white wine vinegar. Peel scallions; remove roots and green outer leaves, then slice thinly. Rinse, dry and finely chop parsley.

● In a pan, heat the extra virgin olive oil. Add the sliced onions and cook until transparent. Add shrimp and dry white wine. Cook for 4 to 5 minutes. Drain shrimp using a slotted spoon and set aside.

● Drain artichokes and add to pan. Season with salt and cook for 15 minutes, stirring often with a wooden spoon. Return the shrimp to the pan. Add chopped parsley; cover pan and cook for another 5 minutes. Taste for salt. Remove from heat and serve immediately.

Calamari with lemon

Difficulty **easy**
Preparation time **50 minutes**
Calories **155**

Ingredients *for 4 servings*

Calamari *1 1/4 lbs*
Garlic *1 clove*
Lemons *the juice of 1*
Parsley *1 small bunch*
Extra virgin olive oil *3 tablespoons*
Salt *to taste*

● Empty the calamari; rinse well under running water and slice in rings. In a saucepan, place the extra virgin olive oil, calamari, a pinch of salt and peeled garlic. Cover and cook on very low heat for 20 minutes, after adding a few tablespoons of water when needed. Remove garlic clove.

● When calamari are half cooked, add lemon juice and continue cooking. Rinse, dry and finely chop parsley. Add to calamari. Continue cooking, stirring often. Keep adding hot water if necessary. When the calamari are cooked, remove from heat and transfer to a serving dish. Can be served hot or cold.

Difficulty **easy**
Preparation time **1 hour 15 minutes**
Calories **350**

Cod salad

Ingredients *for 4 servings*

Cod filets *1 lb*

Artichokes *4*

Potatoes *4*

Carrots *3*

Lemons *2*

Scallions *4 large*

Dried oregano *1 teaspoon*

Extra virgin olive oil *4 tablespoons*

Salt *&* **pepper** *to taste*

Andrea's note: You can vary the vegetables. Celery root, fennel and even yams can be colorful and tasty in this recipe.

● Carefully rinse the artichokes; remove external leaves, stems, tips of all leaves and chokes. Cut in small slices and place in cold water mixed with the juice of one lemon.

● Rinse the carrots and potatoes; steam for 20 minutes. Drain and add artichokes to steamer; cook for another 10 minutes. Slice carrots and potatoes.

● In a bowl, mix 3 tablespoons of the vegetable cooking liquid, the juice of half a lemon, a pinch of salt, fresh ground pepper and oregano. Slowly pour in the extra virgin olive oil and whisk until all ingredients are well blended and the sauce thickens.

● Remove the outer leaves from the scallions in one cup of boiling water for 5 minutes. Add the cod filets. Cover and cook on low heat for 8 minutes. On a serving dish, decoratively place the vegetables and fish. Drizzle with prepared sauce and serve immediately.

Difficulty **easy**
Preparation time **40 minutes**
Calories **280**

Ingredients *for 4 servings*

Fresh tuna *4 slices*

Green bell peppers *1*

Tomatoes *4, firm and ripe*

Lemons *the juice of 1*

Extra virgin olive oil *3 tablespoons*

Salt *&* **pepper** *to taste*

Andrea's note: This is a very simple and very delicious recipe that can be made with almost any fish you wish to serve. When using a different fish, you will need to adjust cooking time.

Tuna with peppers & tomatoes

● Rinse the bell pepper; cut in half and remove all white parts and seeds, then dice. Rinse and dry tomatoes; cut in half and remove seeds and juices with a small spoon, then dice.

● Carefully rinse and dry tuna slices. Brush a baking dish with 1 tablespoon of extra virgin olive oil. Place tuna slices in the dish. Season with salt and fresh ground pepper. Cover the tuna with diced tomatoes and bell pepper. Drizzle with lemon juice and remaining extra virgin olive oil. Bake in a preheated oven at 400°F for about 20 minutes. Remove from oven and transfer to individual warm dishes. Serve immediately.

Difficulty **average**
Preparation time **45 minutes**
Calories **440**

Tuna rolls

Ingredients *for 4 servings*

Tuna *8, thin slices*

Tuna in oil *4 oz*

Chopped tomatoes *14 oz*

Bread *2 thick slices without crust*

Eggs *1*

Egg yolks *1*

Grated pecorino *1 tablespoon*

Onions *1*

Garlic *1 clove*

Parsley *1 small bunch*

Extra virgin olive oil *4 tablespoons*

Salt *& pepper to taste*

● Soak the bread slices in warm water. Pick, rinse and dry parsley. Peel the garlic and chop with parsley. Boil egg until cooked. Peel onion and slice thinly. In a pan, heat 1 tablespoon of extra virgin olive oil. Add the onion and cook until transparent. Add the tomatoes and 1/4 cup of water; mix well and cook on low heat for 10 minutes.

● Drain the tuna from its oil; chop it and transfer to a bowl with garlic-parsley mixture. Drain and squeeze bread; tear in small pieces and add to bowl. Peel and chop hard-boiled egg; add to bowl. With a wooden spoon, mix in the raw egg yolk and grated pecorino until all ingredients are well blended. Divide the preparation between the tuna slices. Roll the tuna slices onto themselves and attach with kitchen twine.

● In a pan, heat the remaining extra virgin olive oil. Add the tuna rolls and cook on medium heat until brown all around. Pour the tomato sauce in the pan; season with salt and fresh ground pepper. Cook for 5 minutes. Remove from heat; discard twine and transfer tuna rolls on a serving dish. Taste the sauce for salt and serve with tuna rolls.

Difficulty **easy**
Preparation time **50 minutes**
Calories **220**

Sea bream with mushrooms & herbs

Ingredients *for 4 servings*

Sea bream *1, about 1 1/2 lbs, cleaned*

Mushrooms *4 oz*

Tomatoes *1, ripe and firm*

Herbs *1 small bunch (rosemary, thyme, sage)*

Carrots *1*

Onions *1*

Dry white wine *2 tablespoons*

Extra virgin olive oil *3 tablespoons*

Salt *& pepper to taste*

● Rinse the carrot, onion and tomato. Wipe the mushrooms. Dice all vegetables separately. In a pan, heat 2 tablespoons of extra virgin olive oil. Add diced carrots, onions and mushrooms. Cook until onions are tender.

● Brush a baking dish with remaining extra virgin olive oil. Rinse and carefully dry the fish; place in the prepared dish. Transfer the pre-cooked vegetables around and on top of the fish. Season with salt and pepper. Add the dry white wine and bake in a preheated oven at 375°F for 10 minutes. Turn the fish and bake for another 10 minutes.

● Remove from the oven. Add diced tomatoes and chopped herbs. Return to oven and bake until the eyes of the fish are opaque and white. Turn off the oven and leave fish in for 5 minutes. Transfer fish and vegetables to a serving dish; serve immediately.

Scallops au gratin

Difficulty **average**
Preparation time **40 minutes**
Calories **280**

Ingredients *for 4 servings*

Scallops *8*
Parsley *1 small bunch*
Garlic *1 clove*
Breadcrumbs *2 tablespoons*
Dry white wine *2 tablespoons*
Extra virgin olive oil *4 tablespoons*
Salt *&* **pepper** *to taste*

● Rinse and carefully dry parsley, then finely chop. Peel garlic clove and remove the green sprout if necessary. With an oyster knife, open the scallops, remove the edible parts, and the white and orange coral. (If you bought already shelled scallops, rinse well and dry on paper towels.)

● In a pan, heat the extra virgin olive oil. Add the garlic clove and cook for one minute. Discard the garlic clove and add scallops. Cook for a minute;

add dry white wine. Season with salt and fresh ground pepper. Sauté for 3 to 4 minutes.

● Wash 4 scallop shells well. Transfer the sautéed scallops in the shells. Sprinkle with breadcrumbs and chopped parsley. Drizzle the cooking juices. Bake in a preheated oven at 425°F for a few minutes, until top is lightly golden. Transfer to serving dishes and serve.

Sea bream with rosemary & tomatoes

Difficulty **average**
Preparation time **45 minutes**
Calories **205**

Ingredients *for 4 servings*

Sea bream *1, about 1 3/4 lbs*
Tomatoes *4*
Rosemary *1 sprig*
Garlic *2 cloves*
Dry white wine *4 tablespoons*
Extra virgin olive oil *2 tablespoons*
Salt *&* **pepper** *to taste*

● Scale the fish. Clean, debone and remove filets. Cut each filet in two, rinse and carefully dry on paper towels. Rinse and dry rosemary; remove needles and finely chop. Peel garlic cloves and remove green sprout if necessary. Blanch the tomatoes in boiling water; drain, peel and squeeze gently to remove seeds, then chop coarsely.

● In a pan, heat the extra virgin olive oil. Add garlic and cook for one minute. Add rosemary; cook for another minute. Add fish filets, dry white wine and chopped tomatoes. Season with salt and pepper. Cook for about 15 minutes (or until fish is tender), turning it once. Transfer fish to a warm serving dish. Serve with tomatoes and cooking juices.

Difficulty **average**
Preparation time **50 minutes**
Calories **315**

Ingredients *for 4 servings*

Mullet *1 3/4 lbs*

Cucumbers *4 oz*

Peeled tomatoes *6*

Onions *2 oz*

Parsley *1 small bunch*

Garlic *1 clove*

Marjoram *a pinch*

Extra virgin olive oil *5 tablespoons*

Salt *&* **pepper** *to taste*

Mullet with cucumbers

● Scale the fish; open and clean well. Rinse under running water and carefully dry with paper towels.

● Peel the onion and garlic. Rinse and dry parsley. Chop onion with cucumber, parsley and garlic. Transfer half the mixture in a large oven dish. Drizzle with 2 tablespoons of extra virgin olive oil. Season with salt and generous fresh ground pepper. Place the fish over the mixture.

● In a food processor, mix the peeled tomatoes with 3 tablespoons of extra virgin olive oil, marjoram, a pinch of salt and a good pinch of fresh ground pepper. Mix until well blended. Pour the prepared sauce over the fish. Cover with remaining cucumber-onion mixture.

● Bake in a preheated oven at 400°F for 10 minutes. Delicately turn the fish one at a time, and bake for another 10 minutes. Remove from oven and serve immediately, decorated with a few parsley leaves.

Difficulty **average**
Preparation time **1 hour**
Calories **345**

Salmon rolls

Ingredients *for 4 servings*

Salmon filets *12 oz*

Peeled shrimp *4 oz*

Tomatoes *3, firm and ripe*

Chopped chives *1 tablespoon*

Chopped parsley *1 tablespoon*

Chopped chervil *1 tablespoon*

Lemon juice *2 tablespoons*

Balsamic vinegar *1 teaspoon*

Extra virgin olive oil *5 tablespoons*

Salt *&* **pepper** *to taste*

For the jelly

Gelatin *4 teaspoons*

Fish broth *1 cup*

Basil *1 small bunch*

● Prepare the jelly. Dissolve gelatin in 1/4 cup of water. In a saucepan, heat the fish broth; add dissolved gelatin and heat through. Rinse basil and blanch in salted boiling water for a few seconds. Drain and add to gelatin. Mix the preparation in a food processor. Transfer to a bowl and refrigerate.

● In a bowl, mix the lemon juice and a pinch of salt and pepper. Slowly whisk in the extra virgin olive oil until ingredients are well blended. Mix in the chopped chives, parsley and chervil.

● Peel and debone salmon filets; rinse, dry well and cut in thick strips. Transfer to a deep dish and drizzle with a few tablespoons of the herb sauce.

Set aside to marinade for 15 minutes, turning the fish often.

● Steam the peeled shrimp; dice and place in a bowl. Blanch the tomatoes in boiling water; drain, peel and squeeze gently to remove seeds, then dice and place in a bowl. Mix the shrimp with half the herb sauce. Mix tomatoes with remaining herb sauce.

● Drain salmon strips from marinade; roll onto themselves. Coarsely chop gelatin and transfer to a serving dish with tomatoes. Place salmon rolls on top. Garnish with chopped shrimp. Drizzle with balsamic vinegar and serve.

Difficulty **average**
Preparation time **45 minutes**
Calories **260**

Mullet in tomato sauce

Ingredients *for 4 servings*

Mullet *1 1/2 lbs*

Tomatoes *14 oz, firm and ripe*

Parsley *1 small bunch*

Garlic *1 clove*

Lemons *a few thin slices*

Extra virgin olive oil *4 tablespoons*

Salt *&* **pepper** *to taste*

● Peel and crush the garlic. Rinse, dry and chop parsley. In a pan, heat the extra virgin olive oil. Add garlic and parsley; cook on low heat for a few minutes. Rinse the tomatoes; peel and squeeze to remove seeds, then chop coarsely. Add to pan. Season with salt and pepper; cook on medium heat for 15 minutes, stirring often.

● Clean mullets; rinse and delicately dry. In a large pan, place lemon slices and mullets. Cook for 8 to 10 minutes, delicately turning the fish once. Add a few tablespoons of water, if necessary. Season with salt. Remove from heat. Place mullets on a warm serving dish with other raw lemon slices. Pour the cooking juices on the fish. Serve immediately.

Spicy calamari

Difficulty **average**
Preparation time **50 minutes**
Calories **185**

Ingredients *for 4 servings*

Small calamari *1 1/4 lbs*

Tomatoes *1/2 lb*

Onions *1*

Parsley *1 small bunch*

Garlic *1 clove*

Saffron *1/2 teaspoon*

Dry white wine *5 tablespoons*

Extra virgin olive oil *4 tablespoons*

Salt *&* **pepper** *to taste*

● Clean the calamari; peel and keep ink pouches; rinse in cold water and set aside in a colander. Peel onion, rinse, dry and dice. Peel the tomatoes; remove seeds then dice. Pick parsley, rinse, dry and chop.

● In a saucepan, heat the extra virgin olive oil; add garlic and onion; cook until just transparent. Add tomatoes. Season with salt and a pinch of fresh ground pepper. Cook for 10 minutes, stirring often with a wooden spoon.

● Add calamari. Cook for 5 minutes; add the ink pouches, the dry white wine and the saffron diluted in a little hot water. Mix well and cook for 15 minutes. Remove the calamari and keep warm between 2 plates. Add chopped parsley to sauce, stir and cook for 5 minutes. Transfer the calamari on a serving dish. Cover with sauce and serve immediately.

Cold dogfish with lemon

Difficulty **easy**
Preparation time **30 minutes**
+ resting time
Calories **160**

Ingredients *for 4 servings*

Dogfish *4 slices, about 5 oz each*

Lemons *3*

Garlic *1 clove*

Parsley *1 small bunch*

Extra virgin olive oil *4 tablespoons*

Salt *&* **pepper** *to taste*

● Press the lemons and filter juice; set aside. Rinse and dry fish slices. Peel garlic. In a large pan, heat the extra virgin olive oil. Add garlic and cook for one minute. Discard garlic. Add fish slices and cook for 2 minutes on each side.

● Add the filtered lemon juice and enough warm water to just cover the fish. Season with salt and fresh ground pepper. Cover pan and cook for 5 minutes. Delicately turn the fish and cook for another 5 minutes.

● Pick, rinse and dry parsley, then chop finely. Remove fish from heat; add chopped parsley and stir gently. Transfer fish to a warm serving dish and cover with the cooking juices. Set aside to cool a few hours before serving.

Shrimp & asparagus salad

Difficulty **easy**
Preparation time **30 minutes**
Calories **185**

Ingredients *for 4 servings*

Shrimp *1 lb*
Asparagus *20*
Red radicchio *1 head*
Celery *2 stalks*
Orange juice *4 tablespoons*
Extra virgin olive oil *4 tablespoons*
Salt *&* **pepper** *to taste*

● Rinse the shrimp carefully; remove the black vein. In a saucepan, cook the shrimp in lightly salted boiling water. Cut off the hard parts of the asparagus stems. Peel the asparagus with a potato peeler and steam until al dente; drain and set aside.

● Rinse and dry the radicchio carefully; slice in thin strips. Rinse, dry and slice the celery stalks. In a bowl, mix the orange juice, extra virgin olive oil, a pinch of salt and fresh ground pepper. Place all ingredients in a salad bowl; toss delicately with the prepared sauce. Serve immediately.

Venus clams with asparagus

Difficulty **average**
Preparation time **40 minutes**
+ resting time
Calories **265**

Ingredients *for 4 servings*

Venus clams *1 1/2 lbs*
Asparagus *1 lb*
Garlic *1 clove*
Extra virgin olive oil *4 tablespoons*
Salt *&* **pepper** *to taste*

● Place the clams in a large bowl; cover with cold salted water and set aside for at least one hour. Peel the garlic and chop. Cut off the hard part of the asparagus stems. Peel the asparagus, rinse and dry. Slice the stems thinly and the tips in half, lengthwise.

● Drain the clams. In a large pan, heat 2 tablespoons of extra virgin olive oil. Add the clams and cook on high heat, until they are open. Remove the clams and filter the cooking juices.

● In another pan, heat the remaining extra virgin olive oil. Add the garlic and the asparagus, a pinch of salt and fresh ground pepper. Toss well and cook for a few minutes. Add a few tablespoons of the clams cooking juice. Cover and cook on low heat, for 10 minutes.

● Remove clams from shells. Discard any unopened clams. Add shelled clams to the asparagus and toss carefully. Transfer to a warm serving dish. Can be served hot or warm.

Difficulty **average**
Preparation time **50 minutes**
Calories **260**

Grouper with vegetables

Ingredients *for 4 servings*

Grouper filets *4, about 5 oz each*

Red bell peppers *1*

Eggplants *1*

Scallions *2 large*

Tomatoes *2*

Zucchini *2*

Extra virgin olive oil *4 tablespoons*

Salt *&* **pepper** *to taste*

● Remove skin and debone the grouper filets; cut in large pieces. Rinse the bell pepper; cut in half and remove white parts and seeds; cut in one-inch pieces. Rinse, dry and dice the zucchinis and eggplant. Blanch the tomatoes in boiling water; drain, peel and squeeze gently to remove all seeds; then dice.

● Remove roots and outer leaves from scallions; rinse, dry and slice. In a saucepan, heat 2 tablespoons of extra virgin olive oil. Add the scallions and sauté until transparent. Add eggplant and bell pepper. Season with salt and fresh ground pepper. Cook for 10 minutes, stirring often. Add the zucchinis and cook for 5 minutes.

● Mix in the tomatoes and cook for another 10 minutes. Transfer the vegetable preparation to a serving dish and set aside to cool.

● Heat the remaining extra virgin olive oil in a pan. Add the pieces of fish. Season with salt and pepper. Sauté for 10 minutes, or until fully cooked, turning them often. Transfer the fish onto the cool vegetables and serve immediately.

Difficulty **easy**
Preparation time **40 minutes**
Calories **245**

Dogfish in pieces

Ingredients *for 4 servings*

Dogfish filets *1 1/4 lbs*

Onions *1*

Carrots *1*

Celery *1 stalk*

Tomato sauce *4 oz*

Black olives *10*

Parsley *1 small bunch*

Dry white wine *5 tablespoons*

Extra virgin olive oil *5 tablespoons*

Salt *&* **pepper** *to taste*

● Slice the fish in 1 inch cubes. Peel the onion and slice very thinly. Peel the carrot, rinse and dice. Remove the larger fibers from the celery, rinse and cut into sticks. Pick, rinse and dry the parsley, then chop finely. Pit the olives.

● In a pan, heat the extra virgin olive oil. Add the onion, carrot and celery; cook for 5 minutes, stirring often. Add the fish cubes and the olives. Season with salt and fresh ground pepper. Cook for 3 minutes. Add the dry white wine and let evaporate. Add the tomato sauce and mix well with a wooden spoon. Cover and cook on low heat, for 15 minutes.

● If the sauce seems a little too liquid, raise the heat slightly and let evaporate until sauce thickens. Transfer the preparation to a serving dish. Sprinkle with chopped parsley and serve immediately.

Scallops with tomatoes & herbs

Difficulty **average**
Preparation time **30 minutes**
Calories **410**

Ingredients *for 4 servings*

Scallops *12*

Cherry tomatoes *1/4 lb*

Shallots *1*

Herbs *1 small bunch (parsley, chives, basil, chervil)*

Dry white wine *1/2 cup*

Extra virgin olive oil *6 tablespoons*

Salt *&* **pepper** *to taste*

● Open the scallops with an oyster knife and remove the white scallop and its coral, then rinse well. (If you bought already shelled scallops, rinse well and dry on paper towels.) Horizontally slice scallops in half. Blanch the cherry tomatoes in boiling water; drain, peel and squeeze gently to remove seeds.

● Rinse mixed herbs; dry and chop. Peel shallot; rinse, dry and finely chop. In a pan, heat 4 tablespoons of extra virgin olive oil. Add half the chopped mixed herbs and shallot. Cook to just wither the herbs. Add cherry tomatoes. Season with a pinch of salt and

pepper. Cook for 2 to 3 minutes, on medium-high heat.

● During this time, heat the remaining extra virgin olive oil in a non-stick pan. Add the scallops and sauté for 2 minutes. Season with salt and pepper. Add dry white wine and let evaporate on high heat. Sprinkle with the remaining mixed herbs.

● Remove the scallops; place in clean and dry scallop shells, or on individual plates. Cover with herb-tomato preparation, and bake in a preheated oven for 2 minutes. Serve immediately.

Skate wings au gratin

Difficulty **average**
Preparation time **50 minutes**
Calories **265**

Ingredients *for 4 servings*

Skate wings *1 1/2 lbs*

Mushrooms *1/2 lb*

Chopped onions *1 tablespoon*

Chopped parsley *1/2 tablespoon*

Lemons *the juice of 1*

Breadcrumbs *1/2 tablespoon*

Dry white wine *1/4 cup*

Extra virgin olive oil *5 tablespoons*

Salt *&* **pepper** *to taste*

● Peel the skate wing; rinse and cut in 4 pieces. Clean the mushrooms and rinse in a bowl of cold water mixed with lemon juice. Drain and dry well on paper towels, then slice thinly.

● In a pan, heat the extra virgin olive oil. Add onions and cook for a minute. Add sliced mushrooms and cook on very low heat until all the water has evaporated. Season with salt and fresh ground pepper; add chopped

parsley. Remove from heat and transfer the preparation to a baking dish.

● Place the pieces of skate wing on top of the mushrooms. Season with salt and a pinch of pepper. Sprinkle with the breadcrumbs and drizzle with the dry white wine. Bake in a preheated oven at 400°F for about 20 minutes, or until top is golden. Serve immediately.

Difficulty **average**
Preparation time **30 minutes**
Calories **335**

Ingredients *for 6 servings*

Dogfish *6 slices*

Peeled tomatoes *6*

Anchovy filets *6*

White onions *1*

Garlic *1 clove*

Chopped parsley *1 tablespoon*

Capers *1 tablespoon*

Unbleached flour *to taste*

Extra virgin olive oil *6 tablespoons*

Salt *&* **pepper** *to taste*

Sicilian-style dogfish

● Peel the garlic and the onion; chop together. In a pan, heat the extra virgin olive oil. Add garlic and onion; cook until onion is transparent. Roll the fish slices in flour; add to pan. Cook on both sides for a few minutes. Season with salt and fresh ground pepper. With a spatula, carefully transfer the fish to a plate. Cover with another plate to keep warm.

● Chop tomatoes. Rinse anchovies and chop. Add tomatoes and anchovies to the pan. Cook on medium heat for 10 minutes. Return the fish slices to the pan. Add the capers and the parsley. Cook for 5 minutes. Transfer to a warm serving dish and serve immediately.

Difficulty **easy**
Preparation time **1 hour**
Calories **380**

Ingredients *for 4 servings*

Scampi *1/4 lb*

Squid *1/4 lb*

Tomatoes *12 oz, firm and ripe*

Eggplants *14 oz*

Baby onions *1/2 lb*

Onions *1*

Pitted green olives *2 oz*

Celery *1 stalk*

Capers *1 tablespoon*

Hard boiled eggs *1*

Bay leaves *1*

Sugar *1 tablespoon*

White wine vinegar *3 tablespoons*

Extra virgin olive oil *8 tablespoons*

Salt *&* **pepper** *to taste*

Scampi & squid in their sauce

● Rinse, dry and dice eggplants. Place in a colander, sprinkle with salt and set aside over a bowl. Clean and peel the squid; rinse and chop in bite-size pieces. Peel the scampi; remove the black vein and rinse. Blanch the tomatoes in boiling water; drain, peel and squeeze gently to remove seeds, chop finely. Peel the onion and chop. Rinse and chop celery; cook in boiling salted water for 3 minutes, then drain. Rinse the small onions and cook in boiling salted water for 3 minutes, then drain.

● In a pan, heat 3 tablespoons of extra virgin olive oil. Add the rinsed and dried eggplants. Sauté until lightly golden; drain on paper towels. In the same pan, add 2 tablespoons of extra virgin olive oil and cook the onion until transparent. Add tomatoes, celery, small onions and bay leaf. Season with salt and pepper. Cook for 15 minutes. Add green olives, capers, white wine vinegar and sugar. Cook for 4 minutes.

● In another pan, heat the remaining extra virgin olive oil. Add the squid and cook for 3 to 4 minutes. Add scampi and cook for 2 to 3 minutes. Season with salt and pepper. Mix this into the tomato sauce. Remove from heat. Stir in the eggplants. Transfer the preparation to a warm serving dish. Decorate with the sliced boiled egg and serve.

Difficulty **average**
Preparation time **1 hour 20 minutes**
Calories **560**

Ingredients *for 6 servings*

Scorpion fish *1 1/2 lbs*

Grouper *1 lb slice*

Mullet *1 1/4 lbs*

Peeled tomatoes *1 1/2 lbs*

Garlic *3 cloves*

Red hot chili peppers *1*

Dry white wine *1 1/2 cups*

Parsley *1 small bunch*

Bay leaves *2*

Toasted bread *30 small pieces*

Extra virgin olive oil *7 tablespoons*

Salt *to taste*

Puréed fish soup

● Peel the garlic cloves and remove green sprout if necessary. In a large saucepan, heat the extra virgin olive oil and garlic. When garlic starts to brown, remove and discard. Add chopped hot chili pepper, bay leaves and peeled tomatoes. Crush tomatoes with a fork. Mix well and cook for 3 to 4 minutes. Add the dry white wine and cook for 15 minutes. Add 6 cups of hot water and continue cooking on medium heat.

● During this time, clean and scale mullet and scorpion fish. Add grouper and all fish to soup. Season with salt. Cook for 20 minutes. Transfer fish to a large plate. Remove heads and tails; peel and debone all fish.

● Return cleaned fish to soup and cook for 10 minutes. Remove from heat. Pass soup through a food mill or in a food processor. Return the puréed soup to the saucepan and cook for 5 minutes. Taste for salt. Sprinkle with chopped parsley. Transfer the soup into warm individual bowls with 5 pieces of toasted bread each. Serve immediately.

Cacciucco

Difficulty **average**
Preparation time **1 hour 30 minutes**
Calories **770**

Ingredients *for 4 servings*

Mixed fish *2 1/2 lbs (dogfish, mullet, scorpion fish, squid, calamari, shrimp)*
Tomatoes *10 oz, firm and ripe*
Carrots *1*
Celery *1 stalk*
Onions *1*
Parsley *1 small bunch*
Garlic *2 cloves*
Red hot chili peppers *1 small piece*
Day-old Italian-style bread *6-8 slices*
Chianti *1/4 cup*
Extra virgin olive oil *1/4 cup*
Salt *to taste*

● Clean the fish; remove heads and debone; filet all fish, then rinse and dry on paper towels; cut in small pieces. Peel shrimp and devein; rinse and dry. Clean squid and calamari; peel, rinse and chop.

● Blanch the tomatoes in boiling water; drain, peel and squeeze gently to remove seeds, then chop finely. Peel and chop garlic and onion. Peel and chop carrot. Rinse and chop celery. Rinse, dry and finely chop the parsley.

● In a large pan, heat the extra virgin olive oil. Add garlic, onion, carrot, celery and chili pepper. Cook until onion is transparent. Add Chianti and let evaporate. Add chopped tomatoes. Season with salt. Cook for about 5 minutes.

● Add 1/2 cup of hot water and cook for 3 minutes. Add all fish, squid and calamari. Cook for another 15 minutes. Add peeled shrimp and cook for another 5 minutes, stirring often. All fish should be tender. Sprinkle with chopped parsley. Remove from heat and let stand for a few minutes. Rub the slices of toasted bread with a piece of garlic. Serve the "cacciucco" soup in warm individual bowls with the bread.

Pea soup with squid

Difficulty **average**
Preparation time **1 hour**
Calories **215**

Ingredients *for 4 servings*

Squid *1 1/2 lbs*
Fresh peas *1/2 lb*
Tomatoes *1/2 lb, firm and ripe*
Onions *1*
Garlic *1 clove*
Parsley *1 small bunch*
Red hot chili peppers *1 small piece*
Extra virgin olive oil *4 tablespoons*
Salt *& pepper to taste*

● Blanch the tomatoes in boiling water; drain, peel and squeeze gently to remove seeds, then chop coarsely. Peel the garlic and onion; rinse, dry and chop finely. Clean the squid; remove tentacles; discard beak and eyes; peel, cut in strips, rinse and dry. Rinse the parsley, dry and chop.

● In a large saucepan, heat the extra virgin olive oil. Add the chopped onions, garlic and chili pepper. Cook until onion is just transparent. Add squid and cook until their water has evaporated, stirring often with a wooden spoon. Season with salt and generous fresh ground pepper.

● Add peas and cook for a few minutes. Add chopped tomatoes and a pinch of salt. Cook on low heat for about 30 minutes. When the squid is tender and sauce is still liquid enough, sprinkle with chopped parsley. Serve the soup in individual bowls with toasted bread.

Difficulty **average**
Preparation time **1 hour 10 minutes**
Calories **330**

Ingredients *for 4 servings*

Shrimp *1/2 lb*

Small calamari *1/4 lb*

Eel *1/4 lb*

Fresh cod *1/4 lb*

Mussels *12, large*

Peeled tomatoes *1/4 lb*

Dry white wine *1/4 cup*

Red hot chili peppers *1/2*

Garlic *1 clove*

Chopped parsley *1 tablespoon*

Extra virgin olive oil *6 tablespoons*

Salt *to taste*

Spicy fish soup

● Clean and carefully rinse fish and calamari. Peel the shrimp. In a large pan, heat the extra virgin olive oil. Sauté all fish (not the mussels) one by one in the oil. When ready, transfer the fish to a deep large plate.

● In the same pan, cook the crushed garlic until golden; remove and discard. Add the tomatoes and crush them with a fork. Season with salt and cook for 15 minutes. Add a few tablespoons of water, if the sauce reduces too much.

● In a mortar, crush the chili pepper. Mix the tomato sauce. Add the dry white wine; mix well. Add pre-cooked fish. Cover the pan and cook on low heat for a few minutes. Set aside.

● Carefully brush and rinse mussels. Place them in a pan and cook on high heat, shaking the pan until mussels are open. Detach mussels from their shells and serve with fish soup. Sprinkle with chopped parsley. Serve the soup directly from the pan or transfer to a warm serving dish.

Seafood soup

Difficulty **average**
Preparation time **40 minutes**
+ resting time
Calories **430**

Ingredients *for 6 servings*

Mussels *2 1/2 lbs*

Little neck clams *1 3/4 lbs*

Razor shells *1 1/2 lbs*

Tomatoes *12 oz, firm and ripe*

Garlic *2 cloves*

Parsley *1 small bunch*

Day-old Italian-style bread *6 slices*

Dry white wine *1/4 cup*

Extra virgin olive oil *5 tablespoons*

Salt *&* **pepper** *to taste*

● Rinse clams and razor shells. In separate bowls, soak them in cold water for at least 2 hours. Carefully brush and rinse the mussels under running water. Blanch the tomatoes in boiling water; drain, peel and squeeze gently to remove seeds, then slice in thin strips. Rinse, dry and finely chop the parsley.

● Drain clams and razor shells. In a large pan, place the clams, razor shells, mussels, dry white wine and 2 tablespoons of extra virgin olive oil. Cook on high heat, shaking often until all shells are open. Remove from heat. Remove mollusks from their shells and place in a bowl. Filter the cooking liquid and set aside.

● Peel the garlic and remove the green sprout if necessary. In a pan, heat the remaining extra virgin olive oil. Add garlic and cook until it becomes golden. Remove and discard garlic. Add tomato strips, filtered cooking liquid and cook for 10 minutes, on medium-low heat, stirring often with a wooden spoon. Add clams, razor shells and mussels. Season with salt and pepper to taste. Cook for a few minutes. Sprinkle with chopped parsley. Transfer to individual bowls and serve with toasted slices of bread.

Anchovy soup

Difficulty **easy**
Preparation time **40 minutes**
Calories **380**

Ingredients *for 4 servings*

Anchovies *1 1/4 lbs*

Tomatoes *1/2 lb, firm and ripe*

Carrots *1*

Celery *1 stalk*

Onions *1*

Parsley *1 small bunch*

Garlic *1 clove*

Red hot chili peppers *1 small piece*

Day-old Italian-style bread *4 slices*

Dry white wine *1/4 cup*

Fish or vegetable broth *2 cups*

Extra virgin olive oil *4 tablespoons*

Salt *&* **pepper** *to taste*

● Clean the anchovies; remove heads; rinse carefully under running water and dry on paper towels. Peel the onion and garlic; chop finely. Peel and chop the carrot. Rinse and chop the celery. Rinse, dry and chop parsley.

● Blanch the tomatoes in boiling water; drain, peel and squeeze gently to remove seeds, then chop coarsely. In a pan, heat the extra virgin olive oil. Add onion, carrot, garlic and celery; cook until onions are just transparent.

Add chili pepper and dry white wine; let evaporate on high heat. Stir in the chopped tomatoes. Season with salt and pepper. Cook for about 8 minutes.

● Add vegetable or fish broth, and bring to boil. Add anchovies. Taste for salt and season with more fresh ground pepper. Cook for 10 minutes, on medium heat. Sprinkle the soup with chopped parsley. Serve immediately with lightly toasted bread slices.

Dogfish & zucchini broth

Difficulty **easy**
Preparation time **30 minutes**
Calories **215**

Ingredients *for 4 servings*

Dogfish *1 1/2 lbs*
Zucchini *1/2 lb*
Tomatoes *1/2 lb, firm and ripe*
Shallots *1*
Basil *1 small bunch*
Parsley *1 small bunch*
Red hot chili peppers *1*
Tarragon *2 sprigs*
Dry white wine *1/4 cup*
Fish or vegetable broth *1 1/2 cups*
Extra virgin olive oil *4 tablespoons*
Salt *to taste*

● Rinse the dogfish; dry on paper towels and cut in small cubes. Rinse, dry and dice zucchini. Rinse, dry and chop basil, parsley and tarragon. Peel, dry and finely chop shallot. Chop chili pepper. Blanch the tomatoes in boiling water; drain, peel and squeeze gently to remove seeds, then chop coarsely.

● In a large pan, heat the extra virgin olive oil. Add shallot and cook until just transparent. Add zucchini and fish.

Sauté on high heat for a few minutes, until lightly brown. Season with a pinch of salt. Sprinkle with chopped chili pepper. Add the dry white wine and let evaporate on high heat, stirring often.

● Add tomatoes and fish or vegetable broth. Cook on medium heat for 5 minutes, stirring often. Sprinkle with chopped herbs. Serve hot with toasted country-style bread.

Fisherman's soup

Difficulty **average**
Preparation time **1 hour 15 minutes**
Calories **775**

Ingredients *for 4 servings*

Mullet *4*
Eel *2 lbs*
Squid *2*
Tomatoes *1/4 lb, firm and ripe*
Onions *1 small*
Leeks *1*
Celery *1 stalk*
Bay leaves *1*
Parsley *1 small bunch*
Thyme *1 small bunch*
Garlic *2 cloves*
Day-old Italian-style bread *8 slices*
Dry white wine *1 cup*
Salt *&* **pepper** *to taste*

● Clean the eel; peel and rinse well; dry on paper towels and cut in large pieces. Blanch the tomatoes in boiling water; drain, peel and squeeze gently to remove seeds, then pass through a strainer.

● Peel and coarsely chop onion. Rinse leek; remove roots and hard leaves, then chop. Chop celery. Tie the parsley, thyme and bay leaf with kitchen twine.

● In a large saucepan, pour the dry white wine and 5 cups of water. Add eel, vegetables, herbs, tomato purée

and a good pinch of salt and pepper. Cover and bring to boil. Lower the heat and cook on medium heat, for 30 minutes. Remove the tied herbs. Pass the preparation through a food mill and transfer into a saucepan.

● During this time, clean and scale mullet; debone and rinse well. Clean the squid; remove eyes, beak and skin; rinse and slice. Return puréed soup to heat. Bring to boil. Add mullet and squid. Cook until tender. Serve soup with toasted bread rubbed with garlic.

Difficulty **average**
Preparation time **1 hour 10 minutes**
Calories **395**

Buridda from Genova

Ingredients *for 4 servings*

Mixed fish *1 lb*

Mixed shellfish *1 lb*

Tomatoes *4, firm and ripe*

Garlic *1 clove*

Onions *1*

Carrots *1*

Celery *1 stalk*

Parsley *1 small bunch*

Pine nuts *2 oz*

Anchovies *2*

Day-old Italian-style bread *4 slices, toasted*

Extra virgin olive oil *4 tablespoons*

Salt *&* **pepper** *to taste*

● Rinse, dry and chop garlic, onion, carrot, celery and parsley. In a mortar, mash the pine nuts. Rinse and debone anchovies. Peel tomatoes, and cut in quarter. In a pan, heat the extra virgin olive oil. Add the chopped vegetables and pine nuts. Cook on medium heat for 2 to 3 minutes. Add anchovies and tomatoes.

● Cook for a few minutes. Add 1/2 cup of hot water and cook on medium heat for about 20 minutes.

● During this time, clean and scale the fish; remove heads and tails; rinse and cut in pieces. Rinse the mixed shellfish several times in cold water; place together in a large pan.

● Cook the shellfish on high heat, shaking the pan until shells are open. Discard any unopened shells. Transfer shellfish to a plate and filter cooking liquids. Return shellfish to pan; add pieces of fish and filtered liquid. Season with salt and pepper. Cook for about 15 minutes, on low heat. Place one slice of bread in each individual soup bowl. Pour soup over bread and serve immediately.

Difficulty **average**
Preparation time **30 minutes**
Calories **280**

Fish fricassee

Ingredients *for 4 servings*

Mussels *1 1/2 lbs*

Sole filets *1/2 lb*

John Dory filets *1/2 lb*

Shrimp *4*

Parsley *1 small bunch*

Garlic *1 clove*

Egg yolks *2*

Lemons *the juice of 1*

Dry white wine *1/4 cup*

Extra virgin olive oil *4 tablespoons*

Salt *&* **pepper** *to taste*

● Peel and devein shrimp; rinse and dry. Rinse and dry fish filets. Peel garlic and crush. Rinse, dry and finely chop parsley. Carefully brush and rinse mussels in cold water.

● In a pan, place mussels, one tablespoon of extra virgin olive oil, dry white wine, one garlic clove and a pinch of parsley. Cook on high heat until mussels are open. Remove from heat; remove mussels from shells and transfer to a bowl. Discard any unopened shells. Filter cooking liquid and pour in a saucepan. Add remaining extra virgin olive oil and garlic clove. Bring to boil. Add fish filets, shrimp, a pinch of salt and pepper. Cook on medium heat for 8 minutes. Remove garlic. Add the mussels and cook for 2 minutes. Transfer the fish to a serving dish.

● Filter the liquid and pour into a small saucepan. In a bowl, whisk the egg yolks with lemon juice, remaining parsley, a pinch of salt and pepper. Pour into the saucepan and mix rapidly with a wooden spoon. When the preparation is just creamy, pour over the fish and serve immediately.

Meat

Difficulty **easy**
Preparation time **1 hour 30 minutes + resting time**
Calories **270**

Ingredients *for 4 servings*

Veal *1 1/4 lbs*

Peeled tomatoes *4*

Eggplants *1*

Zucchini *1*

Bell peppers *2*

Frozen green beans *1/4 lb*

Onions *1*

Garlic *1 clove*

Chopped herbs *1 tablespoon (parsley, sage, basil)*

Vegetable broth *4 cups*

Extra virgin olive oil *3 tablespoons*

Salt *&* **pepper** *to taste*

Veal & vegetable stew

● Thaw the green beans. Peel the eggplant, slice lengthwise and place in a colander; sprinkle with coarse salt and set aside for 30 minutes to remove excess moisture. Dry and dice.

● Peel onion; chop finely. Cut the veal in cubes. In a large pot, heat the extra virgin olive oil. Add onion and cook until transparent; add meat and cook for 10 minutes, mixing often.

● Trim and rinse the other vegetables. Cut the peppers in large pieces. Dice the zucchini and tomatoes. Add zucchini, peppers and green beans to the meat.

● Cook for 5 minutes. Add the chopped herbs, tomatoes, garlic, salt and pepper. Cover with vegetable broth; cook on low heat for 45 minutes, adding more broth if necessary. Taste for salt and transfer to a deep serving bowl. Serve immediately.

Veal rolls with artichokes

Difficulty **easy**
Preparation time **40 minutes**
Calories **390**

Ingredients *for 4-6 servings*

Veal slices *12, about 3 oz each*

Artichokes *2*

Peeled tomatoes *1/2 lb*

Cooked ham *1/4 lb*

Onions *1*

Lemon juice *1 tablespoon*

Dry white wine *1/4 cup*

Extra virgin olive oil *5 tablespoons*

Salt *&* **pepper** *to taste*

● Remove stems and outer leaves from the artichokes; cut in half, discard chokes, slice thinly and soak in water mixed with lemon juice. Drain and dry well. In a skillet, heat 1 tablespoon of extra virgin olive oil and sauté the artichokes. Add 3 or 4 tablespoons of water and mix well. Season with salt and pepper. Cook for about 8 minutes on medium heat or until tender.

● Beat the veal with a meat tenderizer. Finely chop the ham. In the center of each slices of veal, place 2 pieces of artichokes and a little ham; fold the meat and with the back of a knife, press the border so it closes well.

● Peel the onion; chop finely. In a pan, heat the extra virgin olive oil; cook the onion until transparent. Add the veal rolls and brown, on each side. Add the wine and let evaporate on high heat. Season with salt and pepper. Cook for 7 minutes; stir in the crushed tomatoes and cook for 8 minutes. Serve very hot.

Veal rump with eggplant

Difficulty **easy**
Preparation time **30 minutes**
Calories **225**

Ingredients *for 4 servings*

Veal rump *1 lb in thin slices*

Eggplants *10 oz*

Tomatoes *3, firm and ripe*

Green olives *2 oz*

Basil *1 small bunch*

Extra virgin olive oil *3 tablespoons*

Salt *&* **pepper** *to taste*

● Blanch the tomatoes in boiling water; drain, peel and squeeze gently to remove seeds, then dice. Pit the olives and slice. Trim, rinse, dry and dice the eggplant.

● In a non-stick pan, heat 1 tablespoon of extra virgin olive oil. Cook the eggplant for 4 to 5 minutes, on high heat, stirring often; drain and set aside. In the same pan, add 1 tablespoon of extra virgin olive oil and cook the tomatoes for about 10 minutes; season with salt and pepper.

● During this time, in another non-stick pan, heat the remaining extra virgin olive oil. Add the veal rump. Season with salt and pepper. Cook on high heat on both sides for a few minutes. Drain and place in a baking dish.

● Add the olives, basil and eggplant to the tomatoes. Mix well and pour over the slices of veal. Bake in a preheated oven at 400°F for about 4 minutes. Remove from oven and serve immediately.

Sicilian-style veal kebabs

Difficulty **easy**
Preparation time **40 minutes**
Calories **350**

Ingredients *for 4-6 servings*

Veal *12, about 3 oz each*
Raisins *1 tablespoon*
Pine nuts *1 tablespoon*
Small onions *8*
Bay leaves *8*
Basil *12 leaves*
Sharp caciocavallo cheese *1/4 lb*
Breadcrumbs *1 tablespoon*
Dry white wine *1/4 cup*
Extra virgin olive oil *3 tablespoons*
Salt *& pepper to taste*

● Soak the raisins in warm water. Peel the small onions; cook in boiling water for 5 minutes; drain and dry on a towel. Slice the caciocavallo cheese in sticks.

● In a non-stick pan, toast the breadcrumbs briefly. Flatten the veal with a meat tenderizer. On each piece, place a little breadcrumb, a stick of cheese, a few raisins, a few pine nuts and one basil leaf. Roll the slices of meat onto themselves.

● Prepare 4 kebabs. On each stick, place 3 rolls separated by bay leaves and onions. Season with salt and pepper. In a non-stick pan, heat the extra virgin olive oil. Add the kebabs and brown the meat on all sides. When golden, season again with a little salt and pepper. Add the wine and let evaporate on high heat.

● Cover and cook for another 10 minutes, on low-medium heat, adding a little hot water if necessary. When meat is tender, transfer to a serving dish. Serve very hot with mixed vegetables.

Veal cutlets with sun-dried tomatoes

Difficulty **easy**
Preparation time **30 minutes**
Calories **355**

Ingredients *for 4 servings*

Veal cutlets *1 lb*
Sun-dried tomatoes in oil *12*
Shallots *1/4 lb*
Pine nuts *2 oz*
Basil *1 small bunch*
Unbleached flour *2 tablespoons*
Dry white wine *1/4 cup*
Extra virgin olive oil *4 tablespoons*
Salt *& pepper to taste*

● Peel the shallots and slice thinly. In a pan, heat 2 tablespoons of oil; cook the shallots until just transparent. In a non-stick pan, toast the pine nuts until lightly golden.

● Flatten the veal; roll in flour. In a pan, heat the remaining extra virgin olive oil. Add the veal and brown on both sides. Drain on paper towels and keep warm between 2 plates. Drain and slice the tomatoes.

● In the same pan, add the wine and boil for one minute. Add the shallots, pine nuts and tomatoes. Cook on medium heat, until wine is almost evaporated. Remove from heat. Sprinkle with chopped basil.

● Transfer the veal to individual plates. Serve very hot with the prepared sun-dried tomato sauce.

Difficulty **easy**
Preparation time **45 minutes**
+ resting time
Calories **305**

Ingredients *for 4 servings*

Turkey breast *1 lb*
Carrots *2*
Onions *2*
Bay leaves *3*
Sage *2 leaves*
Cloves *3*
Dry white wine *1/2 cup*
White wine vinegar *1/2 cup*
Extra virgin olive oil *5 tablespoons*
Salt *&* **peppercorns** *to taste*

Sweet-and-sour turkey

● Rinse and dry the turkey. Trim, peel and slice the carrots. Peel and slice thinly the onions. In a pot, place the carrots, one onion, one bay leaf, a few peppercorns and cloves; add 3 tablespoons of vinegar and 4 cups of water. Bring to boil for 15 minutes.

● Add a pinch of salt and turkey breast. Cook for 20 minutes on low heat. Drain the vegetables and turkey with a slotted spoon; cool briefly; cut the turkey in pieces.

● In a non-stick pan, heat the extra virgin olive oil and cook the remaining onion until transparent. Add the sage and remaining bay leaves. Add the turkey and brown on all sides. Stir in the drained vegetables, a pinch of salt and pepper. Add the remaining vinegar and dry white wine. Boil for a few minutes.

● Transfer the preparation to a deep serving bowl and set aside to cool, stirring often. Cover and refrigerate for one day. Bring to room temperature before serving.

Difficulty **easy**
Preparation time **20 minutes**
Calories **320**

Ingredients *for 4 servings*

Turkey breast *3/4 lb*
Pitted green olives *4 oz*
Onions *1*
Garlic *1 clove*
Basil *1 small bunch*
Unbleached flour *2 tablespoons*
Dry white wine *1/4 cup*
Extra virgin olive oil *4 tablespoons*
Salt *&* **pepper** *to taste*

Turkey with olives

● Slice the turkey breast thinly; roll in flour. In a pan, heat 2 tablespoons of extra virgin olive oil. Add the turkey slices and brown on both sides; season with salt and pepper. Drain and keep warm between 2 plates. Peel and chop garlic and onion.

● In the same pan, heat the remaining extra virgin olive oil. Add garlic and onion; cook until transparent. Return the turkey to the pan, add wine and let evaporate on high heat. Add olives, half chopped and half whole.

● Cover the pan and cook on medium heat for about 8 minutes, adding a little water if necessary. Sprinkle with the chopped basil. Transfer the preparation to a warm serving dish. Serve immediately.

Difficulty **easy**
Preparation time **40 minutes**
Calories **355**

Ingredients *for 4 servings*

Turkey breast *8 slices*

Cooked ham *3 oz*

Mozzarella *2 oz*

Red bell peppers *1*

Yellow bell peppers *1*

Tomatoes *1/2 lb, firm and ripe*

Basil *1 small bunch*

Sage *2 leaves*

Dry white wine *1/4 cup*

Extra virgin olive oil *4 tablespoons*

Salt *&* **pepper** *to taste*

Turkey rolls with pepper sauce

● Rinse, dry and tear the basil. Rinse and cut the peppers in half; remove seeds and white parts; cut in pieces. Rinse and cut the tomatoes in half; remove seeds and chop coarsely.

● In a pan, heat 2 tablespoons of extra virgin olive oil. Add the pieces of peppers (keep 8 pieces aside) and sauté on high heat for about 3 minutes. Add the tomatoes, salt and pepper. Cover pan; cook for about 15 minutes. Add basil and cook for 5 minutes.

● During this time, flatten the turkey with a meat tenderizer. Cover each slice with one slice of ham, one piece of mozzarella and one piece of pepper. Roll the turkey and close with a toothpick. In a pan, heat the remaining extra virgin olive oil with the sage. Add the rolls and brown on all sides. Season with salt and pepper.

● Add the wine and let evaporate on high heat. Cover the pan and cook on medium heat for about 10 minutes. Remove the rolls and slice them. Transfer to a serving dish. Can be served hot or warm with the prepared pepper sauce.

Difficulty **easy**
Preparation time **50 minutes**
Calories **250**

Ingredients *for 4 servings*

Turkey breast *3/4 lb*

Carrots *1/3 lb*

Green beans *1/4 lb*

Potatoes *1/4 lb*

Zucchini *1/4 lb*

Cauliflower *1/4 lb*

Arugula *2 bunches*

Extra virgin olive oil *4 tablespoons*

Salt *&* **pepper** *to taste*

Turkey with steamed vegetables

● Rinse, dry and season the turkey with salt and fresh ground pepper. Steam for 15 to 20 minutes; cool and slice thinly.

● During this time, trim, peel the carrots and potatoes. Trim the zucchini. Rinse the cauliflower and divide in flowerets. Turn or cut in julienne the carrots, potatoes and zucchini. Rinse all vegetables and steam separately.

● Rinse and dry the arugula on a kitchen towel. Tear in small pieces and place on a serving dish. Cover with turkey slices and steamed vegetables. Season with salt and drizzle with extra virgin olive oil. Serve immediately.

Difficulty **average**
Preparation time **40 minutes**
Calories **360**

Ingredients *for 4 servings*

Chicken breast *1 lb*
Red grapes *1/2 lb*
Oranges *1*
Avocado *1*
Pink grapefruit *1*
Lemons *the juice of 1*
Chervil *1 small bunch*
Extra virgin olive oil *4 tablespoons*
Salt & **pepper** *to taste*

Chicken breast with fruit

● Cut off the top of orange and grapefruit; remove the pulp with a grapefruit knife; divide in segments and peel; place in a bowl.

● In a non-stick pan, heat 1 tablespoon of extra virgin olive oil. Add the chicken breasts and cook for 7 minutes; season with salt and pepper. Remove and drain on paper towels; cool completely.

● Rinse and dry the grapes; cut in half and remove seeds. Cut the avocado in half, peel, pit and dice pulp. Toss with 2 tablespoons of lemon juice.

● In a bowl, whisk a pinch of salt, remaining lemon juice and a pinch of pepper. When salt is dissolved, slowly whisk in the olive oil, until well blended and the sauce thickens.

● Chop the chicken in large cubes and transfer to a salad bowl. Add the orange and grapefruit segments, the avocado and grapes. Toss with the prepared sauce. Cover and set aside for 15 minutes. Sprinkle with the chopped chervil and serve.

Difficulty **easy**
Preparation time **40 minutes**
Calories **205**

Ingredients *for 4 servings*

Chicken breast *1 lb*
Carrots *1*
Leeks *1*
Celery *1 stalk*
Bay leaves *2*
Fennel leaves *a few*
Thyme *1 sprig*
Mint *4 sprigs*
Grated lemon peel *1 tablespoon*
Dry white wine *1/2 cup*
Extra virgin olive oil *3 tablespoons*
Salt *&* pepper *to taste*

Chicken breast with vegetables & herb sauce

● Rinse and dry the chicken on paper towels. Peel the carrots. Trim the leek; remove hard leaves and roots. Rinse all vegetables and slice or thickly cut in julienne.

● In a pan, heat the extra virgin olive oil. Add all vegetables and sauté for about 5 minutes. With a slotted spoon, transfer to a plate. In the same pan, brown the chicken breasts on both sides. Add the dry white wine, bay leaves and cooked vegetables. Cover and cook on low heat for about 15 minutes.

● Drain the chicken breasts and vegetables. (Discard bay leaves.) Place on a warmed serving dish. Cover with aluminum foil to keep warm.

● Rinse the fennel leaves, basil, thyme and mint; dry and chop. Add herbs to the cooking liquids. Mix in the lemon peel and season with salt and pepper. Cook for 5 minutes or until the sauce is reduced by half. Pour over the chicken breasts and serve.

Difficulty **easy**
Preparation time **1 hour 10 minutes**
Calories **290**

Ingredients *for 4 servings*

Chicken *1, about 2 lbs*
Rosemary *1 sprig*
Sage *2 leaves*
Coarse sea salt *about 4 lbs*
Pepper *to taste*

Chicken in salt crust

● Rinse the exterior and interior of the chicken; dry well. Fill the cavity with the rosemary, sage leaves, a pinch of salt and fresh ground pepper. Attach the chicken legs with kitchen twine, so it keeps its shape during the cooking.

● Line a deep oven casserole (not much bigger than the chicken) with a layer of coarse sea salt, 1/2-inch thick.

Place the chicken on top of salt. Pour the remaining salt around the chicken so it is all completely covered.

● Bake in a preheated oven at 475°F and break the crust with the handle of a knife. Remove the chicken and brush any remaining salt from it. Transfer to a serving dish and serve with a green salad.

Spicy chicken

Difficulty **easy**
Preparation time **1 hour + marinating time**
Calories **415**

Ingredients *for 4 servings*

Chicken *1, about 2 1/2 lbs*

Tomatoes *3/4 lb, firm and ripe*

Lemons *1*

Red hot chili peppers *1 small*

Oregano *a pinch*

Cinnamon *1 small stick*

Cloves *1*

Dry white wine *1/2 cup*

Extra virgin olive oil *2 tablespoons*

Salt *&* **peppercorns** *to taste*

● Press the lemon in a bowl. Rinse and dry the chicken; cut in 8 pieces. Place in a bowl and toss with the lemon juice; season with salt. Add peppercorns and marinate at room temperature for 1 hour. Turn the chicken pieces often.

● Blanch the tomatoes in boiling water; drain, peel and squeeze gently to remove seeds, then chop coarsely. In a pan, heat the extra virgin olive oil. Add the drained chicken and brown on all sides. Add the dry white wine and let evaporate on high heat. Drain the chicken and place in a baking dish.

● In another pan, bring to boil the tomatoes with the chili pepper, oregano, cinnamon stick, a few peppercorns and the cloves. Cook on high heat for 20 minutes, stirring often. Pour the sauce over the chicken; cover with aluminum foil. Bake in a preheated oven at 400°F for 30 minutes. Serve directly from the baking dish.

Chicken in milk

Difficulty **easy**
Preparation time **50 minutes
+ marinating time**
Calories **385**

Ingredients *for 4 servings*

Chicken *1, about 2 lbs*

Onions *1/2 lb*

Whole milk *1/2 cup*

Bay leaves *2*

Juniper berries *4*

Extra virgin olive oil *2 tablespoons*

Salt *&* **pepper** *to taste*

● Rinse the chicken carefully and dry well; cut in 8 pieces and remove skin. Place in a bowl; drizzle with extra virgin olive oil. Add juniper berries, chopped bay leaves and generous fresh ground pepper. Set aside to marinate for 30 minutes, turning the chicken often.

● Peel the onions and slice thinly; place at the bottom of a saucepan and drizzle with a few tablespoons of milk.

Place pieces of chicken on top of onions, with the entire marinade. Season with salt and pepper. Add remaining milk. Cover the saucepan and cook on low heat for 30 minutes.

● When the chicken is tender, turn up the heat and brown the chicken, turning them often. Transfer to a warm serving dish. Serve with mashed or baked potatoes.

Guinea fowl with vegetables

Difficulty **easy**
Preparation time **1 hour**
Calories **300**

Ingredients *for 4 servings*

Guinea fowl *1, about 2 lbs*
Tomatoes *1, ripe and firm*
Carrots *1*
Celery *1/2 stalk*
Onions *1/2*
Thyme *1 sprig*
Dry white wine *1/2 cup*
Extra virgin olive oil *3 tablespoons*
Salt *&* **pepper** *to taste*

● Carefully rinse and dry the guinea fowl; cut in 8 pieces. Season all sides of all pieces with salt and pepper.

● Blanch the tomatoes in boiling water; drain, peel and squeeze gently to remove seeds, then chop coarsely. Peel the onion. Trim and peel the carrot. Rinse, dry and finely chop onion, carrot and celery.

● In a pan, heat the extra virgin olive oil. Add the pieces of guinea fowl and brown on all sides. Add dry white wine and evaporate on high heat. Add the chopped onion, carrot, celery and the thyme. Cook on low heat, until just tender. Add the tomatoes and mix well. Taste for salt and pepper.

● Cover the pan and cook for 40 minutes on low heat, stirring often. When meat is tender, remove the thyme. Transfer to a warm serving dish. Serve immediately.

1 *Brown the pieces of guinea fowl on all sides.*

2 *Add the chopped onion, carrot, celery and the thyme; cook briefly.*

3 *Add the coarsely chopped tomato and mix well.*

Difficulty **easy**
Preparation time **50 minutes**
Calories **285**

Chicken with spinach & ham

Ingredients *for 4 servings*

Chicken breast *1 lb*
Cooked ham *3 oz, sliced*
Spinach *1/2 lb*
Onions *1*
Dry white wine *1/4 cup*
Beef broth *1/2 cup*
Extra virgin olive oil *4 tablespoons*
Salt *&* **pepper** *to taste*

● Rinse the spinach several times in cold water; scald in boiling water; drain and transfer to ice water to cool rapidly. Drain again and place the leaves on a kitchen towel to dry. Peel the onion and chop finely.

● Cut the chicken breasts in 8 slices; flatten lightly with a meat tenderizer; season with a pinch of salt and pepper. On each slice, place 2 spinach leaves and one slice of ham. Roll the chicken and close with a toothpick.

● In a non-stick pan, heat the extra virgin olive oil. Add the rolls and brown on all sides. Add dry white wine and evaporate on high heat. Drain the rolls and keep warm.

● In the same pan, add the chopped onion and cook until just transparent. Return the rolls to the pan; add the hot broth and cook for 20 minutes. Drain the rolls and slice. Serve with its cooking juices.

Difficulty **easy**
Preparation time **45 minutes**
Calories **400**

Chicken chunks

Ingredients *for 4 servings*

Chicken *1*
Tomatoes *1/2 lb, firm and ripe*
Basil *1 small bunch*
Garlic *1 clove*
Dry white wine *1/4 cup*
Extra virgin olive oil *4 tablespoons*
Salt *&* **pepper** *to taste*

● Clean, rinse and dry the chicken with a towel; cut in 8 pieces. Blanch the tomatoes in boiling water; drain, peel and squeeze gently to remove seeds, then chop coarsely. Rinse, dry and tear the basil.

● In a pan, heat 3 tablespoons of extra virgin olive oil. Add the chicken and brown all around. Add dry white wine and let evaporate on high heat. Remove the chicken pieces and keep warm.

● In the same pan, add the remaining oil and garlic. When garlic browns, add the tomatoes and basil. Season with a pinch of salt and pepper. Cook for about 6 minutes.

● Return the chicken to the pan. Cover the pan and cook on medium heat for 25 to 30 minutes, adding a little water if necessary. When tender, serve immediately.

Curried chicken with apples

Difficulty **easy**
Preparation time **1 hour**
Calories **505**

Ingredients *for 4 servings*

Chicken *1, about 2 1/2 lbs*
Garlic *1 clove*
Chopped onions *1 tablespoon*
Apples *2*
Lemons *the juice of 1*
Curry powder *1 teaspoon*
Dry white wine *1/4 cup*
Chicken broth *1/2 cup*
Unbleached flour *2 tablespoons*
Butter *2 oz*
Extra virgin olive oil *2 tablespoons*
Salt *to taste*

● Rinse and peel the apples; core and slice thinly. Toss with lemon juice.

● Clean, rinse and dry the chicken; cut in pieces. In a pan, melt half the butter in the extra virgin olive oil. Add the chicken and brown on all sides; season with salt. Add the dry white wine and let evaporate on high heat. Transfer to a plate.

● In the same pan, add remaining butter and garlic. Cook until it starts to brown. Remove the garlic; add the chopped onion, apples and curry powder; cook for a few minutes.

● Return the chicken to the pan. Add hot broth. Cover and cook for about 30 minutes, on medium heat, stirring often. Add more broth if necessary. Taste for salt. Transfer the chicken with its sauce on a warm serving dish. Serve immediately

Chicken with lemon

Difficulty **easy**
Preparation time **1 hour**
Calories **365**

Ingredients *for 4 servings*

Chicken *1*
Lemons *4*
Extra virgin olive oil *3 tablespoons*
Salt & **pepper** *to taste*

● Clean, rinse and dry the chicken. Rinse and slice 1 lemon. Press the other 3 lemons in a bowl; mix in 1/4 cup of water. Season the chicken with salt and pepper inside and out. Stuff with lemon slices. Close the cavity with kitchen twine and attach the chicken legs.

● In a deep oven pan, heat the extra virgin olive oil. Brown the chicken on high heat, until golden on all sides. Add the diluted lemon juice and bake in a preheated oven at 400°F for 40 minutes. Baste often with the cooking juices.

● Remove from the oven. Transfer the chicken to a serving dish. Serve immediately with a mixed salad or steamed vegetables.

Difficulty **easy**
Preparation time **1 hour**
+ marinating time
Calories **270**

Ingredients *for 6 servings*

Veal chops *6*

Artichokes *6*

Tomatoes *3*

Lemons *1*

Garlic *2 cloves*

Bay leaves *2*

Cloves *2*

Basil *1 small bunch*

Parsley *1 small bunch*

Red hot chili peppers *2*

White wine vinegar *3/4 cup*

Dry white wine *3/4 cup*

Extra virgin olive oil *about 1 1/2 cups*

Peppercorns *1 teaspoon*

Salt *&* **pepper** *to taste*

Veal chops & artichokes

● Cut off tips, stems and hard outer leaves from the artichokes; keep the hearts and remove the chokes; soak in water mixed with the lemon juice.

● In a saucepan, heat the vinegar with 3/4 cup of water, the peppercorns, a pinch of salt, bay leaves, cloves and parsley. Bring to boil; add the drained artichokes and cook for 5 to 7 minutes. Drain the artichokes again.

● During this time, rinse and cut the tomatoes in quarters; remove seeds. In a glass jar, layer the tomatoes, a few leaves of basil and artichokes, until all ingredients are used. Cover with extra virgin olive oil. Add peeled garlic and chili pepper. Close the jar and marinate for 3 days.

● In a skillet, heat 1 tablespoon of extra virgin olive oil. Add the chops. Season with salt and pepper. Brown; reduce the heat and cook for 6 to 7 minutes on each side. Remove the chops and keep warm. Pour the fat out of the pan; add the dry white wine and reduce a little, stirring all the time. Pour over the chops. Serve with the marinated tomatoes and artichokes.

Difficulty **easy**
Preparation time **20 minutes**
Calories **160**

Ingredients *for 4 servings*

Veal cutlets *3/4 lb*
Capers *1 tablespoon*
Parsley *1 small bunch*
Basil *1 small bunch*
Unbleached flour *1 tablespoon*
Lemon juice *2 tablespoons*
Extra virgin olive oil *3 tablespoons*
Salt *&* **pepper** *to taste*

Veal cutlets with capers

● Flatten the cutlets a little, with a meat tenderizer, placing them between 2 pieces of waxed paper. Roll them in flour. Rinse, dry and chop the parsley and basil separately. In a pan, heat the extra virgin olive oil. Brown the veal; season with salt and pepper. Cook until golden on all sides; drain and keep warm between 2 plates.

● Pour the fat out of the pan; add lemon juice and 4 tablespoons of water; stir with a wooden spoon. Add capers, parsley and basil; cook for one minute. Return the veal cutlets to the pan and cook for about 2 minutes, turning them once with a spatula. Taste for salt and pepper.

● Serve immediately with buttered steamed spinach.

Difficulty **easy**
Preparation time **40 minutes**
Calories **300**

Ingredients *for 4 servings*

Veal slices *12*
Lean pancetta *12 slices*
Onions *1*
Unbleached flour *2 tablespoons*
Capers *1 tablespoon*
Dry white wine *1/2 cup*
Extra virgin olive oil *4 tablespoons*
Salt *&* **pepper** *to taste*

Veal rolls with lemon

● Peel the onion and chop finely. Rinse and dry the lemon; grate the peel; press the juice; filter into a bowl.

● Brush the meat with the lemon juice; season with salt and fresh ground pepper. Cover with a piece of pancetta. Roll onto themselves and fix with toothpicks. Roll in flour. In a pan, heat the extra virgin olive oil. Add the veal rolls and on high heat, brown on all sides. Remove from the pan and keep warm.

● In the same pan, cook the onion until transparent. Return the rolls to the pan. Add the dry white wine, lemon peel, capers, a pinch of salt and pepper. Cover the pan and cook on medium heat for 15 to 20 minutes. When the meat is tender, serve immediately.

Difficulty **easy**
Preparation time **1 hour 15 minutes**
Calories **210**

Veal tidbits with scallions & carrots

Ingredients *for 6-8 servings*

Veal *2 lbs, from shoulder*
Scallions *12*
Baby carrots *1 lb*
Dry Marsala *1/4 cup*
Fennel seeds *1 tablespoon*
Red hot chili peppers *1*
Bay leaves *1*
Beef broth *1 cup*
Unbleached flour *2 tablespoons*
Extra virgin olive oil *2 tablespoons*
Salt *to taste*

● Cut the meat in bite-size cubes. Remove roots and outer leaves from the scallions; rinse and slice. Trim, peel, rinse and dice the carrot. Roll the veal cubes in flour.

● In a pan, heat the extra virgin olive oil with the chili pepper. Add the veal cubes and brown on all sides. Season with salt. Remove the chili pepper.

● Add Marsala and let evaporate on high heat. Add scallions and carrots. Sauté for a minute. Add bay leaf and fennel seeds. Add hot broth; cover the pan and cook on medium heat, for 50-60 minutes.

● Remove from heat. Transfer the preparation to a warm serving dish. Serve with white rice.

Difficulty **easy**
Preparation time **40 minutes
+ resting time**
Calories **300**

Barbecued turkey meatballs

Ingredients *for 4 servings*

Ground turkey *1 1/4 lbs*
Lean pancetta *8 slices*
Egg yolks *2*
Garlic *1 clove*
Oregano *a pinch*
Sage *8 leaves*
Cognac *1 tablespoon*
Extra virgin olive oil *2 tablespoons*
Salt *& pepper to taste*

● In a bowl, mix the turkey, egg yolks, chopped garlic, oregano, cognac, a pinch of salt and pepper. Mix with a wooden spoon. Cover and refrigerate for about 1 hour.

● In aluminum foil, cut 8 rectangles of 6 x 8 inch; brush with extra virgin olive oil. In each rectangle, place one sage leaf. Remove the preparation from the refrigerator; make 8 meatballs. Roll each in a slice of pancetta. Place one on each sage leaf. Close the aluminum foil around the meatballs.

● Preheat a barbecue grill. Cook the meatballs in aluminum for 7 to 8 minutes; turn them and cook for another 7 minutes. Serve hot with a mixed salad.

Duck breast with oranges

Difficulty **easy**
Preparation time **30 minutes**
Calories **205**

Ingredients *for 4 servings*

Duck breast *1, about 3/4 lb*
Orange juice *10 tablespoons*
Oranges *the peel of 1 small*
Beef broth *1/2 cup*
Red wine *1/2 cup*
Extra virgin olive oil *2 tablespoons*
Salt *&* **pepper** *to taste*

● Separate the duck breast in its two parts. Season with salt and fresh ground pepper. Slice orange peel in thin strips; scald in boiling water and drain.

● In an oven casserole, heat the extra virgin olive oil. Brown the duck breasts on all sides. Add 4 tablespoons of orange juice and broth. Bake in a preheated oven at 375°F for 15 minutes, basting often with the cooking juices. Remove duck from the casserole, cover with aluminum foil and set aside for a few minutes.

● Remove the fat from the casserole. Add the red wine and reduce a little, stirring all the time with a wooden spoon. Add remaining orange juice and orange peel strips. Bring to boil and cook for 2 to 3 minutes. Slice the duck breasts and serve with the sauce, and if you wish, sweet marinated onions.

Young chicken with anchovies

Difficulty **easy**
Preparation time **50 minutes + resting time**
Calories **385**

Ingredients *for 4 servings*

Young chickens *2, about 1 lb each*
Rosemary *1 sprig*
Sage *3 leaves*
Parsley *1 small bunch*
Capers *1 tablespoon*
Anchovies *4*
Beef broth *1/2 cup*
Dry white wine *1/4 cup*
Extra virgin olive oil *3 tablespoons*
Salt *&* **pepper** *to taste*

● Rinse the parsley, rosemary and sage; chop together and mix in a small bowl with a pinch of salt and pepper. Rub the mixture inside and outside the chickens. Set aside for 30 minutes. Rinse the anchovies; debone, filet and chop.

● In an oven pan, heat the extra virgin olive oil and brown the chickens on all sides. Bake in a preheated oven at 350°F for 15 minutes, basting often with the cooking juices. Add the dry white wine and cook for another 15 minutes. Remove from oven and keep the chickens warm.

● Remove fat from the pan. Add capers and chopped anchovies. Add hot broth and mix with a wooden spoon. Cook on medium heat until sauce reduces a little. Place the chickens on a serving dish and serve with the anchovy sauce.

Guinea fowl with tea

Difficulty **easy**
Preparation time **40 minutes**
Calories **215**

Ingredients *for 4 servings*

Guinea fowl breasts *4*

Black tea *6 tablespoons*

Mixed fresh fruit in season *3/4 lb*

Vegetable broth *1/2 cup*

Extra virgin olive oil *2 tablespoons*

Salt & **pepper** *to taste*

Andrea's note: It can also be prepared with pheasant or Cornish hens.

● Season the guinea fowl with salt and pepper. In a pan, heat the extra virgin olive oil. Add breasts and on high heat, brown on all sides. Add 3 table-spoons of tea and cover the pan. Cook on medium heat for 20 minutes. Remove from heat. Transfer the guinea fowl breasts to aluminum paper; wrap them and set aside for 5 minutes.

● During this time, add remaining tea to the pan. Season with a pinch of salt and fresh ground pepper. Let reduce on medium heat. Place the guinea fowl breasts on a serving dish with the sliced mixed fruits. Serve with the warm sauce.

Turkey breast skewers

Difficulty **easy**
Preparation time **30 minutes
+ marinating time**
Calories **310**

Ingredients *for 4 servings*

Turkey breasts *1 1/4 lbs*

Small vine-ripened tomatoes *2*

Red bell peppers *1*

Onions *1*

Juniper berries *a few*

Sage *a few leaves*

Dry white wine *1/4 cup*

Extra virgin olive oil *4 tablespoons*

Salt & **peppercorns** *to taste*

● Cut the turkey meat in cubes. Place in a bowl with the wine, the juniper berries, the peppercorns and 2 table-spoons of olive oil; toss well, cover and set aside for 30 minutes.

● During this time, rinse the tomatoes; quarter and remove the seeds. Rinse the pepper; halve and remove seeds and white parts; cut in small cubes. Peel the onion and slice thinly.

● Drain the turkey cubes and filter the marinade. On skewers, alternate a piece of meat with the vegetables and the sage leaves. Brush a cookie sheet with oil; place the skewers on it. Season with salt and pepper.

● Bake in a preheated oven at 450°F for about 15 minutes, turning the skewers often. Baste often with the marinade. Remove from oven and serve with a mixed salad.

Difficulty **easy**
Preparation time **1 hour 10 minutes**
Calories **360**

Ingredients *for 4 servings*

Rabbit   *2 1/2 lbs*
Green bell peppers   *1*
Garlic   *3 cloves*
Parsley   *1 small bunch*
Unbleached flour   *2 tablespoons*
Vegetable broth   *1 cup*
Extra virgin olive oil   *3 tablespoons*
Salt   *&* **pepper**   *to taste*

Rabbit with peppers

● Cut the rabbit in pieces; rinse and dry well; roll in flour. In a non-stick pan, heat the extra virgin olive oil. Add the pieces of rabbit and brown on all sides. When golden, remove the rabbit and drain on paper towels; transfer to a deep pan.

● Rinse, dry and chop the parsley. Peel and crush the garlic. Rinse, dry and chop the pepper coarsely, removing seeds. Cook in the non-stick pan in which the rabbit was cooked, for a minute. Add parsley and garlic; season with salt and fresh ground pepper. Add broth and bring to boil.

● Transfer the pepper preparation to the pan with rabbit. Cook on medium heat for 30 to 40 minutes, stirring often and adding more broth if needed. When rabbit is tender, transfer to a warm serving dish. Serve very hot.

Difficulty **easy**
Preparation time **20 minutes**
Calories **450**

Ingredients *for 4 servings*

Skinless chicken breasts *2*

Garlic *2 cloves*

Capers *1 tablespoon*

Parsley *2 tablespoons, chopped*

Anchovy fillets *2, chopped*

Tomato sauce *16 oz*

Oregano *1 tablespoon*

Extra virgin olive oil *5 tablespoons*

Salt *& pepper* *to taste*

Chicken breast pizzaiola

● Divide the chiciken breasts in two, lengthwise; to flatten, beat with the back of a large knife.

● In a large skillet, heat the extra virgin olive oil. Add the flattened chicken breasts and cook for about 10 minutes, turning twice.

● Peel the garlic cloves and add to the skillet with the chicken. Add the anchovies, the capers and the parsley; sauté for a few seconds.

● Stir in the tomato sauce; lower the heat. Add salt and fresh ground pepper to taste. Simmer for 5 minutes. Add the oregano and mix well; cook for another 3 minutes.

● Remove from heat and set aside for 2 minutes before serving.

Difficulty **easy**
Preparation time **50 minutes**
Calories **360**

Ingredients *for 4 servings*

Rabbit thighs *8*

Tomatoes *1/2 lb, firm and ripe*

Rosemary *1 sprig*

Basil *1 small bunch*

Dry white wine *1/4 cup*

Extra virgin olive oil *3 tablespoons*

Salt *& pepper* *to taste*

Neapolitan-style rabbit thighs

● Rinse and dry the rabbit thighs on a kitchen towel. Blanch the tomatoes in boiling water; drain, peel and squeeze gently to remove seeds, then dice the pulp.

● In a pan, heat the extra virgin olive oil. Add the rabbit thighs and brown on all sides. Season with salt and pepper. Add the wine and let evaporate on high heat. Remove the rabbit and keep warm between 2 plates.

● In the same pan, add the diced tomatoes, rosemary, shredded basil and a pinch of salt and pepper. Bring to boil. Return the rabbit to the pan and cover. Cook for 30 minutes, stirring often. Transfer to a serving dish and serve immediately.

Difficulty **average**
Preparation time **1 hour**
+ resting time
Calories **290**

Rabbit with vegetables

Ingredients *for 4-6 servings*

Rabbit *1, about 2 lbs*
Carrots *1/2 lb*
Zucchini *1/2 lb*
Eggplants *1*
Parsley *1 small bunch*
Chives *1 bunch*
Shallots *2*
Coriander seeds *1 teaspoon*
Dry white wine *1/4 cup*
Extra virgin olive oil *4 tablespoons*
Salt *&* **pepper** *to taste*

● Trim and rinse the eggplant; cut in strips and place in a colander; sprinkle with coarse salt and set aside for 20 minutes to remove excess moisture.

● Cut the rabbit in pieces; rinse well and dry on a kitchen towel. Peel and finely slice shallots. Trim, rinse and slice carrots and zucchini in strips. Rinse and dry parsley and chives; chop together. Rinse eggplants and dry well.

● In a non-stick pan, heat 2 table-spoons of extra virgin olive oil. Add shallots and cook until just transparent.

Add the pieces of rabbit; season with salt and pepper. Brown on all sides. Add the white wine and let evaporate on high heat. Drain the rabbit and keep warm.

● Remove the fat from the pan. Add the remaining oil, the coriander seeds, carrots, zucchinis and eggplants. Sauté for a few minutes. Add 3 table-spoons of water, the reserved rabbit, a pinch of salt and pepper. Cook on medium heat for 30 minutes. Sprinkle with parsley and chives; serve immediately.

Difficulty **average**
Preparation time **1 hour 15 minutes**
Calories **445**

Rabbit with olives

Ingredients *for 4 servings*

Rabbit *1, about 2 1/2 lbs*
Pitted black olives *4 oz*
Tomatoes *3/4 lb, firm and ripe*
Onions *1*
Celery *1 stalk*
Carrots *1*
Garlic *1 clove*
Rosemary *1 sprig*
Red wine *1/4 cup*
Extra virgin olive oil *4 tablespoons*
Salt *&* **pepper** *to taste*

● Rinse and carefully dry the rabbit; cut in pieces. In a skillet, heat 2 table-spoons of extra virgin olive oil. Add the rabbit on high heat, brown on all sides, turning the pieces often with a spatula.

● Rinse, dry and finely chop the carrot, onion and celery. In a pan, heat the remaining extra virgin olive oil and cook the vegetables until onion is transparent. Add the rabbit pieces. Season with salt and pepper. Add the

wine and let evaporate on high heat.

● Blanch the tomatoes in boiling water; drain, peel and squeeze gently to remove seeds, then chop coarsely. Add tomatoes to the pan with the chopped rosemary. Cover the pan and cook for 45 minutes, stirring often.

● Add the olives and cook covered on low heat for 15 minutes. Transfer to a serving dish and serve immediately.

Difficulty **easy**
Preparation time **1 hour 10 minutes**
+ marinating time
Calories **295**

Ingredients *for 4-6 servings*

Rabbit pieces *2 1/4 lbs*

Small onions *3/4 lb*

Carrots *2*

Celery *1 stalk*

Thyme *2 sprigs*

Rosemary *1 sprig*

Parsley *1 bunch*

Bay leaves *1*

Garlic *1 clove*

Dry white wine *1/2 cup*

Extra virgin olive oil *4 tablespoons*

Salt *&* **pepper** *to taste*

Rabbit with onions

● Rinse the rabbit and place in a bowl with one sprig of thyme, half a sprig of rosemary, a little parsley, crushed garlic and the bay leaf. Toss with the dry white wine and set aside for 2 hours, stirring often.

● Rinse the small onions. Trim, peel and dice the carrot. Rinse and dice the celery. Blanch the small onions, carrots and celery in boiling water for 2 to 3 minutes; drain well.

● In an oven pan, heat the extra virgin olive oil. Add the drained pieces of rabbit. (Keep the marinade aside.) Brown on all sides on high heat. Add the vegetables and mix well.

● Cover the pan and bake in a pre-heated oven at 350°F for about 45 minutes. After 15 minutes, add the marinade and keep in the oven. Remove from oven. Transfer to a serving dish and sprinkle with the thyme, parsley and rosemary chopped together.

Vegetables

Grilled vegetables

Difficulty **easy**
Preparation time **1 hour**
Calories **210**

Ingredients *for 6 servings*

Eggplants *2*

Tomatoes *3*

Potatoes *2*

Red radicchio *2 heads*

Yellow bell peppers *1*

Red bell peppers *1*

Zucchini *3*

Artichokes *2*

Fennel bulbs *2*

Lemons *the juice of 2*

Garlic *2-3 cloves*

Extra virgin olive oil *1/4 cup*

Salt *&* **pepper** *to taste*

● Rinse the vegetables. Trim the zucchini and the eggplants and slice lengthwise. Remove the branches from the fennel and cut into strips. Discard the outer hard leaves and the stems from the artichokes, cut in half and remove the chokes. Keep only the hearts and cut them in half. Rinse and quarter the radicchio. Peel the potatoes and slice thickly. Cut the tomatoes in half, horizontally and remove the seeds.

● Peel the garlic, remove the green sprout and chop finely. In a bowl, mix the olive oil, the garlic, the lemon juice, a pinch of salt and freshly ground pepper; whisk well with a fork until well blended.

● Rinse and dry the whole peppers, put on a hot grill and sear all over; remove the skin wiping with a paper towel to remove any remaining pieces; cut open and remove the seeds and the white parts. Cut in slices and arrange on a serving dish. Grill the other vegetables and lay out on the serving dish as they are ready. Serve with the prepared sauce.

Baked eggplant 'caponata'

Difficulty **easy**
Preparation time **1 hour**
+ resting time
Calories **100**

Ingredients *for 6 servings*

Eggplants *1 lb*
Small vine-ripened tomatoes *1/2 lb*
Red bell peppers *2*
Yellow bell peppers *2*
Onions *1*
Garlic *1 clove*
Basil *a few leaves*
Dry white wine *1/2 cup*
Extra virgin olive oil *4 tablespoons*
Salt *&* pepper *to taste*

● Rinse and trim the eggplants, dice and put into a colander; sprinkle with salt, cover with a weight and leave for about an hour to drain the moisture; rinse quickly and dry carefully.

● Clean the peppers; halve and remove the seeds and the white parts; cut into thin strips; Scald the tomatoes in boiling water; drain, peel and gently squeeze to remove all seeds and cut into strips. Peel the onion, rinse, dry and slice. Peel the garlic, remove the green sprout and chop together with the rinsed basil.

● Brush a baking dish with a tablespoon of olive oil; arrange the peppers, onion, tomatoes, eggplants, chopped garlic and basil in the dish. Season with a pinch of salt and fresh ground pepper and drizzle with the remaining olive oil.

● Bake at 350°F for about 40 minutes; after 20 minutes, remove from oven, mix the vegetables and pour on the wine. When finished baking and the wine has been absorbed, remove from oven and let cool before serving in the same dish.

Eggplants in tomato sauce

Difficulty **easy**
Preparation time **1 hour**
Calories **205**

Ingredients *for 4 servings*

Eggplants *4*
Garlic *3 cloves*
Basil *1 small bunch*
Pecorino *3 oz*
Salt *to taste*

For the sauce

Roma tomatoes *1 1/4 lbs*
Onions *1 small*
Basil *6 leaves*
Extra virgin olive oil *4 tablespoons*
Salt *&* pepper *to taste*

● Rinse and dry the eggplants, trim the ends, and make 3 lengthwise incisions in each eggplant, equally distanced from the ends. Peel the garlic cloves and cut in half or in quarters if the cloves are very large. Rinse and dry the basil leaves. Cut the pecorino into slices. In each incision, insert a slice of pecorino, a piece of garlic and a leaf of basil that has been sprinkled with salt.

● Prepare the sauce. Scald the tomatoes in boiling water; drain, peel and gently squeeze to remove all seeds; chop coarsely. Peel the onion and chop finely.

● In a casserole, cook the onion in olive oil until transparent; add the tomatoes, basil leaves, a dash of salt, generous fresh ground pepper and bring to a boil. Add the eggplants so they are almost completely covered by the sauce; cover the pot and cook over moderate heat for about 40 minutes adding a few tablespoons of water from time to time if the sauce thickens too much; before removing from the heat, season with salt. Serve the eggplants while hot or warm accompanied by the cooking sauce.

Eggplant rolls

Difficulty **average**
Preparation time **40 minutes
+ resting time**
Calories **260**

Ingredients *for 4 servings*

Long eggplants *4*
Desalted anchovy filets *2*
Pitted black olives *3 oz*
Garlic *2 cloves*
Parsley *1 bunch*
Mozzarella *1 small*
Unbleached flour *a few tablespoons*
Extra virgin olive oil *enough for frying*
Salt *to taste*

● Dice the mozzarella and let drain in a colander. Rinse, trim the eggplants, then cut into slices lengthwise. Place the eggplant slices in a colander alternating with layers of coarse salt; leave for 30 minutes to drain off the excess moisture.

● Rinse quickly and dry the eggplant slices; dip in flour, shake off the excess flour and fry in abundant olive oil; remove with a slotted spoon and place on paper towels to drain the excess oil.

● Peel the garlic cloves and remove the green sprout; trim and rinse the parsley. Finely chop the parsley with the garlic and the anchovy filets. Use this mixture to cover each eggplant slice and top with a piece of mozzarella.

● Roll the eggplant slices and secure them with a toothpick; place on a hot grill for a few minutes, turning them with a spatula so the mozzarella melts inside. Transfer to a serving dish and serve while very hot.

Baked eggplants

Difficulty **easy**
Preparation time **1 hour 20 minutes
+ resting time**
Calories **270**

Ingredients *for 4 servings*

Eggplants *2 1/2 lbs*
Pitted black olives *6 oz*
Salted anchovies *3 oz*
Capers in vinegar *2 tablespoons*
Tomatoes *2, firm and ripe*
Day-old Italian-style bread *1 slice, crumbled*
Oregano *1/4 teaspoon*
Parsley *1 small bunch*
Garlic *1 clove*
Extra virgin olive oil *4 tablespoons*
Salt *to taste*

● Rinse the eggplants, halve lengthwise; with a spoon, remove the central seedy pulp. Using a pointed knife slice crosswise diagonally to form a sort of net. Sprinkle with salt and place face down in a strainer to drain the excess moisture.

● Rinse the anchovies under running water, debone and chop finely. Rinse the parsley, peel the garlic and chop finely with the oregano leaves. Blanch the tomatoes, peel and cut in half; squeeze gently to remove the seeds and slice into strips. In a bowl, combine the olives, capers, chopped anchovies, chopped herbs, bread and 2 tablespoons of olive oil; season with salt, and mix with a wooden spoon until well blended.

● Rinse the eggplants, squeeze gently and dry. Brush a baking dish with olive oil. Lay out the eggplants side by side, concave side up. Fill the eggplant halves with the prepared mixture, cover with the tomato strips, drizzle with olive oil and bake at 350°F for about an hour. Arrange the eggplants on a serving dish and serve, decorating, if you wish, with thin slices of tomato.

Sweet-and-sour artichokes

Difficulty **easy**
Preparation time **40 minutes**
Calories **185**

Ingredients *for 4 servings*

Artichokes *8*
Anchovies *5*
Onions *1*
Parsley *1 small bunch*
Unbleached flour *1 tablespoon*
Sugar *1/2 tablespoon*
Lemons *1*
Orange juice *1 cup*
Extra virgin olive oil *4 tablespoons*
Salt *to taste*

● Cut the artichoke stems, remove the outer leaves and discard the chokes. In a bowl, cover the artichokes with water and the juice of 1/2 lemon. In a pot, boil abundant salted water with a little of the remaining lemon juice; add the artichokes and boil for 20 minutes. Remove with a slotted spoon and arrange on a serving dish with the leaves pointing upward.

● Peel the onion and chop finely; season with salt. Cook in a pan with the olive oil. Rinse the parsley and chop; desalt the anchovies, debone and chop. When the onion starts to turn lightly brown, add the anchovies and let dissolve over low heat, mashing them with a fork. Remove from heat.

● Pour on the orange juice and the rest of the lemon juice and, stirring constantly, add the flour; put the sauce back on low heat and let it reduce being careful to not let it boil. Add the sugar, the parsley, a pinch of salt and mix carefully; stir with a wooden spoon until the sugar is melted, remove from heat, pour the sauce over the artichokes and serve at once.

Artichokes cooked with white wine vinegar

Difficulty **easy**
Preparation time **1 hour**
Calories **125**

Ingredients *for 4 servings*

Artichokes *6*
Onions *1/2 lb*
Tomato paste *1 tablespoon*
Parsley *1 small bunch*
Lemons *2, the juice*
White wine vinegar *3 tablespoons*
Extra virgin olive oil *4 tablespoons*
Salt *& pepper to taste*

● Trim the artichokes, eliminating the stems and the hard outer leaves; with a sharp knife, remove the rest of the hard parts and the tips, cut in half, remove the chokes and slice thinly; immerse one by one in water mixed with the juice of 2 lemons.

● Peel the onions, slice thinly and fry in a skillet with the olive oil; add the artichokes, well dried, and the parsley, trimmed, rinsed and chopped. When lightly cooked, add the tomato paste, dissolved in 1/2 cup of hot water. Season with salt, add a dash of ground pepper. Boil over high heat for a few minutes.

● Add the white wine vinegar, cook over high heat until evaporated and continue cooking over low heat for about 1/2 hour adding, from time to time, a little hot water, and stirring often. When done, remove from heat and let cool completely before serving.

Artichokes with mozzarella

Difficulty **easy**
Preparation time **45 minutes**
Calories **260**

Ingredients *for 4 servings*

Artichokes *8*
Mozzarella *5 oz*
Lemons *the juice of 1*
Parsley *1 small bunch*
Salted anchovies *1*
Eggs *1*
Grated grana cheese *1 tablespoon*
Breadcrumbs *1 tablespoon*
Extra virgin olive oil *4 tablespoons*
Salt *&* pepper *to taste*

● Trim the artichokes, remove the hard outer leaves, cut the tips, the stem and discard the chokes. As you finish each one, immerse them right away in cold water mixed with the lemon juice.

● Rinse the parsley, dry and chop. Rinse the anchovy, debone and chop finely. In a bowl, using a wooden spoon, mix the parsley, the mozzarella diced into 1/2 inch cubes, the grated grana cheese, the egg, and season with salt and pepper.

● Pour the olive oil in a skillet, add a cup of water and arrange the well dried artichokes with leaves lightly open; fill the center cavity with the cheese and parsley mixture, add a piece of anchovy and sprinkle the top with breadcrumbs. Cover and cook over low heat for about 30 minutes. Transfer to a serving dish and serve immediately.

Artichokes with pecorino

Difficulty **easy**
Preparation time **40 minutes**
Calories **230**

Ingredients *for 4 servings*

Artichokes *8*
Pecorino *2 oz, diced*
Lemons *1*
Garlic *1 clove*
Breadcrumbs *4 tablespoons*
Oregano *a pinch*
Extra virgin olive oil *4 tablespoons*
Salt *to taste*

● Carefully prepare the artichokes, removing the external hard leaves and the stems; with a sharp knife, cut the spines, quarter the artichokes and remove the chokes; immerse in water mixed with lemon juice.

● In a large pan, add the olive oil and cook the peeled garlic clove cut in half; remove the garlic when slightly golden. Drain the artichokes; add to the pan; season with salt. Cover and cook on low heat for about 15 minutes mixing now and then with a wooden spoon and adding a little water from time to time, if needed.

● Add the breadcrumbs, the diced pecorino and the oregano; season with salt and mix well. Cook for 5 minutes. Transfer to a serving dish and bring to the table while still hot.

Difficulty **easy**
Preparation time **1 hour**
Calories **175**

Ingredients *for 4 servings*

Artichokes *4*
Shelled peas *3/4 lb*
Baby onions *1/2 lb*
Garlic *1 clove*
Parsley *1 small bunch*
Basil *a few leaves*
Mint *a few leaves*
Dry white wine *4 tablespoons*
Lemons *1*
Extra virgin olive oil *4 tablespoons*
Salt *&* pepper *to taste*

Artichokes & vegetables

● Rinse and dry the lemon; grate only the yellow part of the peel and press the juice into a small bowl. Clean the artichokes, remove the stems, the spines and the hard outer leaves; rinse, dry, remove the chokes and sprinkle with the lemon juice to prevent discoloring.

● Peel the garlic and remove the green sprout. Rinse and dry the parsley, the basil and the mint; chop all finely and mix in a bowl with the grated lemon peel, a pinch of salt and a dash of ground pepper. Fill the artichokes with this mixture.

● Place the artichokes in a pot, add the peas and the peeled and rinsed onions; drizzle with the olive oil and the dry white wine. Cover the pot and cook over moderate heat for 40-50 minutes or until the juices have reduced. Transfer the artichokes to a warm serving dish and serve at once.

Beans & potatoes

Difficulty **easy**
Preparation time **1 hour 30 minutes**
+ resting time
Calories **395**

Ingredients *for 4 servings*

Fresh shelled beans *1 3/4 lbs*
Yellow potatoes *10 oz*
Garlic *2 cloves*
Parsley *1 small bunch*
Basil *1 small bunch*
Mint *1 sprig*
Extra virgin olive oil *6 tablespoons*
Salt *to taste*

● Fill a pot with abundant salted water, add 2 tablespoons of olive oil and bring to a boil. In the meantime, shell the beans, rinse and as soon as the water begins to boil, drop in the beans, cover and cook over medium heat for about 1 hour.

● Peel the potatoes, rinse and dice. Peel the garlic. Trim and rinse the parsley, the mint and the basil; tie all into a bunch.

● Add the rest of the ingredients to the beans and continue cooking for another 1/2 hour. Drain and let rest for 1/2 hour; discard the herbs and the garlic. Transfer to a serving dish, season with salt, drizzle with extra virgin olive oil, toss and serve.

Warm salad with broccoli & kidney beans

Difficulty **easy**
Preparation time **1 hour 40 minutes**
+ soaking time
Calories **270**

Ingredients *for 4 servings*

Dried kidney beans *1/2 lb*
Broccoli *1 1/4 lbs*
Hot chili powder *a pinch*
Extra virgin olive oil *4 tablespoons*
Salt *to taste*

● Place the beans in a bowl, cover with abundant water and let soak for 12 hours. At the end of this time, drain, transfer to a pot and cover with water to about 2 inches above the beans. Cover and cook over medium heat for about an hour and 1/2 from the start of boiling.

● In the meantime, rinse the broccoli. Cut into pieces and cook in a pot with abundant boiling salted water until just tender and still firm. Drain and set aside.

● In a skillet, heat the olive oil. Add the beans and the broccoli. Season with salt, sprinkle with the chili powder and cook for a few minutes on medium heat, stirring often with a wooden spoon. Remove from heat, transfer to a serving bowl and serve while hot.

Cannellini beans & cabbage

Difficulty **easy**
Preparation time **2 hours**
+ soaking time
Calories **290**

Ingredients *for 4 servings*

Dried cannellini beans *1/2 lb*
Cabbage *1 1/4 lbs*
Wild fennel *4 branches*
Tomato sauce *1/2 lb*
Onions *1*
Garlic *1 clove*
Extra virgin olive oil *4 tablespoons*
Salt *to taste*

● Soak the beans in warm water for 12 hours. Drain, place in a pot and cover with water. Cover the pot, and cook over low heat for about 1 1/2 hours. Peel the onion and chop. Remove the leaves from the wild fennel, rinse and chop coarsely. Trim the cabbage, rinse, remove the heart and the hard stems and cut the leaves into strips.

● When the beans are cooked and almost dry, add the vegetables and the tomato sauce, season with salt and cook another 20 minutes, stirring from time to time with a wooden spoon. Peel the garlic and chop; lightly cook in the olive oil and add to the beans before removing from heat. Mix thoroughly, season with salt, transfer to a serving dish and serve while hot.

Cannellini beans with oregano

Difficulty **easy**
Preparation time **1 hour 15 minutes**
+ soaking time
Calories **325**

Ingredients *for 4 servings*

Dried cannellini beans *12 oz*
Garlic *2 cloves*
Oregano *1 teaspoon*
Red hot chili peppers *1*
Extra virgin olive oil *4 tablespoons*
Salt *to taste*

● Soak the beans in a bowl with abundant lukewarm water for at least 12 hours. Peel 1 garlic clove, remove the central sprout and crush lightly.

● Drain the soaked beans, rinse, place in a pot with the unpeeled garlic clove. Cover with abundant cold water; slowly bring to a boil and without adding salt, let cook over low heat for an hour or until tender. Season with salt when almost cooked. Discard the garlic clove.

● In a pan, heat the olive oil. Add the remaining garlic clove with the chili pepper. Cook until lightly golden. Add the drained beans, simmer a few minutes, stirring with a wooden spoon. Add a few ladles of cooking broth from the beans. Sprinkle with the oregano and let thicken slightly. Remove the chili pepper; transfer the beans to a serving dish and serve while hot.

Baked vegetables

Difficulty **easy**
Preparation time **45 minutes**
Calories **260**

Ingredients *for 4 servings*

Eggplants *2*
Yellow potatoes *3*
Zucchini *2*
Tomatoes *2, firm and ripe*
Red bell peppers *1*
Onions *1*
Extra virgin olive oil *5 tablespoons*
Salt *to taste*

● Roast the pepper in a hot oven, cut in half, remove the seeds, the white parts and the skin; slice into strips. Trim and eggplants and the zucchini and peel the potatoes; rinse these vegetables , dry and dice.

● Peel the onion, slice thinly. In a large saucepan, heat the olive oil. Add the onions and cook on low heat until just transparent. Add the prepared vegetables, but not the sliced pepper; mix well and sauté over medium heat for a few minutes.

● Scald the tomatoes, peel and squeeze gently to remove the seeds; dice and add to the saucepan. Mix well, season with salt and continue cooking for about 20 minutes; add a little water if the preparation become too dry. When the potatoes are cooked, add the peppers. Season with salt and let simmer for a few minutes. Serve in the cooking dish.

Basilicata-style vegetables

Difficulty **easy**
Preparation time **1 hour**
+ resting time
Calories **165**

Ingredients *for 4 servings*

Tomatoes *2, large*
Onions *2, large*
Eggplants *3*
Red and/or yellow peppers *3*
Garlic *2 cloves*
Basil *a handful of leaves*
Parsley *a handful of leaves*
Extra virgin olive oil *4 tablespoons*
Salt *to taste*

● Rinse the eggplants, trim and cut into chunks; sprinkle with salt, place in a colander, cover with a weight and let the excess moisture drain off for about an hour. When ready to use, rinse quickly and wipe dry. Rinse the peppers, trim and cut in half; remove the seeds and the white parts; slice into strips. Peel the onions and slice thinly. Scald the tomatoes, peel, squeeze gently to remove the seeds and dice.

● In a saucepan, heat the olive oil. Add the onions and cook until just lightly golden. Add the eggplants, the peppers and the tomatoes. Season with salt, cover and cook covered over low heat for about 40 minutes. Peel the garlic. Rinse and dry the basil and the parsley and chop with the garlic. After 30 minutes of cooking, add the chopped herbs and raise the heat. Reduce the cooking juices, remove from heat, transfer to a serving dish and serve at once.

Vegetable 'caponata'

Difficulty **easy**
Preparation time **1 hour**
Calories **190**

Ingredients *for 4 servings*

Spinach *10 oz*

Chicory lettuce *10 oz*

Cauliflower *1*

Chard *1/2 lb*

Curly lettuce *1 head*

Celery *1/2 lb*

Capers *4 tablespoons*

Lemons *a few slices*

Anchovy filets in oil *6*

Breadcrumbs *2 tablespoons*

White wine vinegar *4 tablespoons*

Extra virgin olive oil *6 tablespoons*

Salt *to taste*

● Trim, rinse and dry the spinach, chicory, cauliflower, curly lettuce and the celery. Boil the vegetables in separate pots in little water, lightly salted.

● Drain well, then sauté for a few minutes in a skillet with 4 tablespoons of olive oil; just before finishing, add the white wine vinegar. As soon as done, transfer to a serving dish.

● In a non-stick pan, heat the remaining olive oil and toast the breadcrumbs for a couple of minutes; distribute on the vegetables in the serving dish and decorate with chopped anchovies.

● Desalt the capers under running water, dry well. Cut the lemon slices into eight wedges and lay out on top of the vegetables. The vegetable 'caponata' is best served cold.

Vegetable 'ciambrotta'

Difficulty **easy**
Preparation time **1 hour**
Calories **190**

Ingredients *for 4 servings*

Yellow potatoes *1/2 lb*

Eggplants *1/2 lb*

Red and/or yellow peppers *1/2 lb*

Tomatoes *1/2 lb*

Celery *1 stalk*

Green olives *2 oz*

Onions *1*

Extra virgin olive oil *4 tablespoons*

Salt *to taste*

● Rinse all the vegetables. Peel the potatoes and cut lengthways into slices. Scald the tomatoes, peel and squeeze gently to remove the seeds, then dice. Trim the celery, remove the bigger fibers and dice. Remove the seeds and the white parts of the peppers and cut into strips. Trim the eggplants and cut into slices, not too thin and then quarter them.

● Peel and chop the onion. In a skillet, heat the olive oil. Cook the onions until golden. Add the vegetables and the olives, well drained. Season with salt. Cover and cook over low heat adding a little water if needed. When the vegetables are cooked and still al dente, pour the preparation onto a serving dish and serve immediately.

Fried potatoes with parsley

Difficulty **easy**
Preparation time **45 minutes**
Calories **95**

Ingredients *for 4 servings*

Potatoes *1 lb*
Onions *1*
Parsley *1 small bunch*
Vegetable broth *6 tablespoons*
Extra virgin olive oil *4 tablespoons*
Salt *to taste*

● Peel the potatoes, rinse, dice and leave in a bowl of cold water for 5 minutes. In the meantime, trim the parsley, rinse, dry and chop finely. Peel the onion and slice thinly.

● Heat the olive oil in a frying pan. Cook the onion until transparent. Drain and dry the potatoes. Add to the onion and sauté for a few minutes.

Cook on medium heat, stirring from time to time, add vegetable broth and stir with a wooden spoon.

● A few minutes before removing from heat, season with salt and sprinkle with the chopped parsley. Transfer the preparation to a warm serving dish and serve at once.

Ciammotta

Difficulty **easy**
Preparation time **1 hour**
+ resting time
Calories **250**

Ingredients *for 4 servings*

Eggplants *1/2 lb*
Potatoes *1/2 lb*
Bell peppers *1/2 lb*
Tomatoes *1/2 lb*
Garlic *1 clove*
Extra virgin olive oil *enough for frying*
Extra virgin olive oil *2 tablespoons*
Salt *to taste*

● Rinse the eggplants, cut into slices about 1/2 inch thick, sprinkle with coarse salt and place in layers in a colander. On the last layer, place a dish with a weight on it. Let drain the excess moisture for 40 minutes, then rinse to remove the salt and dry with a clean kitchen towel.

● Wash and peel the potatoes and dice them. Rinse the peppers, dry, remove the stem, the seeds and the white parts, then cut into strips. Heat sufficient oil in a pan and separately fry

the eggplants, the potatoes and the peppers; lay them out on paper towels to absorb the excess oil.

● Scald the tomatoes; drain, peel, squeeze gently to remove the seeds and chop. Heat the olive oil in a skillet. Add the garlic clove and cook until lightly golden, then discard. Add the tomatoes and season with salt. Add the eggplants, the potatoes and the peppers; mix well, cover and simmer on low heat until all the ingredients are done. Serve while hot.

Filled zucchini, Cagliari-style

Difficulty **easy**
Preparation time **1 hour**
Calories **370**

Ingredients *for 4 servings*

Zucchini *2 1/4 lbs*
Tomatoes *1/4 lb, firm and ripe*
Eggs *3*
Basil *a few leaves, chopped*
Grated pecorino *4 oz*
Breadcrumbs *2 oz*
Extra virgin olive oil *6 tablespoons*
Salt *& pepper to taste*

● Trim and rinse the zucchini; cut lengthways in half; sprinkle with salt and let the excess moisture drain. Remove the seeds and the center pulp with a teaspoon and chop the pulp.

● Heat 2 tablespoons of olive oil in a skillet and fry the zucchini pulp until mostly dry. Scald the tomatoes; peel and squeeze gently to remove the seeds; cut in thin strips. To the fried pulp, add the tomatoes, 2 tablespoons of oil and the chopped basil. Continue cooking over medium heat for 10 minutes, stirring from time to time with a wooden spoon.

● Pour the mixture into a bowl. Add the pecorino, the eggs, and the breadcrumbs. Season with salt and pepper; mix well and fill the zucchini with the mixture. Brush a baking dish with 1 tablespoon of the remaining olive oil; place the filled zucchini in the dish, drizzle with the remaining olive oil and bake in a preheated oven at 400°F for about 30 minutes. Serve in the baking dish. Can be served hot or cold.

Zucchini & tomatoes

Difficulty **easy**
Preparation time **45 minutes**
Calories **205**

Ingredients *for 4 servings*

Zucchini *1 1/2 lbs*
Tomatoes *3/4 lb, firm and ripe*
Onions *1*
Fresh mint *a few leaves*
Grated pecorino *2 tablespoons*
Extra virgin olive oil *4 tablespoons*
Salt *to taste*

● Trim the zucchini, rinse, dry and cut into chunks. Scald the tomatoes, peel, gently squeeze to remove the seeds and chop. Rinse the mint leaves, dry and chop. Peel the onion, chop and fry in a skillet with the olive oil. Add the zucchini and brown lightly; add the tomatoes and the mint leaves.

● Season with salt. Cover and cook over medium heat for about 20 minutes, stirring from time to time with a wooden spoon. When done, transfer the preparation onto a warm serving dish, sprinkle with abundant pecorino and serve immediately.

Tuna-filled zucchini

Difficulty **easy**
Preparation time **40 minutes**
Calories **205**

Ingredients *for 6-8 servings*

Zucchini *2 1/2 lbs*

Tomatoes *14 oz, firm and ripe*

Basil *4 leaves*

Extra virgin olive oil *3 tablespoons*

Salt *&* **pepper** *to taste*

For the filling

Tuna in oil *1/2 lb*

Chopped parsley *2 tablespoons*

Breadcrumbs *3 tablespoons*

Eggs *3*

Garlic *1 clove*

Salt *&* **pepper** *to taste*

● Trim the zucchini, rinse and cut in half, lengthways. With a teaspoon, remove the pulp. Drain the tuna; peel the garlic and remove the central sprout. In a food processor, blend the zucchini pulp with the tuna and the garlic.

● Transfer the mixture to a bowl, add the breadcrumbs, the parsley, the eggs, freshly ground pepper and a little salt. Blend well and fill the zucchini with this mixture.

● Pass the tomatoes through a food mill. Heat the olive oil in a skillet. Place the zucchini in the skillet and simmer over very low heat for 2 minutes.

● Raise the heat to high, add the tomato purée, a pinch of salt and a dash of freshly ground pepper and the basil leaves. Cover and continue cooking over medium heat for 20 minutes. The filled zucchini can be served hot or cold.

Zucchini & eggplants with basil

Difficulty **easy**
Preparation time **30 minutes**
+ resting time
Calories **130**

Ingredients *for 4 servings*

Zucchini *2*

Eggplants *2*

Basil *1 small bunch*

Extra virgin olive oil *5 tablespoons*

Salt *to taste*

● Trim the basil, rinse, chop and mix with the oil in a small bowl. Rinse the zucchini and the eggplants, dry and trim; cut into slices, place in a non-stick pan with just a little salted water and cook for about 20 minutes over medium heat, pressing the vegetables with the back of a fork to extract their moisture and to cook without adding any water.

● Transfer the vegetables onto a serving dish, drizzle with the basil flavored olive oil and a pinch of salt, if needed. Let stand in a cool place (do not refrigerate) for a few hours before serving.

Difficulty **easy**
Preparation time **1 hour 10 minutes**
Calories **545**

Stuffed peppers

Ingredients *for 4 servings*

Red bell peppers *2*
Yellow bell peppers *2*
Tomato sauce *8 tablespoons*
Olives *1/2 lb*
Anchovy filets in oil *8*
Capers *2 tablespoons*
Raisins *2 oz*
Chopped parsley *2 tablespoons*
Breadcrumbs *1/2 lb*
Extra virgin olive oil *7 tablespoons*
Salt *&* **pepper** *to taste*

● Soak the raisins in a bowl of warm water for 20 minutes. Rinse and dry the peppers, cut in half lengthways, remove the seeds and the white parts. Pit the olives and chop. Cut the anchovy filets into small pieces. Rinse and dry the capers.

● In a pan, heat 2 tablespoons of olive oil and toast the breadcrumbs, stirring with a wooden spoon. Remove, transfer to a bowl, add the parsley, the olives, the anchovies, the capers, the raisins (squeezed dry), a little salt and pepper. Blend thoroughly and fill the peppers with the mixture.

● Brush a baking dish with 2 tablespoons of olive oil and fill with the stuffed peppers, one next to the other. On each pepper half, place 1 tablespoon of tomato sauce and drizzle with the remaining olive oil. Bake in a preheated oven at 320°F for about 20 minutes, then raise the heat to 375°F to finish the baking. This dish can be served hot or at room temperature.

Difficulty **easy**
Preparation time **40 minutes**
Calories **200**

Fried peppers

Ingredients *for 4 servings*

Bell peppers *6*
Tomatoes *8, firm and ripe*
Onions *2*
Extra virgin olive oil *4 tablespoons*
Salt *to taste*

● Rinse the peppers, cut in half, remove the seeds and cut into large pieces. If you want to peel them, place on the end of a fork, sear the skin of each piece over high heat and then remove the peel

● Peel the onions, rinse, dry with paper towels, slice thinly and fry in a skillet with the olive oil over very low heat until transparent.

● In the meantime, scald the tomatoes; peel, squeeze gently to remove the seeds; chop and add to the onions. Cook for a few minutes, then add the peppers. Season with salt. Cover and continue cooking over low heat for about 20 minutes, stirring often with a wooden spoon. Remove from heat, transfer onto a serving dish and serve at once.

Soft peppers

Difficulty **easy**
Preparation time **30 minutes**
Calories **270**

Ingredients *for 4 servings*

Bell peppers *1 1/2 lbs*
Grated pecorino *2 oz*
Breadcrumbs *1/4 cup*
Capers *1 tablespoon*
Oregano *a pinch*
Extra virgin olive oil *1/2 cup*
Salt *to taste*

● Rinse the peppers, dry well with a clean kitchen towel and quarter; remove the seeds, the stem, and the white parts; rinse the capers in running water to remove the salt and dry on paper towels.

● Heat the olive oil in a skillet. Add the peppers and sauté until they are softened; discard most of the frying oil and add the capers, the pecorino, the breadcrumbs, and the oregano.

● Season with a pinch of salt and mix thoroughly. Cover and cook over low heat for about 10 minutes, stirring often with a wooden spoon. When done, remove from heat, transfer the peppers onto a warm serving dish and serve at once.

Peperonata

Difficulty **easy**
Preparation time **1 hour**
Calories **165**

Ingredients *for 4 servings*

Bell peppers *4*
Tomatoes *6, firm and ripe*
Onions *1*
Garlic *1 clove*
Basil *a few leaves*
Extra virgin olive oil *4 tablespoons*
Salt *& pepper to taste*

● Peel the onion, rinse and slice. Heat the olive oil in a skillet and add the onion; cover and brown lightly; add a few tablespoons of water, remove the cover and continue cooking until the water has evaporated.

● Sear the peppers over high heat, peel, cut open, remove the seeds and the white parts, rinse, dry with paper towels and cut into strips. Blanch the tomatoes in boiling water; peel, squeeze gently to remove the seeds and chop.

● When the onion is cooked, add the peppers and cook for 15 minutes over medium heat, then add the tomatoes, season with salt and pepper. Peel the garlic, remove the green sprout and add to mixture.

● Cook until the olive oil is completely absorbed by the vegetables. Just before serving, transfer the preparation to a serving dish, add the cleaned and chopped basil leaves and serve at once.

Sweet-and-sour zucchini

Difficulty **easy**
Preparation time **40 minutes**
Calories **110**

Ingredients *for 4 servings*

Zucchini *3/4 lb*
Garlic *1 clove*
Pine nuts *1 oz*
Raisins *2 tablespoons*
Anchovies *2*
White wine vinegar *2 tablespoons*
Extra virgin olive oil *2 tablespoons*
Salt *to taste*

● Rinse the zucchini, trim and cut in half, lengthwise; remove the seeds in the middle with a teaspoon and slice into strips. Soak the raisins in a bowl of warm water for 15 minutes. Rinse, debone and filet the anchovies.

● Peel the garlic. Heat the olive oil in a skillet; add the garlic; discard when golden; add the zucchini and sauté briefly before seasoning with salt.

● Add a few tablespoons of water and the vinegar and cook over medium heat until the liquid is reduced. Add the pine nuts, the drained raisins and the anchovy filets. Mix well and let simmer a few minutes. Transfer the preparation when ready to a serving dish and serve immediately.

Ciaudedda

Difficulty **easy**
Preparation time **1 hour**
Calories **220**

Ingredients *for 4 servings*

Artichokes *4*
Fresh lima beans *1 1/2 lbs*
Yellow potatoes *10 oz*
Onions *1*
Pancetta *2 oz*
Lemons *1/2*
Extra virgin olive oil *3 tablespoons*
Salt *to taste*

● Trim the artichokes, remove the hard outer leaves, cut off the spines and the stems, remove the chokes; rinse, cut into pieces and spray with the lemon juice to prevent discoloring. Shell the beans and remove the peel.

● Peel the potatoes, rinse dry and slice. Chop the pancetta. Peel the onion and slice thinly. Heat the oil in a saucepan and cook the pancetta and the onion on low heat.

● When the onions are transparent, add the potatoes, the artichoke pieces and the beans. Season with salt and cook on low heat for about 30 minutes adding a few tablespoons of hot water to keep the preparation moist. Place on a serving dish and serve at once.

Baked stuffed potatoes

Difficulty **easy**
Preparation time **1 hour 20 minutes**
Calories **410**

Ingredients *for 4 servings*

Potatoes *4, large*
Cooked ham *3 oz, in 1 slice*
Mushrooms *1/2 lb*
Eggs *1*
Garlic *1 clove*
Chopped parsley *1 tablespoon*
Grated grana cheese *2 tablespoons*
Butter *2 tablespoons*
Extra virgin olive oil *3 tablespoons*
Salt *&* **pepper** *to taste*

● Carefully brush the potatoes, under running water. Place on a cookie sheet and bake in a preheated oven at 375°F for 35 to 40 minutes. Remove from oven. Cut potatoes in half, lengthwise. Empty potatoes without breaking the skins. Pass the potatoes through a potato ricer; place in a large bowl. Set aside.

● Quickly rinse the mushrooms in cold water; drain, dry and chop. Peel garlic and crush. In a pan, heat 2 tablespoons of extra virgin olive oil. Add garlic and cook for 1 minute. Discard garlic. Add mushrooms and cook on high heat, stirring often, until mushrooms are almost dry. Mix mushrooms with mashed potatoes. Mix in the chopped ham, chopped parsley and egg. Season with salt and fresh ground pepper.

● Fill the potato skins with the mixture. Brush a baking dish with the remaining extra virgin olive oil. Place the filled potatoes in the dish. Sprinkle with the grated parmigiano. Place one small piece of butter on each. Bake in a preheated oven at 400°F for about 15 minutes. Serve immediately.

Nonna's potatoes

Difficulty **easy**
Preparation time **45 minutes**
Calories **365**

Ingredients *for 4 servings*

Potatoes *8*
Peeled tomatoes *6*
Unbleached flour *a few tablespoons*
Garlic *1 clove*
Sage *a few leaves*
Rosemary *1 sprig*
Vegetable broth *2 cups*
Extra virgin olive oil *4 tablespoons*
Salt *&* **pepper** *to taste*

● Peel the garlic. Rinse and dry herbs. Brush and rinse potatoes; cut in large pieces and roll them twice in the flour. In a large pan, heat the extra virgin olive oil. Add garlic, sage and rosemary.

● When the garlic turns brown, add floured potatoes. Season with salt and fresh ground pepper. Sauté for about 10 minutes, until brown on all sides. Pour in the vegetable broth.

● Cover and cook for 15 minutes. Add tomatoes and mix well. Cook for 5 minutes, or until sauce is reduced a little. Transfer to a warm serving dish and serve hot.

Potato tart

Difficulty **easy**
Preparation time **1 hour**
Calories **255**

Ingredients *for 4 servings*

Potatoes *1 1/2 lbs*
Tomatoes *1/2 lb, firm and ripe*
Onions *1*
Black olives *2 tablespoons*
Anchovy filets in oil *4*
Capers *1 tablespoon*
Extra virgin olive oil *3 tablespoons*
Salt *to taste*

● Blanch the tomatoes in boiling water; drain, peel and squeeze gently to remove seeds, then crush with a fork. Peel, rinse, dry and chop onion. In a pan, heat 2 tablespoons of extra virgin olive oil. Add onion and cook until just transparent. Add tomatoes and cook on high heat for 10 minutes.

● During this time, brush, rinse and cook potatoes for about 30 minutes. Drain and peel; pass through a food mill. Transfer to a bowl. Season with salt and mix well.

● Rinse capers carefully. Slice olives in half. Drain the anchovy filets. Brush a baking dish with remaining extra virgin olive oil. Place half the crushed potatoes in the dish. Cover with the tomato sauce, anchovies, capers and olives. Cover with remaining potatoes. Bake in a preheated oven at 375°F for about 15 minutes. Serve immediately.

Potato & tomato dish

Difficulty **easy**
Preparation time **1 hour**
Calories **185**

Ingredients *for 4 servings*

Yellow potatoes *14 oz*
Tomatoes *1 lb*
Garlic *3 cloves*
Parsley *1 small bunch*
Extra virgin olive oil *4 tablespoons*
Salt *to taste*

● Peel the potatoes; rinse and cut in 1/4-inch slices. Rinse the tomatoes and cut in thick slices. Rinse and dry parsley. Peel the garlic and remove the green sprout if necessary; chop with parsley.

● Brush a deep casserole with a little extra virgin olive oil. Place a layer of tomatoes in the dish. Sprinkle with some of the garlic-parsley mixture. Season with salt. Drizzle with a little extra virgin olive oil. Cover with a layer of potatoes, tomatoes and garlic-parsley mixture.

● Continue to alternate layers until all ingredients are used; finish with a layer of tomatoes; add salt and drizzle with extra virgin olive oil. Cover and cook for 40 minutes, on low heat. Remove the cover and continue cooking until juices have reduced a little. Transfer to a serving dish.

Onions filled with tuna

Difficulty **easy**
Preparation time **1 hour**
Calories **450**

Ingredients *for 4 servings*

Onions *4*
Tuna in oil *1/2 lb*
Day-old bread *4 oz*
Tomato paste *4 oz*
Grated grana cheese *4 tablespoons*
Breadcrumbs *1 tablespoon*
Marjoram *1 sprig*
Garlic *1 clove*
Oregano *a pinch*
Eggs *1*
Milk *a few tablespoons*
Extra virgin olive oil *4 tablespoons*
Salt *&* **pepper** *to taste*

● Peel the onions. Dip in boiling salted water and cook for 10 minutes; drain well and slice in half horizontally; remove center and set aside.

● Soak bread in warmed milk for a few minutes; drain and squeeze. Chop the bread with tuna and half the reserved onion flesh. Peel the garlic. Rinse and dry the marjoram; chop with the garlic; mix into the tuna mixture. Add the parmigiano, egg, a pinch of salt and pepper. Mix well and add a little extra virgin olive oil if mixture seems to become dense.

● Fill the onion halves with the preparation. Sprinkle with breadcrumbs and oregano. Drizzle with half the extra virgin olive oil. Brush a baking dish with remaining extra virgin olive oil. Place the onions in the dish. Add tomato sauce, mixed with 2 tablespoons of water. Bake in a preheated oven at 375°F for about 30 minutes. Remove from oven. Transfer to a serving dish and cool lightly before serving.

Onions with marsala

Difficulty **easy**
Preparation time **1 hour**
Calories **120**

Ingredients *for 4 servings*

Onions *4*
Capers *2 oz*
Marsala *1 cup*
Thyme *a pinch*
Oregano *a pinch*
Cloves *4*
Extra virgin olive oil *4 tablespoons*
Salt *&* **pepper** *to taste*

● Peel the onions; remove outer layers; leave whole and prick each one with a clove. In a pan, heat the extra virgin olive oil. Add onions and cook on low heat until they are lightly brown on all sides. Preheat the oven at 370°F.

● When the onions are golden. Add 1 cup of hot water, a pinch of salt and fresh ground pepper, thyme and oregano. Continue cooking until water has evaporated.

● Transfer onions to a baking dish. Add Marsala. Cover with aluminum foil. Bake in the oven for about 20 minutes or until liquid has reduced. Remove from oven. Mix in the capers and cook the liquid on high heat, if necessary to reduce more. Serve immediately.

Sicilian croquettes

Difficulty **easy**
Preparation time **1 hour 20 minutes**
Calories **410**

Ingredients *for 4-6 servings*

Potatoes *1 lb*
Cooked ham *2 oz*
Eggs *2*
Caciocavallo cheese *2 oz*
Breadcrumbs *1/4 cup*
Grated pecorino *2 oz*
Parsley *1 small bunch*
Unbleached flour *a few tablespoons*
Extra virgin olive oil *enough for frying*
Extra virgin olive oil *2 tablespoons*
Salt *&* **pepper** *to taste*

Andrea's note: Caciocavallo cheese may be difficult to find. It can be replaced by provolone or even aged cheddar for a different taste.

● Rinse the potatoes; place in a saucepan, cover with water and cook for 30 to 35 minutes. Pick, rinse, dry and chop parsley with cooked ham. Grate the caciocavallo cheese.

● Drain potatoes and while still hot, peel and pass through a potato ricer. Set aside in a large bowl. Separate the eggs. Mix in the yolks with potatoes. Place mixture in a saucepan; add extra virgin olive oil and stirring all the time, cook on low heat for a few minutes.

● Add ham-parsley mixture, grated caciocavallo and pecorino. Season with salt and pepper; mix well. Form small cylinders about 2 inch long, with the preparation. In a bowl, whisk the egg whites. Roll the croquettes in flour, then in beaten egg whites and finally in the breadcrumbs.

● Heat abundant olive oil in a deep pan, or a deep-fryer. When hot, add potato croquettes, a few at a time. Fry until golden on all sides. Drain and place on paper towels. Salt lightly and serve very hot.

Stuffed onions

Difficulty **easy**
Preparation time **1 hour**
Calories **215**

Ingredients *for 4 servings*

Onions *4*
Grated pecorino *4 tablespoons*
Eggs *1*
Nutmeg *1/4 teaspoon*
Extra virgin olive oil *4 tablespoons*
Salt *to taste*

● Peel the onions; rinse, dry and cook in boiling salted water, for about 20 minutes. Drain and slice in half horizontally. With a teaspoon, remove most of the interior; chop and set aside in a bowl.

● Add grated pecorino, egg, a pinch of salt and nutmeg to the chopped onion; mix well. Fill the onions with this preparation.

● Place filled onions in a baking dish brushed with extra virgin olive oil. Drizzle with remaining extra virgin olive oil. Bake in a preheated oven at 350ºF for about 30 minutes, or until top is brown. Transfer to a serving dish and serve immediately.

Difficulty **easy**
Preparation time **1 hour**
Calories **340**

Ingredients *for 4 servings*

Yellow & red bell peppers *1 1/2 lbs*

Capers *1 tablespoon*

Pine nuts *1 tablespoon*

Raisins *2 tablespoons*

Anchovy filets in oil *4*

Breadcrumbs *1/2 cup*

Chopped parsley *1 tablespoon*

Extra virgin olive oil *7 tablespoons*

Salt *&* **pepper** *to taste*

Rolled peppers

● Preheat the oven to 475ºF. Roast the peppers all around. Cut in half, remove seeds, peel and trim to make large rectangles.

● Rinse and drain capers. Soak raisins in warm water and drain. Rinse, dry and chop anchovies. Rinse, dry and chop parsley. In a large bowl, mix pine nuts, capers, raisins, anchovies, parsley and breadcrumbs with 3 tablespoons of extra virgin olive oil. Season with salt and fresh ground pepper. Mix until ingredients are well blended.

● Spread the prepared filling in the rectangles of pepper. Roll onto themselves. Brush a baking dish with 3 tablespoons of extra virgin olive oil. Place the pepper rolls in the dish. Drizzle with remaining extra virgin olive oil. Bake in a preheated oven at 400ºF for 15 minutes. Transfer to a serving dish and serve very hot.

Difficulty **easy**
Preparation time **1 hour**
Calories **415**

Broccoli Sicilian-style

Ingredients *for 4 servings*

Broccoli *2 1/2 lbs*
Desalted anchovy filets *5*
Sharp provolone cheese *3 oz*
Pitted black olives *4 oz*
Onions *1*
Dry red wine *1/2 cup*
Extra virgin olive oil *1/4 cup*
Salt *to taste*

● Cut off hard part of broccoli stems. Divide the broccoli in flowerets; rinse and drain carefully. Chop the anchovy filets. Peel and thinly slice the onion. Slice the provolone cheese in strips. Cut the olives in quarter.

● Brush a deep dish with 1 tablespoon of extra virgin olive oil. Spread the bottom with a layer of broccoli flowerets. Cover with a layer of onion slices, a few olives and half the anchovies.

● Drizzle with a little extra virgin olive oil and season with salt. Repeat layers and add provolone cheese, until all ingredients are used. Finish with a layer of broccoli. Drizzle with remaining extra virgin olive oil and dry red wine.

● Cover the casserole and cook on low heat, without mixing or moving it, until wine has evaporated and broccoli is just tender. Serve very hot, directly in its cooking dish.

Difficulty **easy**
Preparation time **50 minutes**
Calories **135**

Simply broccoli

Ingredients *for 4 servings*

Broccoli *2 lbs*
Garlic *2 cloves*
Extra virgin olive oil *4 tablespoons*
Salt *& pepper to taste*

● Remove external leaves and hard part of stem from broccoli. Separate into flowerets; rinse well and set aside to drain in a colander.

● During this time, peel the garlic and remove the green sprout if necessary; crush lightly. In a pan, heat the extra virgin olive oil and garlic for a few minutes.

● When the garlic starts to brown, add broccoli flowerets. Season with salt and pepper; mix well. Cover pan and cook on low heat for about 30 minutes, adding a little water if necessary.

● When the broccoli is cooked softly, remove from heat. Transfer to a warm serving plate.

Difficulty **easy**
Preparation time **30 minutes**
Calories **135**

Broccoli with oranges

Ingredients *for 4 servings*

Broccoli *1 1/2 lbs*

Oranges *1*

Shallots *1*

Extra virgin olive oil *4 tablespoons*

Salt *&* **pepper** *to taste*

● Rinse and dry the orange. Remove half the orange peel and slice in strips. Press the orange and strain the juice. Rinse the broccoli and separate in flowerets; cook in abundant salted boiling water for 5 minutes. Drain; soak in ice water; drain again and dry in a kitchen towel. Peel and chop the shallot.

● In a small saucepan, reduce the orange juice on high heat. In another pan, heat the extra virgin olive oil. Add shallot and orange peel strips. Cover and cook on medium heat for 10 minutes, stirring often. Add reduced orange juice, cooked broccoli, a pinch of salt and pepper. Heat through and transfer to a serving dish.

Difficulty **easy**
Preparation time **1 hour**
Calories **145**

Turnip tops in red wine

Ingredients *for 4 servings*

Turnip tops *3 lbs*

Garlic *2 cloves*

Bay leaves *1*

Red wine *1/2 cup*

Extra virgin olive oil *4 tablespoons*

Salt *&* **peppercorns** *to taste*

● Carefully rinse the turnip tops several times; drain. Cook in a saucepan without other water than the one on the turnips. During the cooking, remove the liquid rejected by the turnip tops because it can give them a bitter taste.

● When the turnip tops do not reject any more liquid (about 30 minutes),

season with salt and fresh ground pepper. Reduce the heat to very low. Add the peeled garlic, the red wine and the bay leaf.

● Mix well and cover the saucepan, on low heat, for 15 minutes. Transfer the turnip tops to a warm serving dish. Must be served very hot.

Bean salad

Difficulty **easy**
Preparation time **1 hour**
Calories **180**

Ingredients *for 4 servings*

Fresh broad beans *3 lbs*
Day-old Italian-style bread *2 slices*
Anchovy paste *2 teaspoons*
Garlic *1 clove*
Dijon mustard *1 teaspoon*
Cider vinegar *1 tablespoon*
Extra virgin olive oil *4 tablespoons*
Salt *&* **pepper** *to taste*

● Shell and peel the beans. In a saucepan, bring 8 cups of water to a boil. Add the beans and cook for 15 minutes. Drain and set aside to cool.

● During this time, cut the Italian-style bread into cubes. Peel and crush the garlic. In a pan, heat 2 tablespoons of olive oil. Add the garlic and cook until it begins to brown. Discard the garlic and add the bread. Sauté until lightly brown on all sides.

● In a bowl, mix the anchovy paste, a generous pinch of fresh ground pepper, the cider vinegar and the mustard. Slowly add 2 tablespoons of olive oil, whisking until well blended.

● Transfer the beans and the bread to a serving dish. Pour the prepared sauce over and toss well. Serve immediately.

Beans & chicory lettuce

Difficulty **easy**
Preparation time **1 hour 30 minutes + soaking time**
Calories **435**

Ingredients *for 4 servings*

Dried cannellini beans *14 oz*
Chicory lettuce *1 1/4 lbs*
Onions *2*
White wine vinegar *1 tablespoon*
Extra virgin olive oil *3 tablespoons*
Salt *&* **pepper** *to taste*

● Soak the beans in warm water for 12 hours. Drain and transfer to a saucepan. Cover with water and cook on low heat. Skim if necessary and stir often. When the beans have reached the consistency of a purée, season with salt and pepper.

● During this time, rinse the chicory. Cook in salted boiling water. Peel and slice the onions very thinly. In a pan, heat the oil; add the onions and cook until transparent.

● When chicory is tender, drain and add to the onions. Cook for a few minutes. Add the wine vinegar and mix well. Transfer the beans and the chicory to a serving dish. Drizzle with olive oil and serve very hot.

Frittedda

Difficulty **easy**
Preparation time **45 minutes**
Calories **155**

Ingredients *for 4 servings*

Shelled lima beans *10 oz*
Shelled peas *1/2 lb*
Artichokes *2*
Onions *1*
Mint leaves *5-6*
Lemon juice *1 tablespoon*
Sugar *a pinch*
Extra virgin olive oil *3 tablespoons*
Salt *& pepper* *to taste*

● Remove the hard outer leaves and cut off the tips of the artichokes. Slice in half and remove the chokes. Cut in thin slices. Transfer to a bowl of cold water mixed with the lemon juice.

● Scald the beans in salted boiling water; drain when their peel is wrinkled; peel. Peel the onion; slice thinly. In a pan, heat the oil and cook the onions until just transparent. Add the drained artichokes and cook for a few minutes, stirring often.

● Add the peas and the beans; cook for a few minutes. Pour in 1/2 cup of water. Cover and cook on medium heat for about 10 minutes. Add the sugar, a pinch of salt and fresh ground pepper. Continue cooking for 10 minutes. Remove from heat; add the mint leaves. Cool completely before serving.

Beans & potatoes

Difficulty **easy**
Preparation time **2 hours**
+ soaking time
Calories **295**

Ingredients *for 4 servings*

Dried cannellini beans *1/2 lb*
Potatoes *1/2 lb*
Garlic *2 cloves*
Mint *2 branches*
Parsley *1 small bunch*
White wine vinegar *3 tablespoons*
Extra virgin olive oil *4 tablespoons*
Salt *to taste*

● Soak the beans in warm water for about 24 hours. Drain and place in a saucepan. Cover with cold water and cook for about 2 hours.

● Rinse the potatoes; place in a saucepan; cover with salted cold water and cook for about 45 minutes. Drain, peel and mash.

● Rinse and dry the parsley and the mint. Peel the garlic and remove the green sprout if necessary. In a mortar, mash the herbs and the garlic. Slowly add the oil, the vinegar and a pinch of salt. This can also be done in a food processor.

● When the beans are cooked, drain well and mix into the mashed potatoes. Transfer to a serving dish; drizzle with the prepared sauce and serve.

Cold stuffed zucchini

Difficulty **average**
Preparation time **40 minutes**
Calories **170**

Ingredients *for 4 servings*

Zucchini *4*

Basil *1 bunch*

Garlic *1 clove*

Thyme *2 sprigs*

Marjoram *2 sprigs*

Chopped walnuts *2 oz*

Grated grana cheese *3 oz*

Extra virgin olive oil *4 tablespoons*

Salt & **pepper** *to taste*

● Rinse and dry the basil leaves. Rinse, dry and slice off the ends of the zucchini. Peel the garlic. Rinse and dry the thyme and the marjoram.

● Steam the zucchini for 7 minutes or until just tender. Place in ice water for a few seconds; drain, dry and empty their centers with an apple corer. Finely chop the extracted pulp with the basil leaves, the garlic, the thyme and marjoram.

● Transfer this mixture to a bowl. Add the grated cheese, the chopped walnuts, the oil, a pinch of salt and pepper. Mix well until all ingredients are blended.

● Place the mixture in a pastry bag. Fill the zucchini with the mixture. Diagonally slice the zucchini in thick pieces. Place decoratively on a serving dish. Should be served at room temperature.

2 *Remove the middle with an apple corer.*

1 *Steam the prepared zucchini.*

4 *Fill the zucchini with the preparation.*

3 *Chop the extracted zucchini pulp with the herbs and the garlic.*

Difficulty **easy**
Preparation time **45 minutes**
Calories **200**

Stuffed artichokes

Ingredients *for 4 servings*

Artichokes *4*
Shallots *3*
Anchovy filets in oil *2*
Parsley *1 small bunch*
Nutmeg *a pinch*
Lemon juice *1 tablespoon*
Butter *2 oz*
Salt *&* **pepper** *to taste*

● Remove the hard outer leaves and cut off the tips of the leaves from the artichokes; peel the stems. Cover with cold water mixed with lemon juice.

● Peel, rinse, and dry the shallots. Rinse and dry the parsley. Keep a few sprigs aside and chop the rest with the shallots and the anchovies very finely. Place the mixture in a bowl with half the butter, cut in pieces, a pinch of salt, fresh ground pepper and a pinch of nutmeg. Mix well.

● Drain the artichokes; dry with a kitchen towel and slice in half. Remove the chokes and fill with the prepared mixture. Place them in a saucepan, next to each other, so they do not move during the cooking.

● Add 1/4 cup of water, the remaining parsley, a pinch of salt and pepper and the remaining butter. Cover the saucepan and cook on medium heat for about 30 minutes. (The liquid will be almost all evaporated.) Transfer to a serving dish. Can be served hot or warm.

1 *Finely chop the shallots, parsley and anchovies.*

2 *Add the butter in pieces, to the chopped parsley, anchovies and shallots.*

3 *Fill the emptied artichokes with the preparation.*

4 *Add 1/4 cup of water before cooking the artichokes.*

Difficulty **easy**
Preparation time **2 hours 30 minutes + soaking time**
Calories **585**

Ingredients *for 4 servings*

Dried chickpeas *3/4 lb*

Red bell peppers *1*

Yellow bell peppers *1*

Tuna in oil *1/2 lb*

Capers *2 tablespoons*

Garlic *2 cloves*

Sage *a few leaves*

Eggs *2*

White wine vinegar *2 tablespoons*

Extra virgin olive oil *3 tablespoons*

Salt *&* **pepper** *to taste*

Tasty chickpeas

● Soak the chickpeas in water for at least 12 hours. Rinse the sage leaves. Peel the garlic and place in a large pot. Add the drained chickpeas and the sage. Cover with cold water. Cover and cook on low heat for 2 hours.

● During this time, roast the peppers on a flame or in the oven; peel them and cut into strips. Boil the eggs; peel and cut in quarter. Carefully rinse the capers to remove all salt. Drain the tuna and break with a fork.

● When cooked, season the chickpeas with salt. Drain and let cool. In a serving dish, mix the chickpeas, pepper strips, capers and tuna. Drizzle with the extra virgin olive oil and vinegar. Season with salt and fresh ground pepper. Toss well. Distribute the eggs around the plate before serving.

Cauliflower in tomato sauce

Difficulty **easy**
Preparation time **45 minutes**
Calories **240**

Ingredients *for 4 servings*

Cauliflower *1, about 1 1/4 lbs*
Tomato sauce *4 tablespoons*
Pitted black olives *2 oz*
Pancetta *3 oz*
Onions *1*
Garlic *1 clove*
Bay leaves *1*
Vegetable broth *1/4 cup*
Extra virgin olive oil *2 tablespoons*
Salt *&* **pepper** *to taste*

● Peel the onion; rinse, dry and slice thinly. Peel garlic; remove green sprout and chop. Trim and carefully rinse the cauliflower; divide in flowerets. Slice the olives in half. Finely chop pancetta.

● In a pan, heat the extra virgin olive oil. Add the garlic and onions. Cook until just transparent. Add pancetta and sauté. Add cauliflower, olives, bay leaf, tomato sauce and the vegetable broth. Season with salt and pepper. Cover pan and cook on low heat for 30 minutes, stirring often. Transfer to a warm serving bowl and serve hot.

Country-style cauliflower

Difficulty **easy**
Preparation time **30 minutes**
Calories **130**

Ingredients *for 4 servings*

Cauliflower *1, about 1 1/4 lbs*
Tomatoes *5 oz*
Garlic *1 clove*
Parsley *1 small bunch*
Onions *1*
Extra virgin olive oil *4 tablespoons*
Salt *&* **pepper** *to taste*

● Peel the onion, rinse, dry and slice thinly. Blanch the tomatoes in boiling water; drain, peel and squeeze gently to remove seeds, then chop.

● Trim the cauliflower; divide in flowerets and rinse in cold water; drain well and blanch in salted boiling water for one minute. Drain again.

● Peel the garlic. Rinse and dry parsley; chop half with garlic. In a pan, heat the oil. Add garlic-parsley mixture and onions. Cook until onions are just transparent. Add cauliflower. Season with salt and pepper. Cook on high heat, mixing carefully for a few minutes.

● Add chopped tomatoes. Season again if needed. Cook on medium heat for about 10 minutes, stirring often. When cauliflower is tender and the sauce has thickened, sprinkle with remaining parsley. Serve immediately.

Cauliflower salad

Difficulty **easy**
Preparation time **30 minutes**
Calories **200**

Ingredients *for 4 servings*

Cauliflower *1, about 1 1/2 lbs*
Pitted black olives *2 oz*
Pitted green olives *2 oz*
Capers *2 oz*
Anchovies *4*
Garlic *1 clove*
Parsley *a few sprigs*
White wine vinegar *2 tablespoons*
Extra virgin olive oil *4 tablespoons*
Salt *to taste*

● Carefully rinse the cauliflower; trim and divide in flowerets. Place in a pot; cover with salted water and bring to boil. Cover the pot and cook for 10 minutes.

● During this time, rinse the anchovies under running water; debone and chop. Peel garlic and remove the green sprout. Rinse, dry and chop parsley with half the olives and anchovies.

● Place all prepared ingredients in a bowl. Add capers, remaining olives and extra virgin olive oil. Add salt, pepper and vinegar. Whisk until well blended. Drain the cauliflower and transfer to a large bowl. Pour the prepared sauce over it and toss well. Can be served warm or cold.

Baked cauliflower & potatoes

Difficulty **easy**
Preparation time **1 hour**
Calories **450**

Ingredients *for 4 servings*

Cauliflower *1, about 1 lb*
Potatoes *10 oz*
Spicy Italian sausage *1*
Oregano *a pinch*
Extra virgin olive oil *5 tablespoons*
Salt *to taste*

● Bring two pots of salted water to boil. Rinse the cauliflower; divided in flowerets and cook in one pot for 15 minutes. Rinse the potatoes and cook in the other pot for about 20 minutes. Peel the hot potatoes and cut in thick slices. Peel and chop the sausage.

● In a baking dish, place the drained cauliflower, potatoes and sausage. Sprinkle with oregano. Season with salt. Drizzle with extra virgin olive oil and mix well. Bake in a preheated oven at 375°F for 20 minutes. When the top is lightly brown, remove from oven and serve.

Green beans with tomatoes

Difficulty **easy**
Preparation time **40 minutes**
Calories **220**

Ingredients *for 4 servings*

Green beans *1 lb*
Peeled tomatoes *1/2 lb*
Pine nuts *2 oz*
Garlic *1 clove*
Desalted anchovy filets *2*
Parsley *1 small bunch*
Vegetable broth *1 cup*
Day-old Italian-style bread *4 slices*
Extra virgin olive oil *5 tablespoons*
Salt *to taste*

● Trim and rinse the green beans; blanch in abundant salted boiling water; drain and cut in pieces. Peel the garlic. Rinse and chop parsley with pine nuts. In a saucepan, heat 3 tablespoons of extra virgin olive oil. Add garlic and cook for a minute. Discard the garlic. Add pine nuts, parsley and hot vegetable broth.

● Cook on medium heat until the broth has almost evaporated. Add tomatoes and crush with a fork. Add the chopped anchovy filets. Cook the sauce for 10 minutes, stirring often with a wooden spoon. Add the green beans and taste for salt.

● Cut bread in cubes. In a skillet, heat 1 tablespoon of extra virgin olive oil. Add bread cubes and fry quickly. Brush a baking dish with remaining extra virgin olive oil. Layer the beans in their sauce and bread cubes. Finish with a layer of green beans in sauce. Bake in a preheated oven at 400°F for a few minutes. Remove from oven and serve immediately.

Green beans with anchovies

Difficulty **easy**
Preparation time **30 minutes**
Calories **80**

Ingredients *for 4 servings*

Green beans *1 1/4 lbs*
Anchovies *2*
Garlic *1 clove*
White wine vinegar *1 tablespoon*
Extra virgin olive oil *2 tablespoons*
Salt *&* **pepper** *to taste*

● Trim the green beans; rinse well and drain. Cook in salted boiling water for 7 minutes. Drain. Set aside 3 tablespoons of cooking water.

● Rinse anchovies under running water; debone and chop. Peel the garlic and chop. In a skillet, heat the extra virgin olive oil. Add the garlic and cook for a minute. Add anchovies and vinegar; mix well and cook for a minute.

● Add green beans and cooking liquid. Season with salt and fresh ground pepper. Continue cooking for about 10 minutes, on medium heat, stirring often. Transfer to a serving place and serve at once.

Green beans & peppers with cheese

Difficulty **easy**
Preparation time **40 minutes**
Calories **185**

Ingredients *for 4 servings*

Green beans *1 lb*
Red bell peppers *1*
Yellow bell peppers *1*
Green bell peppers *1*
Onions *1*
Garlic *1 clove*
Basil *1 small bunch*
Grated grana cheese *2 oz*
Extra virgin olive oil *4 tablespoons*
Salt *to taste*

● Cut the peppers in half; remove white parts and seeds; rinse, dry and cut in strips. Trim the green beans; rinse and cut in large pieces. Peel the garlic and the onion; chop finely. Rinse and dry the basil leaves; tear in small pieces.

● In a pan, heat the extra virgin olive oil with half the basil. Add garlic and onions. Cook until onion is just transparent. Add pepper and sauté for 4 to 5 minutes, on medium heat. Add the green beans and remaining basil leaves. Season with salt and cook for 10 to 15 minutes, or until green beans are tender.

● Remove from heat. Mix in half the grated parmigiano. Transfer vegetables on a warm serving dish. Sprinkle with remaining cheese and serve.

Green beans with herbs

Difficulty **easy**
Preparation time **40 minutes**
Calories **85**

Ingredients *for 4 servings*

Green beans *1 lb*
Parsley *a few sprigs*
Basil *a few leaves*
Fresh marjoram *a few sprigs*
Mint *1 leaf*
Garlic *1 clove*
Extra virgin olive oil *3 tablespoons*
Salt *& pepper to taste*

● Peel the garlic and remove the green sprout. Trim the green beans; rinse, dry and blanch in salted boiling water; drain. Rinse, dry and finely chop all herbs together.

● In a pan, heat the extra virgin olive oil. Add garlic and cook until it just begins to brown; discard garlic. Add green beans, 1/2 cup of hot water and chopped herbs. Season with salt and fresh ground pepper.

● Cook uncovered on medium heat for about 15 minutes, or until the liquid has almost evaporated. Stir often. Remove from the heat and transfer to a warm serving dish.

Difficulty **easy**
Preparation time **40 minutes**
+ resting time
Calories **110**

Ingredients *for 4 servings*

Eggplants *3*
Parsley *1 small bunch*
Garlic *1 clove*
White wine vinegar *1 tablespoon*
Extra virgin olive oil *4 tablespoons*
Salt *&* **pepper** *to taste*

Eggplant salad

● Trim the eggplants; cut lengthwise in thin slices. Place in a colander, sprinkle with coarse salt and set aside for one hour.

● Rinse and drain the eggplants. Dry carefully on paper towels. Place on a cookie sheet and bake in a preheated oven at 370°F for about 20 minutes. Turn the eggplants a few times so they cook equally on all sides.

● When the eggplants are tender, remove from oven and peel. Set aside to cool completely. Cut the eggplants in strips lengthwise. Transfer to a serving dish.

● Peel the garlic. Rinse, dry and coarsely chop the parsley with the garlic. In a bowl, mix the extra virgin olive oil, vinegar, garlic and parsley. Season with a pinch of salt and fresh ground pepper. Pour this sauce over the eggplants; toss well. Refrigerate for at least 2 hours before serving.

Baked tomatoes

Difficulty **easy**
Preparation time **1 hour**
Calories **240**

Ingredients *for 4 servings*

Tomatoes *8*

Onions *1*

Breadcrumbs *4 tablespoons*

Capers *1 tablespoon*

Parsley *a few sprigs*

Basil *a few leaves*

Oregano *a pinch*

Extra virgin olive oil *4 tablespoons*

Salt *&* **pepper** *to taste*

● Rinse and dry the tomatoes; cut off top part and remove seeds with a spoon. Salt and pepper the interior of the tomatoes and turn them onto a kitchen towel to drain. Rinse and dry the parsley. Rinse and dry basil leaves.

● Rinse and dry capers. Peel the onion. Chop onion, parsley and basil together; place in a bowl. Mix in the capers, oregano and 3 tablespoons of breadcrumbs. Season with salt and fresh ground pepper. Add 1 tablespoon of extra virgin olive oil and mix with a wooden spoon until well blended.

● Return the tomatoes; fill them with the preparation. Sprinkle the tomatoes with remaining breadcrumbs. Brush a baking dish with a little extra virgin olive oil. Place tomatoes in the dish. Drizzle with remaining extra virgin olive oil. Bake in a preheated oven at 350°F for about 40 minutes. When the tomatoes are tender, remove from oven. This can be served hot or cold.

Tomatoes filled with eggplants

Difficulty **easy**
Preparation time **1 hour**
+ resting time
Calories **185**

Ingredients *for 4 servings*

Tomatoes *8*

Eggplants *2*

Onions *1*

Garlic *1 clove*

Basil *1 small bunch*

Extra virgin olive oil *5 tablespoons*

Salt *&* **pepper** *to taste*

● Trim the eggplants; rinse, dry and dice. Place them in a colander; sprinkle with coarse salt and set aside for 30 minutes.

● Rinse and dry the tomatoes; cut off the top parts and remove the seeds with a spoon. Crush the extracted pulp with a fork and set aside. Salt the interior of the tomatoes. Turn them onto a towel or onto a rack to drain. Peel the garlic, remove green sprout if necessary, and crush. Peel the onion; rinse, dry and finely chop.

● Rinse the eggplants again (to remove salt) and dry on paper towels. Rinse and dry basil. In a pan, heat 4 tablespoons of extra virgin olive oil. Add onion and garlic; cook until onion is transparent; discard the garlic clove. Add the eggplants and sauté for a few minutes. Add the tomato pulp, a pinch of salt and pepper. Cook for 10 minutes, on medium heat, stirring often. Remove from heat. Mix in the basil leaves.

● Distribute the preparation into the tomatoes. Brush a baking dish with remaining extra virgin olive oil. Place tomatoes in the dish. Bake in a preheated oven at 350°F for about 15 minutes. Transfer to a serving dish and serve immediately.

Messina-style filled tomatoes

Difficulty easy
Preparation time 1 hour
Calories 290

Ingredients *for 4 servings*

Tomatoes *8, not too ripe*
Breadcrumbs *3 tablespoons*
Desalted anchovy filets *8*
Chopped parsley *1 tablespoon*
Garlic *1 clove, chopped*
Capers *2 tablespoons*
Fresh oregano *a pinch*
Chopped onions *1*
Extra virgin olive oil *6 tablespoons*
Salt *& pepper to taste*

● Rinse and dry tomatoes; cut in half horizontally. Remove seeds, leaving pulp intact. Salt each piece. Turn tomatoes onto a towel and let drain for 15 minutes. In a pan, heat 1 tablespoon and toast breadcrumbs.

● In a skillet, heat 2 tablespoons of extra virgin olive oil. Add chopped onion, garlic and anchovy filets. When anchovies begin to dissolve, remove skillet from heat. Mix in the capers, oregano, a pinch of salt and pepper. Mix well and fill tomatoes with the preparation.

● Brush a baking dish with 2 tablespoons of extra virgin olive oil. Place the filled tomatoes in the dish. Sprinkle with breadcrumbs and drizzle with remaining extra virgin olive oil. Bake in a preheated oven at 350°F for about 30 minutes. Transfer to a serving dish and serve immediately.

Tomatoes, mozzarella & salad

Difficulty easy
Preparation time 30 minutes
Calories 290

Ingredients *for 4 servings*

Tomatoes *4*
Mozzarella *12 oz*
Lettuce *1 head*
Carrots *1*
Cider vinegar *1 tablespoon*
Extra virgin olive oil *3 tablespoons*
Salt *& pepper to taste*

● Carefully rinse the lettuce; delicately dry with paper towels and set aside. Rinse, dry and slice tomatoes; place in a colander and set aside to eliminate most water. Trim and peel carrot; cut in tiny strips.

● Drain the mozzarella and slice thinly. In a bowl, mix a pinch of salt and vinegar until salt is dissolved. Add fresh ground pepper and slowly whisk in the extra virgin olive oil. Mix until ingredients are well blended.

● On a serving dish, place the lettuce leaves. Cover with tomato slices and mozzarella slices. Add carrot strips and pour the prepared sauce over the vegetables. Serve immediately.

Eggplant 'Parmigiana'

Difficulty **easy**
Preparation time **1 hour 30 minutes + resting time**
Calories **450**

Ingredients *for 4 servings*

Eggplants *3*
Peeled tomatoes *1 lb*
Mozzarella *1/2 lb, in thin slices*
Onions *1 small*
Grated parmigiano *3 oz*
Basil *6 leaves*
Extra virgin olive oil *enough for frying*
Extra virgin olive oil *4 tablespoons*
Salt *& pepper to taste*

● Rinse and dry the eggplants. Cut lengthwise in 1/4-inch slices. Place in a colander; sprinkle with coarse salt and set aside to drain, for about 1 hour. Rinse them under running water and dry carefully on paper towels.

● In a deep pan, heat enough extra virgin olive oil to fry. Add the eggplants and fry on both sides. Drain on paper towels and keep them warm. Peel and finely chop onion. Pass the tomatoes through a vegetable mill. In a saucepan, heat 2 tablespoons of extra virgin olive oil. Add the onion and cook until transparent. Add the tomatoes and season with salt and pepper.

Cook on medium heat for 10 minutes. Add basil and cook for 5 minutes.

● Cover the bottom of a baking dish with a few tablespoons of tomato sauce. Place a first layer of eggplants; season with salt; cover with slices of mozzarella, a few tablespoons of tomato sauce and sprinkle with parmigiano. Repeat layers until all the ingredients are used, finishing with mozzarella, tomato sauce and parmigiano. Drizzle with extra virgin olive oil. Bake in a preheated oven at 325°F for 30 minutes. Remove from oven and serve immediately from the dish.

Eggplant compote

Difficulty **easy**
Preparation time **1 hour**
Calories **230**

Ingredients *for 4 servings*

Eggplants *1 1/4 lbs*
Tomatoes *3/4 lb, firm and ripe*
Onions *1*
Lemons *the juice of 1 of*
Garlic *2 cloves*
Parsley *1 small bunch*
Toasted bread *4 slices*
Extra virgin olive oil *5 tablespoons*
Salt *& pepper to taste*

● Rinse the eggplants; prick with a fork and bake whole and unpeeled in a preheated oven at 350°F for 40 minutes. Remove from oven, cool briefly and peel. Place eggplants in a colander. Cover with a plate and a weight; set aside to eliminate excess moisture. Chop eggplants very finely.

● Blanch the tomatoes in boiling water; drain, peel and squeeze gently to remove seeds, then chop. Rinse, dry and chop parsley. Peel and chop the

onion and garlic. In a pan, heat the extra virgin olive oil. Add garlic and onion; cook on low heat until onion is transparent.

● Add eggplants, tomatoes, lemon juice, a pinch of salt and pepper. Cook on low heat for 5 minutes or until the preparation is creamy. Remove from the heat. Set aside to cool and refrigerate until ready to serve. Transfer to a serving bowl; sprinkle with chopped parsley and serve with toasted bread.

Grilled eggplant rolls

Difficulty **easy**
Preparation time **50 minutes**
Calories **320**

Ingredients *for 4 servings*

Long eggplants *4*

Prosciutto *6 oz, in thin slices*

Pitted black olives *4 oz*

Garlic *2 cloves*

Chopped parsley *1 tablespoon*

Grated pecorino *2 tablespoons*

Extra virgin olive oil *enough for frying*

Salt *to taste*

● Trim and rinse eggplants; slice very thinly lengthwise. Place them in a colander. Sprinkle with coarse salt and set aside for 10 minutes, to remove excess moisture.

● Rinse again and dry on paper towels. In a large pan, heat a large quantity of extra virgin olive oil. Add eggplant slices, a few at a time; fry on both sides. Remove with a slotted spatula and drain on paper towels to remove excess oil.

● Chop the olives, garlic and parsley together. Place in a bowl. Add grated pecorino and mix well. With this mixture, cover the fried eggplant slices

● Place one slice of prosciutto on each eggplant and roll them; close with a toothpick. Place the rolled eggplants on a hot grill for a few minutes, turning once. Transfer to a serving dish. Must be eaten very hot.

Sweet-and-sour eggplants

Difficulty **easy**
Preparation time **50 minutes**
+ resting time
Calories **240**

Ingredients *for 4 servings*

Eggplants *4*

Peeled tomatoes *1 lb*

Capers *2 tablespoons*

Garlic *1 clove*

Red hot chili peppers *1*

Basil *1 small bunch*

Sugar *1 teaspoon*

White wine vinegar *4 tablespoons*

Extra virgin olive oil *enough for frying*

Extra virgin olive oil *2 tablespoons*

Salt *to taste*

● Trim the eggplants; dice and transfer to a colander. Sprinkle with coarse salt and set aside for 20 to 30 minutes. Rinse the capers under running water. Peel the garlic and remove the green sprout. Rinse the basil.

● Drain the eggplants again and dry on paper towels. In a large pan, heat some extra virgin olive oil. Add diced eggplants and sauté for a few minutes. Remove and drain on paper towels.

● In a skillet, heat the extra virgin olive oil. Add garlic and chili pepper; cook for a few minutes. Add the peeled tomatoes and a pinch of salt. Cook until the sauce thickens, stirring often. Remove the garlic and pass the sauce through a sieve.

● Return the sauce to the pan. Add capers, vinegar and sugar; cook for 5 minutes. Remove from heat and mix in the eggplants. Pour the preparation on a serving dish. Sprinkle with basil leaves and serve at room temperature.

Difficulty **easy**
Preparation time **1 hour**
Calories **95**

Mixed cooked vegetables

Ingredients *for 4 servings*

White onions *10 oz*

Peeled tomatoes *1/2 lb*

Bell peppers *2*

Zucchini *2*

Celery *1 stalk*

White wine vinegar *1 tablespoon*

Extra virgin olive oil *2 tablespoons*

Salt *&* **pepper** *to taste*

● Rinse all vegetables. Cut the peppers in half and remove seeds; cut in strips. Slice the zucchini. Chop the celery. Coarsely chop tomatoes.

● Peel the onions, rinse, dry and finely slice. Heat the extra virgin olive oil in a saucepan. Add the onions and cook on low heat until just transparent. Add all other vegetables and vinegar. Season with salt and pepper.

● Cover saucepan; reduce heat to a minimum and cook for about 30 minutes, stirring often with a wooden spoon. Remove from heat and serve directly from the pan.

2 Cook the sliced onions in extra virgin olive oil.

1 Rinse all vegetables; cut the peppers into strips.

4 Season with salt and pepper; add vinegar.

3 When the onions are transparent, add the other vegetables.

Salad with provolone

Difficulty **easy**
Preparation time **20 minutes**
Calories **235**

Ingredients *for 4 servings*

Tomatoes *3*

Curly endive *1 head*

Smoked provolone cheese *1*

Scallions *2, large*

Radishes *1 bunch*

White wine vinegar *2 tablespoons*

Extra virgin olive oil *3 tablespoons*

Salt *&* **pepper** *to taste*

● Carefully rinse the curly endive; dry well and tear into pieces, leaving a few of the large leaves intact. Rinse, dry and cut the tomatoes in quarter. Trim scallions; cut off roots and outside parts; slice. Trim radishes; rinse, dry and slice. Thinly slice provolone cheese.

● In a bowl, mix the extra virgin olive oil, vinegar, a pinch of salt and fresh ground pepper. Whisk until well blended. Transfer all vegetables to a large salad bowl. Pour prepared sauce over vegetables and toss well. Serve immediately.

Fennel with pecorino

Difficulty **easy**
Preparation time **1 hour**
Calories **310**

Ingredients *for 4 servings*

Fennel bulbs *2 lbs*
Young pecorino *4 oz*
Day-old Italian-style bread *4 slices*
Extra virgin olive oil *4 tablespoons*
Salt *to taste*

● Cut the slices of bread in half. In a large pan, heat 2 tablespoons of extra virgin olive oil. Add the bread slices and fry until golden on both sides. Remove the bread and drain on paper towels to remove excess oil.

● Trim and rinse the fennel. Cook in abundant salted boiling water for 320 minutes. Drain the fennel, keeping 1 cup of the cooking liquid. Slice the fennel thinly. Brush a baking dish with a little extra virgin olive oil. Place fried bread in the dish. Cover with a layer of cheese, then a layer of fennel. Pour the reserved cooking liquid over the preparation. Drizzle with remaining extra virgin olive oil.

● Bake in a preheated oven at 350°F for about 20 minutes. Remove from oven and serve immediately, directly from the baking dish.

Fennel with vinegar

Difficulty **easy**
Preparation time **40 minutes**
Calories **150**

Ingredients *for 4 servings*

Fennel bulbs *4*
Anchovies *4*
Black olives *8*
Parsley *a few sprigs*
Lemons *the juice of 1/2*
White wine vinegar *4 tablespoons*
Unbleached flour *1/2 tablespoon*
Extra virgin olive oil *4 tablespoons*
Salt *&* **pepper** *to taste*

● Rinse the anchovies under running water; filet them and dry on paper towels. Trim the fennel; with a sharp knife, make a cross at the root and rinse under running water. Pit the olives and slice in half.

● In a large saucepan, bring 8 cups of water to boil. Add a good pinch of salt, lemon juice and flour. Mix well. Add the fennel and cook for 15 minutes. Drain and cut in quarters. In a large skillet, heat the extra virgin olive oil. Add the fennel and brown on all sides. Season with pepper. Transfer to a serving dish. Place half an anchovy on each piece of fennel.

● Deglaze the skillet with the vinegar. Add the olives and mix well. Transfer the olives to the fennel dish and drizzle the fennel with boiling vinegar. Sprinkle with chopped parsley and serve immediately.

Fennel with herbs

Difficulty **easy**
Preparation time **1 hour**
Calories **80**

Ingredients *for 4 servings*

Fennel bulbs *1 1/2 lbs*

Celery *1 stalk*

Thyme *1 sprig*

Bay leaves *1*

Lemon juice *1 tablespoon*

Parsley *1 small bunch*

Coriander seeds *1 teaspoon*

Fennel seeds *1 teaspoon*

Extra virgin olive oil *3 tablespoons*

Peppercorns *5*

Salt *to taste*

● Trim the fennel; remove the outside leaves and the branches; slice and rinse well. Rinse and dry the parsley. Rinse, dry and chop the celery.

● In a saucepan, place the parsley, the celery, the thyme, the bay leaf, half the coriander seeds, half the fennel seeds and the peppercorns. Add the lemon, the olive oil, a pinch of salt and 3 cups of water.

● Bring to boil and cook for about 10 minutes. Add the fennel and cook for 15 to 20 minutes on medium heat. Remove from the heat. Drain the fennel and transfer to a serving dish. Drizzle with a few tablespoons of the cooking liquid and sprinkle with the remaining fennel and coriander seeds. Serve at once.

Fennel with walnuts

Difficulty **easy**
Preparation time **45 minutes**
Calories **390**

Ingredients *for 4 servings*

Fennel bulbs *4*

Walnuts *12*

Fontina cheese *4 oz*

Grated parmigiano *4 oz*

Whole wheat flour *3 tablespoons*

Nutmeg *a pinch*

Butter *2 tablespoons*

Salt *&* **pepper** *to taste*

● Trim and rinse the fennel; cut in large pieces. Cook the fennel in salted boiling water for 15 minutes; remove the fennel and drain well. Heat the oven to 400°F.

● Butter a baking dish carefully. Sprinkle with the whole wheat flour. Arrange the pieces of cooked fennel in the dish.

● Dice the fontina cheese; arrange on top of the fennel. Finely chop the walnuts in a food processor; sprinkle over the cheese. Sprinkle with the nutmeg and the grated parmigiano. Season with salt and fresh ground pepper.

● Top the prepared dish with a few pieces of butter. Bake for about 15 minutes. Remove from the oven and serve directly from the baking dish.

Artichokes with eggs

Difficulty **easy**
Preparation time **40 minutes**
Calories **140**

Ingredients *for 4 servings*

Artichokes *4*

Eggs *2*

Lemon juice *1 tablespoon*

Garlic *1 clove*

Grated grana cheese *1 tablespoon*

Extra virgin olive oil *3 tablespoons*

Salt *&* **pepper** *to taste*

● Trim the artichokes; discard the outer leaves and the stem; cut off the tips; rinse in cold water; drain, cut in half and remove the chokes; quarter and plunge in a bowl of cold water mixed with the lemon juice.

● Peel the garlic and remove the green sprout if necessary; crush lightly. Drain the artichokes; place in a large pan. Add the garlic, 1/4 cup of water and a pinch of salt. Drizzle with the olive oil. Bring to a boil. Cover and cook for about 20 minutes on medium heat.

● During this time, in a bowl, whisk the eggs with the grated grana cheese. Season with salt and fresh ground pepper. Pour that preparation over the artichokes. Bake in a preheated oven at 400°F until the eggs are cooked but still soft. Serve very hot.

Artichokes & potatoes with herbs

Difficulty **easy**
Preparation time **1 hour**
Calories **250**

Ingredients *for 4 servings*

Artichokes *6*

Yellow potatoes *4*

Garlic *1 clove*

Oregano *a pinch*

Thyme *1 sprig*

Parsley *1 small bunch*

Vegetable broth *1 cup*

Lemons *the juice of 1*

Extra virgin olive oil *4 tablespoons*

Salt *&* **pepper** *to taste*

● Trim the artichokes; remove the outer leaves, the stems and the tips; quarter them and remove the chokes; plunge them into a bowl of cold water mixed with the lemon juice. Rinse the potatoes; peel and cut in 1/4 inch thick slices.

● Peel and crush the garlic clove. In a pan, heat the oil; add the garlic and cook for 2 minutes. Discard the garlic and add the artichokes and the potatoes; cook for a few minutes. Add the vegetable broth. Cover the pan and cook on low heat for 35 to 40 minutes. Add more broth if necessary.

● Rinse and dry the parsley and the thyme; chop together. Season the potatoes and artichokes with salt and pepper; add the chopped herbs and mix well. Remove from heat and serve immediately.

Artichoke & bean stew

Difficulty **easy**
Preparation time **1 hour**
Calories **145**

Ingredients *for 4 servings*

Artichokes *6*
Fresh cannellini beans *2 1/4 lbs*
Boston lettuce *1 head*
Lemons *the juice of 1*
Basil *4-5 leaves*
Parsley *1 small bunch*
Extra virgin olive oil *4 tablespoons*
Salt *& pepper to taste*

● Shell the beans; rinse and drain well. Trim the artichokes; remove the outer leaves, the stems and the tips; quarter them and remove the chokes; place them in a bowl of cold water mixed with the lemon juice.

● Separately rinse and carefully dry the lettuce, the parsley and the basil. Slice the lettuce in strips. Chop the herbs.

● Drain the artichokes. Place in a deep pan with the lettuce, the herbs, the beans, the olive oil, a pinch of salt and fresh ground pepper. Add enough water to cover the ingredients.

● Cook the preparation on medium heat for about 40 minutes or until all water is absorbed. Stir often with a wooden spoon. Remove from the heat; transfer to a serving dish and serve immediately.

Artichoke pie, Sicilian-style

Difficulty **easy**
Preparation time **40 minutes**
Calories **285**

Ingredients *for 4 servings*

Artichokes *6*
Eggs *4*
Milk *3 tablespoons*
Unbleached flour *3 tablespoons*
Lemons *the juice of 1*
Extra virgin olive oil *enough for frying*
Extra virgin olive oil *1 tablespoon*
Salt *& pepper to taste*

● Carefully rinse the artichokes; cut off the outer leaves, the stems and the tips; quarter and remove the chokes. Place them in a bowl of cold water mixed with the lemon juice. Drain well and dry on paper towels; roll in flour.

● In a deep pan (or a deep-fryer), heat a large quantity of olive oil. Add the quartered and floured artichokes. Fry until golden on all sides. Remove with a slotted spatula and drain on paper towels to remove excess oil. Season

with salt while hot.

● Brush a baking dish with the extra virgin olive oil. Place the fried artichokes in the dish. In a bowl, mix the eggs with the milk; season with salt and pepper. Pour this preparation over the artichokes. Bake in a preheated oven at 400°F until the eggs are cooked but still soft. Transfer to a serving dish. Can be served hot or cold.

Difficulty **easy**
Preparation time **50 minutes**
Calories **140**

Ingredients *for 4 servings*

Snow peas *3/4 lb*

Yellow potatoes *10 oz*

Onions *1*

Garlic *2 cloves*

Nutmeg *a pinch*

Extra virgin olive oil *3 tablespoons*

Salt *&* **pepper** *to taste*

Snow peas & potatoes

● Bring 2 pots of salted water to boil. During this time, trim the snow peas; rinse and plunge in a pot of boiling water. Cook for 20 minutes.

● Peel the potatoes; rinse, dice and plunge in the second pot. Cook for 10 minutes. Drain the snow peas and potatoes separately. Dry on kitchen towels.

● Slice the onion and chop one garlic clove. In a pan, heat the oil. Add the onions and garlic; cook until onion is transparent. Add the diced potatoes and fry lightly. Add the snow peas. Season with fresh ground pepper and a pinch of nutmeg. Stir and cook on high heat for a few minutes. Serve immediately.

Savory potato salad

Difficulty **easy**
Preparation time **45 minutes**
Calories **300**

Ingredients *for 4 servings*

Yellow potatoes *1 lb*

Celery *1 branch*

Anchovy filets in oil *4*

Onions in vinegar *2*

Pickles *2*

Bell peppers in vinegar *1*

Capers in vinegar *1 tablespoon*

Eggs *1*

Basil *3 leaves*

Parsley *a handful of leaves*

Extra virgin olive oil *4 tablespoons*

Salt *&* **pepper** *to taste*

● Boil the egg. Brush the potatoes carefully; rinse under running water and cook, unpeeled, in salted water. Rinse the celery. Rinse and dry the basil and the parsley.

● In an electric blender (or a food processor), place the olive oil, the celery, the anchovy filets, the pickles, the onions, the pepper and the capers.

Mix quickly. Add the peeled egg, the basil, the parsley, a pinch of salt and fresh ground pepper. Mix until the sauce is fluid.

● When the potatoes are cooked, drain them and peel while still hot. Transfer to a salad bowl and toss carefully with the prepared sauce. Serve hot.

Potatoes 'all'arrabbiata'

Difficulty **easy**
Preparation time **45 minutes**
Calories **275**

Ingredients *for 4 servings*

Yellow potatoes *1 1/2 lbs*

Garlic *3 cloves*

Rosemary *2 sprigs*

Sage *5-6 leaves*

Extra virgin olive oil *6 tablespoons*

Salt *&* **pepper** *to taste*

● Peel the potatoes; rinse them and quarter twice; dry them well. In a skillet, heat the oil. Add the potatoes and cook on medium heat for about 20 minutes, turning them often so they brown all over.

● Peel the garlic and remove the green sprout; crush lightly. Rinse the rosemary and remove the leaves from the stem. Rinse and dry the sage. Chop all together.

● Add the chopped garlic and herbs to the potatoes. Season with salt and generous fresh ground pepper. Cook on low heat for 5 minutes, stirring often.

● When the potatoes are done, transfer to a warm serving dish with a slotted spoon to drain the excess oil. Taste for salt and season again with fresh ground pepper. Serve immediately.

Baked potatoes & mushrooms

Difficulty **easy**
Preparation time **40 minutes**
Calories **220**

Ingredients *for 4 servings*

Yellow potatoes *1 lb*
Porcini mushrooms *3/4 lb*
Parsley *1 small bunch*
Extra virgin olive oil *5 tablespoons*
Salt & pepper *to taste*

● Peel the potatoes; rinse and slice. Blanch in boiling salted water for 2 to 3 minutes, or steam them. Clean the mushrooms; rinse quickly and cut in thick slices. Rinse, dry and chop the parsley.

● Brush a baking dish with extra virgin olive oil. Arrange a layer of potatoes. Brush with a little extra virgin olive oil. Season with salt and fresh ground pepper. Cover with a layer of mushrooms and a little parsley, salt and pepper. Continue layering potatoes and other ingredients, finishing with a layer of potatoes. Brush with olive oil.

● Cover the dish with aluminum foil. Bake in a preheated oven at 350°F for 20 minutes. Pierce a whole in the aluminum foil and bake for another 10 minutes. Can be served hot or at room temperature.

Potatoes 'pizzaiola'

Difficulty **easy**
Preparation time **40 minutes**
Calories **175**

Ingredients *for 4 servings*

Yellow potatoes *1 1/2 lbs*
Small vine-ripened tomatoes *8*
Garlic *1 clove*
Capers *1 tablespoon*
Anchovy filets in oil *2*
Oregano *a pinch*
Vegetable broth *1/2 cup*
Salt *to taste*

● Peel the potatoes and slice; rinse and dry well. Blanch the tomatoes in boiling water; drain, peel and squeeze gently to remove seeds, then chop coarsely and set aside in a bowl.

● Chop the anchovies. Peel and finely chop garlic. Add anchovies and garlic to tomatoes with capers, a pinch of oregano and salt. Mix well. In a saucepan, place a layer of potatoes. Cover with part of the prepared sauce. Continue layering the ingredients.

● Pour the broth over the potatoes. Cover the saucepan. Cook on low heat, until the potatoes are tender. Add more broth if necessary. Remove from the heat. Taste for salt and serve immediately.

Difficulty **easy**
Preparation time **1 hour 20 minutes + soaking time**
Calories **410**

Ingredients *for 4-6 servings*

Dried cannellini beans *10 oz*

Chicory *2 1/4 lbs*

Tomatoes *5, firm and ripe*

Onions *1*

Garlic *1 clove*

Bay leaves *2*

Parsley *2 sprigs*

Extra virgin olive oil *4 tablespoons*

Salt *&* **pepper** *to taste*

Purée of beans & chicory

● Soak the beans in cold water for 12 hours. Drain and place in a pot with 8 cups of water, peeled garlic and bay leaves. Cook on medium heat for about 1 hour. Drain well and pass through a food mill. Set aside a few whole beans.

● Trim the chicory; remove the hard outer leaves and the stem; cut in pieces and rinse several times in cold water. Cook in boiling salted water for 3 to 4 minutes; drain well. Blanch the tomatoes in boiling water; drain, peel and squeeze gently to remove seeds, then chop coarsely. Peel the onion and chop finely.

● In a pan, heat the extra virgin olive oil. Cook the onion until just transparent. Add tomatoes. Season with salt and fresh ground pepper. Cook for 10 minutes, on medium heat. Add chicory and parsley; cook for 2 minutes. In individual plates, place a serving of chicory and sauce, and a serving of bean purée. Decorate with a few whole beans and serve.

Difficulty **easy**
Preparation time **50 minutes**
Calories **310**

Ingredients *for 4 servings*

Chicory lettuce *1 1/2 lbs*

Smoked scamorza cheese *1/2 lb*

Tomatoes *3/4 lb, firm and ripe*

Eggs *3*

Grated grana cheese *2 tablespoons*

Extra virgin olive oil *3 tablespoons*

Salt *&* **pepper** *to taste*

Chicory tart

● Trim the chicory; remove the hard outer leaves and rinse well. In a pot of boiling water, blanch the chicory; drain and dry on a kitchen towel; chop in small pieces.

● Peel the cheese and slice thinly. Blanch the tomatoes in boiling water; drain, peel and squeeze gently to remove seeds, then dice or slice thinly.

● Brush a baking dish. Place half the chicory in the dish. Cover with half the cheese slices, half the tomatoes and repeat layers with remaining ingredients.

● In a bowl, whisk the eggs, grated cheese, a pinch of salt and pepper. Pour this preparation on the vegetables. Drizzle with remaining extra virgin olive oil. Bake in a preheated oven at 350°F for 20 to 30 minutes. Can be served hot or warm.

Mixed cooked vegetables

Difficulty **easy**
Preparation time **1 hour**
Calories **210**

Ingredients *for 4 servings*

Mixed greens *2 1/4 lbs (chicory, cabbage, beet tops, etc.)*
Yellow potatoes *3*
Garlic *2 cloves*
Red hot chili peppers *1*
Extra virgin olive oil *4 tablespoons*
Salt *to taste*

● Rinse the potatoes; place in a pot, cover with cold water and a pinch of salt. Cook for 40 minutes. Rinse the mixed greens well. Cook them in boiling salted water for 15 minutes, pushing them often under water with a slotted spoon.

● Drain the mixed greens; squeeze gently to remove excess moisture and set aside on kitchen towels to dry a little. When potatoes are done, drain, peel and slice.

● In a pan, heat the extra virgin olive oil. Add unpeeled garlic and chili pepper. Cook for a few seconds. Add potatoes and mixed greens. Season with salt and cook on high heat for 5 to 6 minutes, stirring with a wooden spoon. Serve immediately.

Mixed vegetables with tomatoes

Difficulty **easy**
Preparation time **40 minutes**
Calories **230**

Ingredients *for 4 servings*

Chicory lettuce *1 lb*
Beet tops *3/4 lb*
Cherry tomatoes *10, firm and ripe*
Garlic *1 clove*
Celery *1 stalk*
Parsley *1 small bunch*
Red hot chili peppers *1*
Grated grana cheese *1 tablespoon*
Extra virgin olive oil *5 tablespoons*
Salt *to taste*

● Trim the chicory; remove the outer leaves and cut in pieces; rinse in cold water. Rinse the beet tops. Rinse, dry and chop the celery.

● Cook chicory, celery and beet tops in boiling salted water for a few minutes. Blanch the tomatoes in boiling water; drain, peel and squeeze gently to remove seeds, then chop coarsely. Peel the garlic and crush lightly. Rinse, dry and chop parsley. In a pan, heat the extra virgin olive oil. Add garlic, onion and parsley. Cook for a few minutes; add tomatoes and chili pepper. Season with salt. Cover and continue cooking on medium heat for 10 minutes, stirring from time to time.

● Add the beet tops, chicory and celery. Mix well. Sprinkle with grated parmigiano and serve very hot.

Chunky vegetables

Difficulty **easy**
Preparation time **1 hour**
Calories **175**

Ingredients *for 4 servings*

Round eggplants *2*
Zucchini *2*
Carrots *2*
Bell peppers *2*
Peeled tomatoes *1 lb*
Onions *2*
Garlic *1 clove*
Basil *6 leaves*
Extra virgin olive oil *4 tablespoons*
Salt *&* **pepper** *to taste*

● Trim the eggplants; rinse, dry and dice. Chop the tomatoes. Trim zucchini and carrots; rinse, dry and slice. Cut the peppers in half, remove seeds and white parts; rinse and cut into strips. Peel onions and cut into thick slices.

● Peel the garlic and remove green sprout if necessary. In a large pan, heat the extra virgin olive oil. Add garlic and cook for a few minutes; discard garlic. Add all the prepared vegetables and sauté for a few minutes. Mix in the chopped basil.

● Season with salt and fresh ground pepper. Cover the pan and cook on medium heat for about 40 minutes, stirring from time to time. Transfer the cooked vegetables to a serving bowl. Serve very hot.

Bandiera

Difficulty **easy**
Preparation time **1 hour**
Calories **125**

Ingredients *for 4 servings*

Bell peppers *1 lb*
Tomatoes *1 lb*
Onions *1/2 lb*
Extra virgin olive oil *3 tablespoons*
Salt *&* **pepper** *to taste*

● Peel the onions; rinse, dry and slice thinly. In a saucepan, place the onions, with extra virgin olive oil and a pinch of salt. Cover the pan and cook on low heat until just tender.

● Cut the peppers in half; remove seeds and white parts; rinse, dry and cut in large strips. When the onions are tender, add the peppers and let simmer for 10 minutes.

● Blanch the tomatoes in boiling water; drain, peel and squeeze gently to remove seeds, then crush the pulp. Add tomatoes to peppers. Season with salt and pepper. Cover and cook for another 20 minutes, on low heat, stirring often. Serve hot directly from the cooking pan.

Asparagus & orange salad

Difficulty **easy**
Preparation time **40 minutes**
+ resting time
Calories **220**

Ingredients *for 4 servings*

Romaine lettuce *1 head*
Asparagus *1 bunch*
Oranges *2*
Scallions *1*
Shrimp *10 oz*
Melon *1*
Black olives *2 oz*
Cider vinegar *2 tablespoons*
Dry white wine *1/4 cup*
Extra virgin olive oil *5 tablespoons*
Salt *&* **pepper** *to taste*

● Trim the asparagus; remove the tough parts of stems; peel lightly with a potato peeler; slice in half lengthwise and then in strips. Set aside in cold water; refrigerate overnight.

● Remove the outside leaves from the lettuce; rinse and slice lettuce in strips; dry well. Peel and devein the shrimp. In a pot, bring to boil 1 cup of water and the white wine. Add the shrimp and cook for 2 to 3 minutes; drain and cool.

● Peel the oranges and divide in segments; remove the pith and membrane. Trim the scallion and remove the outside leaves; rinse and slice. Halve the melon and make as many melon balls as you can with a melon baller. Pit the olives. Place the asparagus and the shredded lettuce in a deep serving dish. Add the shrimp, the melon balls, and the oranges. Place the olives in the middle and sprinkle with the scallions.

● In a bowl, mix the vinegar with a pinch of salt and fresh ground pepper. Slowly whisk in the extra virgin olive oil to blend all ingredients well and thicken the sauce lightly. Pour over the salad and toss delicately. Serve.

Citron & lettuce salad

Difficulty **easy**
Preparation time **20 minutes**
Calories **100**

Ingredients *for 4 servings*

Romaine lettuce *1 head*
Citron *2*
Granny Smith apples *2*
Lemons *the juice of 1*
Extra virgin olive oil *4 tablespoons*
Salt *&* **white pepper** *to taste*

● Peel the apples; core, slice thinly and place in a bowl covered with half the lemon juice. Remove yellow peel and white pith from the citrons; slice and mix with apples.

● Remove the exterior leaves from the lettuce; rinse in cold water; drain and dry on a kitchen towel; slice in thin strips.

● In a small bowl, mix the remaining lemon juice with a pinch of salt and fresh ground white pepper until dissolved. Slowly whisk in the extra virgin olive oil. Transfer lettuce, apple and citrons to a salad bowl. Add the prepared sauce and toss well. Serve immediately.

Vegetables in sweet-and-sour sauce

Difficulty **easy**
Preparation time **20 minutes**
Calories **170**

Ingredients *for 4 servings*

Zucchini *3/4 lb*

Red bell peppers *1/2 lbs*

Tomatoes *3/4 lb, firm and ripe*

Bean sprouts *5 oz*

Chives *1 small bunch*

Sugar *1 tablespoon*

White wine vinegar *3 tablespoons*

Extra virgin olive oil *4 tablespoons*

Salt *to taste*

● Trim the zucchini; rinse and cut in thin strips. Cut the peppers in half; remove seeds and white parts; rinse and cut in thin strips. Rinse bean sprouts in cold water; drain well. Blanch the tomatoes in boiling water; drain, peel and squeeze gently to remove seeds, then chop coarsely.

● In a saucepan, melt the sugar in one tablespoon of water; cook until it begins to caramelize. Add vinegar and let caramel melt. Add tomatoes and a pinch of salt. Cook the sauce on high heat for 4 to 5 minutes.

● In a non-stick pan, heat the extra virgin olive oil. Add the peppers and cook for one minute. Mix in the zucchini. Add bean sprouts and cook for 2 to 3 minutes. Pour the prepared sauce over the vegetables and cook for a few minutes, stirring. Remove from the heat and sprinkle with chopped chives. Can be served warm or cold.

Royal salad

Difficulty **easy**
Preparation time **50 minutes**
Calories **220**

Ingredients *for 4 servings*

Mixed lettuce greens *1/2 lb*

Artichokes *4*

Chicken breast *1 lb*

Radishes *4*

Carrots *1*

Onions *1/2*

Celery *half a stalk*

Parsley *a few sprigs*

Black truffle *1 small*

Lemons *the juice of 1/2*

White wine vinegar *3 tablespoons*

Extra virgin olive oil *4 tablespoons*

Salt *& **pepper** to taste*

● Peel and trim the carrot. Peel the onion. Trim the celery. Rinse the parsley. Rinse all and place in a large pot. Cover with water and bring to boil for 20 minutes. Reduce heat; add chicken breasts and cook on very low heat for 20 minutes. Drain chicken and cool before slicing thinly.

● During this time, rinse the lettuce and dry it on a kitchen towel. Cut off stems and outer leaves from the artichokes; cut in half and remove chokes; cut in thin slices and soak in lemon juice. Brush the truffle; rinse and dry well, then slice thinly.

● In a bowl, mix vinegar, a pinch of salt and pepper. Slowly whisk in the extra virgin olive oil. Place lettuce on a serving dish. Drain artichokes and place on the lettuce. Add slices of chicken and of radishes. Cover with truffle slices. Pour the prepared sauce over and serve immediately.

Difficulty **easy**
Preparation time **30 minutes**
Calories **245**

Salad 'deliziosa'

Ingredients *for 4 servings*

Artichokes *2*

Palm hearts *4*

Mushrooms *1/2 lb*

Avocado *1*

Red lettuce *2 heads*

Lemons *2*

Extra virgin olive oil *4 tablespoons*

Salt *&* **pepper** *to taste*

● Remove stems and outer leaves from the artichokes; slice thinly and remove chokes; soak in water mixed with the juice of half a lemon.

● Clean the mushrooms; rinse quickly and pat-dry with a kitchen towel. Slice the mushrooms thinly and place in a serving bowl. Drizzle with juice of half a lemon.

● Slice the palm hearts. Rinse, dry and slice the red lettuce into strips. Peel the avocado and discard the pit; dice the avocado.

● Place all prepared ingredients in the salad bowl, with the mushrooms. In a bowl, mix the juice of the remaining lemon, a pinch of salt and a pinch of fresh ground pepper. Slowly whisk in the extra virgin olive oil. Pour this sauce over the vegetables and toss carefully. Serve immediately.

Eggplants 'capricciose'

Difficulty **easy**
Preparation time **45 minutes**
+ resting time
Calories **235**

Ingredients *for 4 servings*

Eggplants *3*
Green olives *10*
Capers *2 tablespoons*
Onions *1*
Garlic *2 cloves*
Peeled tomatoes *1/2 lb*
Breadcrumbs *2 tablespoons*
Porto *3 tablespoons*
White wine vinegar *4 tablespoons*
Extra virgin olive oil *enough for frying*
Extra virgin olive oil *2 tablespoons*
Salt *to taste*

● Trim and peel the eggplants; cut in julienne and soak in cold water for 30 minutes. During this time, peel the onion and slice thinly. Peel the garlic. Pit the olives and cut in strips. Dice the peeled tomatoes. In a non-stick pan, lightly toast the breadcrumbs.

● Drain the eggplants and dry well on a kitchen towel. In a pan, heat olive oil to fry; fry in the eggplants. Drain on paper towels to remove excess oil.

● In a pan, heat the extra virgin olive oil. Add garlic and onion; cook until just transparent. Mix in the olives and capers; cook for one minute. Add the tomatoes and a pinch of salt. Bring to boil on high heat. Add the fried eggplant and cook for about 5 minutes, stirring often.

● Remove the garlic. Pour the vinegar and the port in the pan and let evaporate on high heat. Stir the preparation. Sprinkle with breadcrumbs. Remove from heat and let cool completely before serving.

Eggplants in hot sauce

Difficulty **easy**
Preparation time **30 minutes**
+ resting time
Calories **40**

Ingredients *for 4 servings*

Eggplants *3/4 lb*
Anchovies *3*
Parsley *a few sprigs*
Oregano *a pinch*
Hot chili powder *a pinch*
Garlic *1 clove*
White wine vinegar *2 tablespoons*
Salt *to taste*

● Trim and rinse the eggplants; slice lengthwise and cook in abundant salted water for 5 minutes. Drain and squeeze to remove excess moisture..

● Rinse, dry and chop the parsley. Peel and slice the garlic. Rinse the anchovies; debone and chop. In a food processor, mix the garlic, parsley, red hot pepper powder, oregano and anchovies, until creamy. Transfer to a bowl and mix with the vinegar.

● Place the eggplants on a serving dish. Add the sauce, toss and refrigerate for 3 hours. Sprinkle with extra virgin olive oil, and garlic, parsley and hot pepper chopped together before serving.

Eggplant surprise

Difficulty **easy**
Preparation time **40 minutes**
Calories **170**

Ingredients *for 4 servings*

Eggplants *4*
Tomatoes *1/2 lb, firm and ripe*
Parsley *1 small bunch*
Basil *1 small bunch*
Garlic *1 clove*
Onions *1*
Breadcrumbs *1 tablespoon*
Extra virgin olive oil *5 tablespoons*
Salt *&* **pepper** *to taste*

● Rinse, dry and cut the eggplants in half lengthwise. With a spoon, remove half the pulp and dice. Salt the interior of the eggplant halves. Brush a baking dish with extra virgin olive oil; place eggplants and bake in a preheated oven at 350ºF for 10 to 15 minutes.

● Blanch the tomatoes in boiling water; drain, peel and squeeze gently to remove seeds, then chop. Peel the onion and a garlic clove; finely chop together. In a pan, heat 3 tablespoons of extra virgin olive oil and cook onion and garlic for a few minutes. Rinse, dry and chop parsley and basil.

● Add diced eggplants. Season with salt and pepper. Sauté for a few minutes. Add tomatoes and half the parsley and basil. Cook for 10 minutes, stirring often.

● Chop the remaining garlic and mix with parsley and basil. Remove eggplants from oven; fill with tomato preparation. Sprinkle with garlic-herb mixture and breadcrumbs. Return to oven, at 400ºF, or under the grill for a few minutes. Can be served warm or cold.

Eggplants in tuna sauce

Difficulty **easy**
Preparation time **30 minutes
+ resting time**
Calories **155**

Ingredients *for 4 servings*

Round eggplants *2*
Tuna in oil *3 oz*
Anchovy filets in oil *4*
Basil *10 leaves*
Sage *2 leaves*
Mint *a few leaves*
Lemons *the juice of 1*
Extra virgin olive oil *3 tablespoons*
Salt *&* **peppercorns** *to taste*

● Trim, rinse and slice the eggplants; place in a colander, sprinkle with coarse salt and set aside for 30 minutes. In a blender, mix the tuna, anchovy filets, basil, extra virgin olive oil, lemon juice and peppercorns, until sauce is smooth.

● Rinse eggplants and dry on paper towels. Place on a very hot grill for 2 minutes; turn and cook completely. Transfer to a serving dish. Cover with the prepared sauce. Decorate with the mint and sage leaves. Can be served hot or at room temperature.

Difficulty **easy**
Preparation time **30 minutes**
Calories **225**

Ingredients *for 4 servings*

Artichokes *8*
Garlic *2 cloves*
Dry white wine *a few tablespoons*
Breadcrumbs *2 oz*
Grated pecorino *2 oz*
Lemons *the juice of 1*
Fresh oregano *1 bunch*
Extra virgin olive oil *5 tablespoons*
Salt *&* **pepper** *to taste*

Artichokes with fresh oregano

● Remove the outer leaves and stems from the artichokes; slice and remove the chokes. Soak in a bowl of cold water mixed with the lemon juice.

● In a saucepan, heat 2 tablespoons of extra virgin olive oil. Add garlic, one branch of oregano and drained artichokes. Season with salt. Cover the pan and cook on low heat for 10 minutes, adding the dry white wine after 5 minutes.

● When the artichokes are tender, remove from the pan and transfer to an oiled oven dish. Mix the breadcrumbs with grated pecorino and chopped oregano, salt and pepper. Sprinkle over the artichokes. Drizzle with remaining extra virgin olive oil. Bake in a preheated oven, at 400°F for 5 minutes. Can be served hot or cold.

Difficulty **easy**
Preparation time **45 minutes**
Calories **150**

Ingredients *for 4 servings*

Artichokes *6*
Onions *1/2 lb*
Tomato sauce *4 oz*
Parsley *a few sprigs*
Lemons *the juice of 2*
White wine vinegar *3 tablespoons*
Extra virgin olive oil *5 tablespoons*
Salt *&* **pepper** *to taste*

Marinated artichokes

● Trim the artichokes; remove stems and outer leaves; slice in half and remove the chokes; place in cold water mixed with lemon juice.

● Peel onion and slice. In a pan, heat the extra virgin olive oil. Add onions, drained artichokes and chopped parsley. Season with salt and pepper. Sauté for a few minutes.

● Add the tomato sauce and vinegar. Let evaporate on high heat. Continue cooking on low heat for 20 minutes, adding a few tablespoons of hot water if needed; stir often. Remove from the heat and let cool completely before serving.

Artichokes & peas

Difficulty **easy**
Preparation time **45 minutes**
Calories **190**

Ingredients *for 4 servings*

Artichokes *8*
Unshelled peas *1 1/2 lbs*
Onions *1*
Lemons *the juice of 1*
Vegetable broth *1 to 2 cups*
Extra virgin olive oil *4 tablespoons*
Salt *&* **pepper** *to taste*

● Remove stems and outer leaves from artichokes; slice thinly and remove chokes. Soak in cold water mixed with lemon juice. Shell the peas.

● Peel and slice the onion thinly. In a pan, heat the extra virgin olive oil. Add onions and cook until just softened. Add peas and cook for a minute, stirring.

● Add one cup of hot broth. Cover and cook for 5 minutes. Add drained artichokes and cook on low heat for about 12 minutes, adding more broth if necessary. Stir often.

● When vegetables are tender, season with salt and generous fresh ground pepper. Transfer to a serving dish and serve hot.

Raw artichoke salad

Difficulty **easy**
Preparation time **20 minutes**
+ resting time
Calories **115**

Ingredients *for 4 servings*

Artichokes *8*
Fresh mint *a few leaves*
Garlic *1 clove*
Lemons *2*
Extra virgin olive oil *4 tablespoons*
Salt *to taste*

● Rinse the artichokes; remove the tips, stems and outer leaves; cut in quarter and remove chokes. Soak in cold water mixed with the juice of one lemon.

● Rinse, dry and chop the mint. Place in a bowl with the juice of the remaining lemon; mix with the olive oil and a pinch of salt.

● Peel the garlic and remove the green sprout; slice thinly or crush; place in a salad bowl. Add drained artichokes, sliced very thinly. Pour the prepared sauce over the artichokes and toss well. Cover the bowl and set aside for one hour before serving.

Pinzimonio

Difficulty **easy**
Preparation time **30 minutes**
Calories **245**

Ingredients *for 4 servings*

Celery *2 stalks*
Fennel bulbs *2*
Red bell peppers *1*
Yellow bell peppers *1*
Belgian endives *2 heads*
Carrots *4 small*
Young artichokes *2*
Radishes *8*
White wine vinegar *a few tablespoons*
Extra virgin olive oil *1/2 cup*
Salt *&* **pepper** *to taste*

Andrea's note: A terrific way to taste a very good olive oil, it also makes a quick, easy and tasty starter for any meal. Make sure you only use easy-to-handle vegetables and excellent oil.

● Trim all vegetables; rinse and carefully dry. Cut celery in half. Cut carrots, artichokes and peppers in strips. Cut the fennel halves in quarter. Slice the radishes and separate the leaves of the Belgian endives. Place vegetables decoratively on a large serving plate.

● In a bowl, mix the extra virgin olive oil with white wine vinegar, a generous pinch of salt and fresh ground pepper. Whisk until well blended. Pour this sauce in 4 individual small bowls. Every guest needs only to dip the chosen vegetables in his bowl of extra virgin olive oil before eating.

Difficulty **easy**
Preparation time **40 minutes**
Calories **175**

Ingredients *for 4 servings*

Curly endive *2 1/4 lbs*
Pitted black olives *2 oz*
Capers *2 oz*
Anchovy filets *6*
Garlic *3 cloves*
Extra virgin olive oil *5 tablespoons*
Salt *to taste*

Endive with capers & olives

● Trim the curly endive; detach the outer leaves and rinse with the heart. Slice dark leaves and tender leaves separately. Peel and crush garlic. In a pan, heat the extra virgin olive oil and cook the garlic for a minute. Add the hard outer leaves of the endive. Cover and cook on low heat for 10 minutes. Add remaining leaves and cook for 5 minutes, adding a little water, if necessary.

● Rinse the capers and anchovies. Debone and chop the anchovies. Add capers, olives and a pinch of salt to the pan. Cook uncovered on low heat for 10 minutes.

● Add anchovies and mash with a fork until dissolved. Transfer the preparation to a serving dish. Serve very hot.

Difficulty **easy**
Preparation time **30 minutes**
Calories **110**

Ingredients *for 4 servings*

Chicory *2 1/4 lbs*
Garlic *1 clove*
Extra virgin olive oil *4 tablespoons*
Salt *to taste*

Chicory, garlic & olive oil

● Trim and rinse the chicory under running water; drain and cook in abundant salted boiling water until al dente; drain again.

● Peel the garlic and remove the green sprout. In a skillet, heat the extra virgin olive oil and cook the garlic on medium heat until golden. Discard the garlic.

Reduce the heat and add chicory, still lightly wet.

● Season with salt and cook for about 10 minutes, or until chicory is dry, stirring often with a wooden spoon. Remove from heat. Transfer to a serving dish. Serve at once.

Stewed chicory

Difficulty **easy**
Preparation time **30 minutes**
Calories **130**

Ingredients *for 4 servings*

Chicory *1 3/4 lbs*
Tomato sauce *10 oz*
Garlic *1/2 clove*
Red hot chili peppers *1 small*
Extra virgin olive oil *4 tablespoons*
Salt *to taste*

● Carefully rinse the chicory. Cook in abundant boiling salted water for 5 minutes; drain and squeeze-dry.

● Peel the garlic, removing the green sprout if necessary; lightly crush. In a pan, heat the extra virgin olive oil. Add garlic and chili pepper. When the garlic starts to brown, discard. Add chicory and cook for 5 minutes.

● Add tomato sauce and a pinch of salt. Cover and cook on low heat, for about 10 minutes. Stir often. Transfer to a serving dish and serve immediately.

Arugula with black-eyed beans

Difficulty **easy**
Preparation time **2 hours 30 minutes + soaking time**
Calories **205**

Ingredients *for 4 servings*

Arugula *2 1/4 lbs*
Black-eyed beans *5 oz*
Garlic *2 cloves*
Extra virgin olive oil *4 tablespoons*
Salt *&* **pepper** *to taste*

● Soak the black-eyed beans in cold water for 12 hours. Drain and cook in abundant water for 2 hours.

● Carefully rinse the arugula. Cook in salted boiling water for 5 minutes; drain and squeeze-dry.

● When the beans are cooked, add generous coarse salt and mix. Drain well. In a large pan, heat the extra virgin olive oil and cook the crushed garlic clove. Add arugula, beans, a pinch of salt and fresh ground pepper. Mix well and cook for a few minutes before serving.

Eggplant 'peperonata'

Difficulty **easy**
Preparation time **50 minutes**
Calories **180**

Ingredients *for 4 servings*

Assorted peppers *1 lb*
Eggplants *3/4 lb*
Tomatoes *3/4 lb*
Onions *2*
Yellow potatoes *1*
Garlic *1 clove*
Celery *1 stalk*
Parsley *1 small bunch*
Tarragon *a few leaves*
Basil *a few leaves*
Marjoram *1 sprig*
Reduced vegetable broth *3/4 cup*
Extra virgin olive oil *4 tablespoons*
Salt *to taste*

● Trim, rinse and dry the peppers, tomatoes, eggplants, parsley, tarragon, basil, marjoram and celery. Peel and rinse the onion, garlic and potato.

● Cut the peppers, tomatoes, celery and eggplant in pieces. Grate the potato. Thinly slice the onion and garlic. Chop the herbs together. In a large pan, heat the extra virgin olive oil and broth. Add all vegetables, herbs and a pinch of salt. Cover and cook on low heat for 30 minutes.

● Remove the cover and let the liquid evaporate; remove from heat. Transfer peperonata to a serving dish. Can be served hot or cold.

Peppers with almond sauce

Difficulty **easy**
Preparation time **40 minutes**
Calories **205**

Ingredients *for 4 servings*

Yellow bell peppers *1 3/4 lbs*
Tomato sauce *14 oz*
Peeled almonds *2 oz*
Raisins *2 oz*
Sugar *1/2 tablespoon*
White wine vinegar *4 tablespoons*
Extra virgin olive oil *2 tablespoons*
Salt *to taste*

● Rinse the peppers; cut in half, remove seeds and cut in strips. In a pan, heat the extra virgin olive oil. Cook the peppers, with a pinch of salt, on low heat, for about 20 minutes, adding a little hot water if necessary.

● During this time, soak the raisins in hot water for 15 minutes. Blanch the almonds for one minute; drain, peel, dry and slice thinly.

● When the peppers are tender, add the almonds, drained raisins, tomato sauce, sugar and vinegar. Season with salt and mix well. Cook for 5 minutes, on medium-high heat. Serve very hot.

Baked peppers

Difficulty **easy**
Preparation time **50 minutes**
Calories **300**

Ingredients *for 4 servings*

Yellow bell peppers *1 3/4 lbs*
Pitted green olives *3 oz*
Oregano *a pinch*
Garlic *1 clove*
Parsley *1 small bunch*
Capers *2 tablespoons*
Breadcrumbs *4 tablespoons*
Extra virgin olive oil *5 tablespoons*
Salt *&* **pepper** *to taste*

● Rinse the peppers and remove the stem. Place in a preheated oven, at 495°F for 10 minutes. Remove from the oven; peel, cut in half and remove the seeds; cut in thin strips.

● Rinse the parsley; peel the garlic and chop together. Rinse the capers under running water and dry on paper towels. Brush a baking dish with extra virgin olive oil. Place the peppers in the dish. Cover with the olives and the capers.

● Sprinkle with garlic and parsley, oregano, a pinch of salt and fresh ground pepper. Cover with the breadcrumb. Drizzle with remaining extra virgin olive oil and bake in a preheated oven at 400°F for about 20 minutes. Can be served hot or at room temperature.

Pepper filets

Difficulty **easy**
Preparation time **40 minutes**
Calories **365**

Ingredients *for 4 servings*

Red, green and yellow peppers *2 lbs*
Capers *2 oz*
Parsley *1 small bunch*
Grated pecorino *1/2 lb*
Breadcrumbs *4 tablespoons*
Extra virgin olive oil *3 tablespoons*
Salt *to taste*

● Rinse the capers under running water; dry and chop. Brush a baking dish with 1 tablespoon of extra virgin olive oil. Cover the peppers; remove the seeds and white parts; cut in large pieces. Rinse and chop parsley.

● Place the peppers in the dish. Cover with breadcrumbs, grated pecorino, capers and parsley. Season with salt.

● Drizzle the preparation with remaining extra virgin olive oil. Bake in a preheated oven, at 425°F for about 30 minutes. Can be served warm or cold, directly from the baking dish.

Difficulty **easy**
Preparation time **30 minutes**
Calories **485**

Ingredients *for 4 servings*

Tomatoes *3*

Leeks *3*

Cucumber *1*

Basil *a few leaves*

Garlic *1 clove*

Mozzarella *1*

Day-old bread *10 oz*

White wine vinegar *1 tablespoon*

Extra virgin olive oil *4 tablespoons*

Salt *&* **pepper** *to taste*

Baker's salad

● Remove the crust from the bread. Dice bread. In a non-stick pan, heat the extra virgin olive oil and fry the bread. When golden, remove and transfer to a salad bowl.

● Rinse the tomatoes; dry and cut in quarters. Peel the cucumber; cut in half and then in slices. Cut off the roots and outer leaves from the leeks; rinse, dry and slice thinly. Peel the garlic. Rinse the basil; dry it and tear in small pieces. Dice the mozzarella.

● Add all prepared ingredients to the salad bowl; mix with bread. In a bowl, mix the extra virgin olive oil, vinegar, a pinch of salt and fresh ground pepper, with a fork until well blended. Toss with salad and serve.

Sweets &
Desserts

Difficulty **easy**
Preparation time **1 hour**
Calories **175**

Cherry sorbet

Ingredients *for 4 servings*

Cherries *1 lb*

Sugar *3 oz*

Lemons *1*

Kirsh *2 tablespoons*

Egg whites *1*

Andrea's note: Try using very ripe and very large cherries, like the Vignola cherries available in springtime in Northern Italy.

● Rinse and dry lemon; remove its skin. Press the lemon juice in a bowl. Rinse the cherries, drain and pit. In a saucepan, place the lemon peel, lemon juice and cherries. Cook on high heat, for about 4 minutes, stirring often with a wooden spoon.

● Remove from the heat; drain the cherries carefully; discard the lemon peel. Cool completely. Transfer the cherries to a food processor. Mix into a fine purée; add Kirsch. In a saucepan, melt the sugar in 1/2 cup of water; slowly bring to boil and cook for 2 to 3 minutes. Remove and cool completely.

● When cold, add to the puréed cherries and mix well. Pour into an ice cream machine and follow the manufacturer's instructions. Halfway through, add the egg white and continue process. When ready, serve in cold individual bowls.

Mint granita with syrup

Difficulty **easy**
Preparation time **40 minutes**
Calories **190**

Ingredients *for 4 servings*

Mint syrup *5 tablespoons*
Sugar *1/2 cup*
Wild berries *1/2 lb (blueberries, raspberries, or blackberries)*
Apricots *4*

● Blanch the apricots in boiling water; drain, divide in half, pit and slice. Rinse the wild berries in ice water; drain on a kitchen towel and dry delicately.

● Pour 1 1/2 cups of water in a pot. Add sugar and bring to boil. Stirring, cook until sugar is completely dissolved. Remove the syrup from the heat and cool.

● Mix 4 tablespoons of mint syrup with syrup; pour into ice cream machine. Work for a few minutes at a time, stopping the machine often for 30 seconds, until the granita is ready.

● Divide the remaining mint syrup into cold individual bowls. Place a ball of granita in each bowl. Serve covered with the apricots and mixed wild berries.

Coffee granita

Difficulty **easy**
Preparation time **40 minutes**
Calories **185**

Ingredients *for 4 servings*

Espresso *9 tablespoons*
Sugar *3 oz*

To decorate

Whipping cream *1/2 cup*
Coffee beans *4*

● In a saucepan, place sugar and 1 cup of water. Bring to boil and cook for 2 to 3 minutes, stirring until dissolved and the syrup is dense and transparent. Remove from heat and set aside to cool.

● Add the coffee to cold syrup. Pour the mixture into the ice cream machine. Work for 1 minute; stop the machine for 1 minute and start over. Repeat until granita is ready.

● During this time, whip the cream with an electric mixer; transfer to a pastry bag with a star tip. Place the granita in individual cold bowls. Decorate with the whipped cream and coffee beans. Serve immediately.

Pineapple & lemon granita

Difficulty **average**
Preparation time **40 minutes**
Calories **125**

Ingredients *for 4 servings*

Pineapples *1*
Lemon juice *1 tablespoon*
Sugar *4 oz*

● Pour 1 cup of water in a saucepan. Add the sugar and bring to boil. Cook for 1 to 2 minutes, until completely dissolved, stirring. Remove from heat and place saucepan in a bowl of ice water to cool.

● Remove top of pineapple; empty pineapple and refrigerate the shell. Discard the hard core. Weigh 12 oz of the pulp and dice it; mix in a food processor with lemon juice; pass through a sieve; add to prepared syrup.

● Pour the preparation in an ice cream machine; work for a few minutes. Stop the machine for 30 seconds and start again. Repeat this operation until the granita is ready. Remove the pineapple shell from refrigerator; fill with granita. Decorate with Maraschino cherries and serve immediately.

Green tea granita

Difficulty **easy**
Preparation time **45 minutes**
Calories **100**

Ingredients *for 4 servings*

Green tea leaves *1 tablespoon*
Sugar *4 oz*
Vanilla extract *1/2 teaspoon*
Lemons *1*
Lemon balm *1 sprig*

● In a saucepan, boil 1 cup of water. In a cup, pour the water over the tea leaves. Cover and set aside for 10 minutes. Pass tea through a sieve and cool completely.

● In a saucepan, bring to boil 1 cup of water, the sugar and grated peel of 1 lemon. Cook for a few minutes, stirring until sugar is dissolved.

● Remove syrup from heat. Mix in the green tea, lemon juice and vanilla. Cool completely before pouring into the ice cream machine. Work the machine for a few minutes; stop for 30 seconds and start again. Repeat until granita is ready. Distribute among 4 cold glasses. Garnish with lemon balm leaves and serve.

Difficulty **easy**
Preparation time **50 minutes**
Calories **570**

Ingredients *for 4 servings*

Cherries *1/2 lb*

Apricots *3/4 lb*

Milk *2 cups*

Egg yolks *4*

Potato starch *2 oz*

Sugar *1 cup*

Grand Marnier *1/4 cup*

Cinnamon *1 stick*

Andrea's note: The recipe can also be made with frozen fruits for an excellent ending to a light winter dinner. Easy to do, it is a guaranteed success.

Fruit compote with Grand Marnier

● Whisk the egg yolks with 1/2 cup of sugar, until creamy and white. Slowly mix in the sifted potato starch. Whisk in the milk. Pour the mixture in a saucepan and cook on very low heat, stirring all the time, until it thickens. Remove from heat, mix in the Grand Marnier and transfer to a baking dish.

● Rinse and dry the apricots; cut in half and discard the pit. Rinse, dry and pit the cherries. Melt remaining sugar in a saucepan, with 1/2 cup of water and the cinnamon. Boil until syrup covers a wooden spoon. Add apricots and cherries; cook for 5 minutes on high heat.

● Drain the fruits from the syrup and place on top of the prepared cream. Reduce the syrup; remove the cinnamon stick and pour over the fruits. Bake under the grill for a few minutes and serve immediately.

Orange sorbet

Difficulty **easy**
Preparation time **40 minutes**
Calories **240**

Ingredients *for 4 servings*

Oranges *4*
Sugar *1/2 cup*
Egg whites *1/2*

To decorate

Candied oranges *2 oz*
Whipping cream *1/2 cup*

● In a small saucepan, boil the sugar in 1/2 cup of water for 10 minutes. Remove from heat and immerse the saucepan in ice water to cool.

● Rinse and dry oranges; remove top and empty orange pulp with a grapefruit knife. Remove white pith, being careful not to break orange skins. Freeze orange shells.

● Pass the orange pulp in a food mill. Weigh 11 oz of the pulp; add to syrup and mix. Pour the mixture in an ice cream machine. Follow manufacturer's instructions. Halfway through, add beaten egg white and continue.

● Remove the orange shells from the freezer. Fill with sorbet and return to freezer for at least 30 minutes. Cut the candied oranges into thin strips. Whip the cream and transfer to a pastry bag. Before serving, decorate the frozen sorbet with whipped cream and strips of candied oranges.

Jasmine sorbet

Difficulty **easy**
Preparation time **45 minutes**
Calories **115**

Ingredients *for 4 servings*

Watermelon *1 small*
Sugar *4 oz*
Vanilla *1 bean*
Jasmine water *1/2 tablespoon*
Egg whites *1*

● In a saucepan, place sugar, 1 cup of water and vanilla bean. Boil for 5 minutes. When sugar is completely dissolved, remove vanilla bean and cool syrup.

● Peel the watermelon; weigh 1 lb of pulp and chop it, removing seeds. Mix in a food processor; add the prepared syrup and jasmine water. Mix well.

● Pour the preparation in an ice cream machine. Follow manufacturer's instructions. Halfway through add the beaten egg white and continue. When ready, serve in cold glasses or bowls.

Kiwi sorbet

Difficulty **easy**
Preparation time **40 minutes**
+ resting time
Calories **170**

Ingredients *for 4 servings*

Kiwis *1 lb*

Sugar *4 oz*

Egg whites *1/2*

To decorate

Kiwis *3*

● In a saucepan, melt the sugar in 1/2 cup of water. Boil for 3 minutes. Remove from heat and cool the syrup. During this time, peel kiwis and dice. Mix in a food processor. Add cold syrup and mix delicately.

● Pour the kiwi preparation in an ice cream machine. Follow manufactur-er's instructions. Halfway through, add beaten egg white and continue. When ready, pour into molds and freeze.

● Before serving, peel the kiwis and slice; divide each slice in 6. Dip molds in hot water for a few seconds; turn onto cold individual plates. Decorate with kiwi pieces and serve.

Lemon yogurt sorbet

Difficulty **easy**
Preparation time **40 minutes**
Calories **165**

Ingredients *for 4 servings*

Lemons *2*

Plain yogurt *1/2 cup*

Sugar *4 oz*

To decorate

Mixed wild berries *5 oz*

Kiwis *2*

Mint *1 sprig*

● In a saucepan, melt sugar in 1 1/2 cups of water. Boil until completely dissolved. Remove from heat and immerse the pan in ice water to cool.

● Press the lemons, filter and mix with cold syrup. Add yogurt and mix well. Pour the preparation in an ice cream machine and follow manufacturer's in-structions.

● Rinse, drain and dry the berries on a kitchen towel; cut the strawberries in quarters. Peel and slice kiwis. Distribute the sorbet in individual bowls. Decorate with berries, kiwi and a few mint leaves.

Difficulty **average**
Preparation time **30 minutes**
+ resting time
Calories **555**

Ingredients *for 4 servings*

Strawberries *2 1/4 lbs*

Sugar *1 lb*

Cold water *3 cups*

Lemons *the juice of 1*

Vanilla *1 bean*

Strawberries in syrup

● Rinse strawberries in cold water mixed with lemon juice. Drain well and place in a bowl. In a saucepan, mix sugar with cold water and vanilla bean. Cook on low heat for a few minutes, stirring slowly.

● When sugar is dissolved, pour syrup over the fruits. Cover the bowl and set aside for at least 30 minutes. Delicately drain the fruits from the syrup. Return syrup to the saucepan and bring to boil; reduce by half. Pour syrup over the fruits and serve.

Difficulty **easy**
Preparation time **30 minutes**
Calories **185**

Ingredients *for 4 servings*

Yellow peaches *1 1/4 lbs*

Dry sparkling wine *1 1/4 cups*

Sugar *5 oz*

Fresh mint *a few leaves*

Peach sorbet

● In a saucepan, melt sugar in the sparkling wine, on low heat, stirring all the time. remove from heat and immerse the saucepan in ice water to cool.

● During this time, rinse, peel and pit peaches. Mix the pulp in a food processor. Add to cold syrup. Pour in an ice cream machine and follow manufacturer's instructions.

● If you do not have an ice cream machine, pour preparation in an ice cube tray, without the separation. Freeze until it just starts to solidify and mix with a fork. Mix often until ready to serve. Serve the sorbet in cold glasses, garnished with mint leaves.

Difficulty **easy**
Preparation time **30 minutes**
+ resting time
Calories **145**

Ingredients *for 4 servings*

Seasonal fruits *1 1/4 lbs (apples, pears, raspberries, strawberries, blackberries, blueberries)*

Gelatin *3 teaspoons*

Sugar *1/4 cup*

Sparkling wine *3 tablespoons*

Lemons *the juice of 1*

Fruits in jelly

● Dissolve gelatin in a few tablespoons of cold water. In a saucepan, dissolve sugar in 1 cup of water; boil for a few minutes, stirring. Add gelatin and mix well. Remove from heat and cool, mixing often. Add sparkling wine and stir.

● Quickly rinse strawberries, blueberries and raspberries in ice water; drain and delicately dry on paper towels. Slice the strawberries. Peel the apples and pears; cut in half, core, slice thinly and pass in lemon juice.

● In a large bowl, pour a layer of liquid but cool gelatin syrup. Refrigerate until solid. Cover with a layer of fruits and cover with some of the remaining syrup. Repeat until all ingredients are used, finishing with syrup. Refrigerate between each layer. Refrigerate for at least 3 hours before serving.

Difficulty **easy**
Preparation time **40 minutes**
+ resting time
Calories **185**

Ingredients *for 4-6 servings*

Nectarines *1 lbs*

Lemons *the juice of 1*

Sugar *1/2 cup*

Gelatin *2 teaspoons*

For the sauce

Oranges *2*

Sugar *1/4 cup*

Mint *a few leaves*

Nectarine molds

● Melt gelatin in a little cold water. Rinse and dry the nectarines; cut in half, pit, dice pulp and purée in a food processor with lemon juice.

● In a saucepan, melt sugar in 1/2 cup of water. Boil on medium heat for about 5 minutes. Remove from heat and mix in the gelatin. Cool briefly and add to purée. Pour preparation in individual molds. Refrigerate for at least 3 hours.

● Press the oranges and pour in a saucepan. Add 1/2 cup of sugar and cook on low heat for 5 minutes. Set aside for 30 minutes and filter. To serve, dip molds into hot water for a few seconds and turn onto a plate. Decorate with mint leaves and serve with prepared orange sauce.

Fruits in gelatin 'bombe'

Difficulty **average**
Preparation time **30 minutes**
+ resting time
Calories **190**

Ingredients *for 4 servings*

Oranges *2 lbs*

Mango *1*

Maple syrup *6 tablespoons*

Gelatin *2 teaspoons*

● Refrigerate an ice cream mold or "bombe." Dissolve the gelatin in a little cold water. Peel the mango; cut in half and pit; slice pulp. Peel orange; divide in segments and set aside on a kitchen towel.

● In a saucepan, pour 2 cups of water and maple syrup. Bring to boil and cook for 30 seconds. Remove from heat; add gelatin and mix well.

● Remove mold from refrigerator. Pour in a light coat of gelatin syrup. Refrigerate again until set. Remove from refrigerator and arrange fruits on the bottom. Cover with a little syrup and refrigerate to set.

● Repeat until ingredients are used. Refrigerate for at least 3 hours. To serve, dip the mold into hot water for a few seconds and turn onto a serving dish.

Grape aspic

Difficulty **average**
Preparation time **30 minutes**
+ resting time
Calories **360**

Ingredients *for 6 servings*

Green grapes *1 lb*

Red grapes *1 lb*

Orange peel *1 piece*

Dry white wine *2 cups*

Sugar *5 oz*

Gelatin *4 teaspoons*

● Refrigerate a mold. Dissolve gelatin in cold water. In a saucepan, mix sugar and orange peel with 2 cups of water. Bring to boil and cook for a few minutes. Remove from heat and stir in the gelatin. Mix in the wine and cool.

● Remove mold from refrigerator; coat with a little gelatin syrup. Refrigerate until set. Rinse and dry grapes. Re-

move mold from refrigerator. Alternate layers of green and red grapes, covered with layers of gelatin. Refrigerate to set between each layer.

● Continue until all ingredients are used. Refrigerate for at least 3 hours. To serve, dip mold in hot water and turn the aspic on a cold serving dish.

Fruit salad with vanilla ice cream

Difficulty **easy**
Preparation time **50 minutes**
+ resting time
Calories **320**

Ingredients *for 6 servings*

Mixed fruits *1 1/2 lbs (strawberries, raspberries, blueberries, gooseberries, kiwis)*

Moscato wine *1 cup*

Sugar *1/2 cup*

For the ice cream

Milk *2 cups*

Egg yolks *4*

Sugar *1/2 cup*

Vanilla *1 bean*

● Quickly rinse and drain the berries; dry on a kitchen towel. Peel the kiwi and slice; cut in pieces and set aside in a bowl. Cut the strawberries in half and mix with kiwis; add other berries.

● Pour the Moscato over the fruits; sprinkle with sugar and mix delicately. Cover with plastic wrap and refrigerate for 30 minutes, stirring often.

● During this time, prepare the ice cream. Bring the milk and vanilla bean to boil. In a bowl, whisk the egg yolks and sugar; slowly whisk in the boiled milk. Return mixture to saucepan and cook, stirring all the time with a wooden spoon until mixture coats the spoon.

● Remove from heat and cool; discard the vanilla bean. Pour in an ice cream machine and follow manufacturer's instructions. To serve, pour fruit salad in bowls and top with a scoop of ice cream.

Pears in syrup

Difficulty **easy**
Preparation time **30 minutes**
+ resting time
Calories **230**

Ingredients *for 4-6 servings*

Pears *2 1/4 lbs*

Sugar *1 cup*

Dry white wine *1/2 cup*

Lemons *the peel of 1/2*

Oranges *the peel of 1/2*

Vanilla *1 bean*

Cinnamon *1 stick*

● Carefully peel the pears. In a pot, pour 4 cups of water, the dry white wine, sugar, cinnamon, vanilla bean, lemon and orange peel. Add pears. Bring to boil for 10 minutes.

● Remove from heat and cool the pears in the cooking liquid. Drain the pears, cut in half and core; cut each piece in quarters. Keep the liquid.

● In a saucepan, melt sugar in 1/4 cup of water; cook until the caramel is golden. Remove from heat and slowly whisk in 1/3 of the pear cooking liquid. Return to heat and boil for one minute.

● Dip the pear pieces in the syrup; remove from heat and cool completely. Cover and set aside for 12 hours. To serve, place the pears in a fan and drizzle with syrup.

Fruit carpaccio with mandarin sorbet

Difficulty **easy**
Preparation time **1 hour**
Calories **310**

Ingredients *for 4 servings*

Persimmons *2*
Pineapples *1/2*
Pink peppercorns *1 teaspoon*
Fresh ginger *1 small piece*
Sugar *1/4 cup*
Mint *a few leaves*

For the sorbet

Mandarin juice *1 1/2 cups*
Grated mandarin peel *1 tablespoon*
Sugar *1/2 lb*

● In a saucepan, melt sugar in 3/4 cup of water. Boil for a few minutes; remove from heat and cool syrup. Add the filtered mandarin juice and grated peel. Pour the preparation in an ice cream machine and follow manufacturer's instructions.

● In a saucepan, melt sugar in 1/2 cup of water. Boil for 2 minutes; remove from heat and cool.

● Peel and core the pineapple; slice thinly. Rinse and dry persimmons; peel and cut in quarters. Place the fruit in a deep bowl. Cover with prepared syrup. Sprinkle with pink peppercorns, thinly sliced ginger and mint leaves. Marinate for at least 15 minutes. Drain the fruit and serve on individual plates, with a scoop of mandarin sorbet.

Fruit salad with pineapples

Difficulty **easy**
Preparation time **40 minutes + resting time**
Calories **185**

Ingredients *for 4 servings*

Pineapples *2*
Red apples *1*
Green apples *1*
White grapes *1/4 lb*
Red grapes *1/4 lb*
Bananas *1*
Oranges *2*
Maraschino liqueur *1/4 cup*
Sugar *1/4 cup*
Lemons *the juice of 1*

● Cut the pineapple in half lengthwise. Remove pulp and refrigerate the empty shell. Cut off the core and slice the pulp. Peel the orange and divide the segments. Rinse and dry the grapes. Peel the banana; slice and place in a bowl, tossing with a little lemon juice.

● Rinse the apples; cut in half, core and slice thinly. Place the apples in a bowl with remaining lemon juice. Add the grapes, pineapple and drained banana slices. Drizzle with Maraschino liqueur and toss delicately. Add orange segments and set aside for 1 hour.

● Sprinkle fruits with sugar; toss to dissolve. Distribute the salad in the empty pineapple shells. Cover with plastic wrap and refrigerate until ready to serve.

Difficulty **easy**
Preparation time **40 minutes**
Calories **460**

Wild strawberry surprise

Ingredients *for 4 servings*

Peaches *4*

Wild strawberries *1/2 lb*

Powdered sugar *1/2 cup*

Whipping cream *1 cup*

Almonds *2 oz*

Cognac *1/4 cup*

● Blanch the peaches in boiling water; drain, peel and cut in half horizontally. Pit and place on a dish; sprinkle with a little sugar and drizzle with cognac.

● Toast the almonds in the oven and peel if necessary. Chop in a food processor and set aside. In a cold bowl, whip the cream.

● Quickly rinse wild strawberries in ice water; dry on paper towels and crush with a fork. Add sugar and whipped cream. Mix carefully so the cream does not deflate.

● With the preparation, fill the peach halves. Sprinkle with chopped almonds. Refrigerate until ready to serve.

Figs in pastry

Difficulty **average**
Preparation time **50 minutes**
Calories **630**

Ingredients *for 4 servings*

Puff pastry *1/2 lb*
Figs *2 lbs*
Powdered cinnamon *1/2 teaspoon*
Breadcrumbs *2 oz*
Eggs *1*
Brown sugar *2 oz*
Powdered sugar *1 tablespoon*
Dry white wine *1/4 cup*

● Peel the figs and cut in quarters. In a non-stick pan, mix the wine, brown sugar, cinnamon and figs. Cook on high heat for 5 minutes, stirring often. Remove from heat and set aside to cool.

● Roll out the puff pastry dough. Cut in 2 rectangles. Place one rectangle on a non-stick cookie sheet, brushed with water. Sprinkle the center of dough with breadcrumbs; brush the border with beaten egg yolk. Distribute the figs on the breadcrumbs.

● Fold the remaining rectangle lengthwise. With a knife, make cuts at equal distance, all along the folded border. Open the rectangle and place on the figs. Close the rectangle carefully, pressing with your fingers.

● Brush the top of dough with the remaining beaten egg yolks. Bake in a preheated oven at 425°F for 15 to 20 minutes. Remove from oven and sprinkle with sugar. Return to oven and bake until top is caramelized. Remove from heat and cool briefly before serving.

Peach pie

Difficulty **average**
Preparation time **1 hour**
Calories **425**

Ingredients *for 6 servings*

Pastry dough *1/2 lb*
Peaches *1 1/2 lbs*
Eggs *3*
Milk *1/2 cup*
Sugar *1/4 cup*
Amaretti *5*
Amaretto liqueur *1 tablespoon*
Unbleached flour *1 teaspoon*
Butter *a dab*

● Rinse the peaches; scald in boiling water for a minute; drain, peel, cut in half and pit; slice in thick pieces. Crumble the amaretti.

● Roll out the dough thinly. Line a buttered and floured a pie dish with the dough. Trim the sides. Keep remaining dough aside. Prick the dough with a fork and sprinkle with crumbled amaretti. Cover with the peaches.

● In a bowl, whisk 2 eggs, milk and the amaretto liqueur. Pour the mixture over the peaches.

● Roll out the remaining dough and make a long roll; place around pie, pressing with a fork. Brush with remaining beaten egg. Bake in a preheated oven at 350°F for 40 minutes. Remove from oven and cool completely before serving.

Whole wheat plum pie

Difficulty **average**
Preparation time **1 hour**
+ resting time
Calories **530**

Ingredients *for 4 servings*

Whole wheat flour *1/2 cup*
Unbleached flour *1/2 cup*
Plums *1 1/4 lbs*
Eggs *3*
Milk *1 cup*
Brown sugar *1/2 cup*
Lemons *the grated peel of 1*
Maraschino liqueur *1/4 cup*
Butter *2 oz*

● Sift both flours together with 1/4 cup of sugar into a large bowl. Make a well in the middle; add eggs, butter and lemon peel. Mix rapidly; form a ball; cover with a humid kitchen towel and set aside to rest for 30 minutes, in the refrigerator.

● Rinse and dry the plums on kitchen towels. Pit and dice the pulp. Place in a bowl with Maraschino liqueur. Roll out the prepared dough. Line a pie dish with wax paper and then with the dough. Prick dough with a fork.

● In a bowl, whisk 2 eggs, remaining sugar and milk. Pour this mixture in the pie dish. Drain the plums and add to the pie. Roll out the dough trimmings; cut in long strips and use them to criss-cross over the pie. Trim dough. Bake in a preheated oven at 350°F for 40 minutes. Cool completely before serving.

Pineapple in puff pastry

Difficulty **average**
Preparation time **50 minutes**
Calories **235**

Ingredients *for 6 servings*

Puff pastry *1/2 lb*
Pineapples *1/2*
Apricot jelly *3 oz*
Candied cherries *2, chopped*

● Roll out the dough thinly; cut an 8-inch square and place on a cookie sheet brushed with water. Along the sides of the square; cut 4 strips, 1/4-inch wide.

● Brush the sides of the square with water. Cover with strips, pressing with a fork, and roll up the ends. Prick the dough with a fork. Bake in a preheated oven at 400°F for 20 minutes. Cool completely.

● During this time, peel the pineapple and cut horizontally in 1/2-inch slices. Remove the core and cut each slice in quarters. Melt the apricot jelly with 2 tablespoons of hot water; brush on the puff pastry square. Cover with pineapple pieces and garnish with candied cherries. Brush the fruits with remaining jelly. Transfer to a serving dish.

Difficulty **easy**
Preparation time **30 minutes**
Calories **205**

Ingredients *for 4 servings*

Ripe figs *8*

Walnuts *8*

Sugar *2 tablespoons*

Cognac *1/4 cup*

Butter *a dab*

Andrea's note: The real fruits of the Mediterranean, figs are a great source of sunshine on the table.

Figs with walnuts

● Rinse the figs; peel and slice in half lengthwise. In a saucepan, melt sugar in a little water, on low heat. Remove from heat; mix in the cognac and set aside.

● Butter a baking dish. Place prepared figs in the dish. Cover with cognac syrup. Place half a walnut on each fig half. Bake in a preheated oven at 350°F for 15 minutes. Remove from oven and serve directly from the baking dish.

Strawberry mousse cake

Difficulty **average**
Preparation time **45 minutes**
+ resting time
Calories **205**

Ingredients *for 10 servings*

For the cake

Peeled almonds *1/4 cup*

White sugar *1/4 cup*

Powdered sugar *1/4 cup*

Unbleached flour *2 tablespoons*

Egg whites *4*

For the mousse

Strawberries *1/2 lb*

Whipping cream *1 cup*

Sugar *1/2 cup*

Lemon juice *1 tablespoon*

Gelatin *2 teaspoons*

For the pan

Butter *1 teaspoon*

Unbleached flour *1 tablespoon*

● Prepare the cake. In a food processor, reduce the almonds to powder. In a bowl, beat the egg whites until firm; delicately mix in the white sugar, powdered sugar, flour and almonds.

● Butter and flour a springform cake pan. Pour the batter in the pan. Bake in a preheated oven at 375°F for about 20 minutes. Remove from oven and cool completely.

● During this time, prepare the mousse. Dissolve the gelatin in 2 tablespoons of hot water. Quickly rinse the strawberries in ice water; drain and dry on a towel; purée in a food processor with sugar and lemon juice.

● Mix the dissolved gelatin with the purée. Whip the cream and delicately fold in the purée. Pour the mousse over the cold cake, in the springform pan. Refrigerate for 4 hours. Open the springform and transfer the dessert on a serving dish. Decorate with a few strawberries before serving.

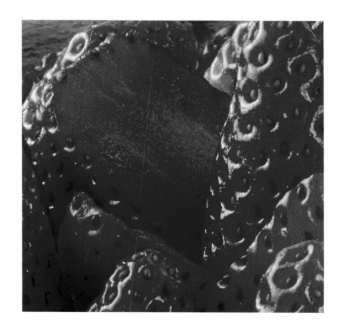

Raspberry tartlets

Difficulty **average**
Preparation time **1 hour**
Calories **315**

Ingredients *for 6-8 servings*

Puff pastry dough *1/2 lb*
Raspberries *1/2 lb*
Apricot jelly *3 tablespoons*
Powdered sugar *1 tablespoon*
Whipping cream *1 cup*

● Roll out the puff pastry dough; cut out 4-inch circles and line individual tartlet molds with it. Prick dough with a fork and refrigerate for 10 minutes.

● Remove from the refrigerator; line with aluminum foil and fill with beans. Bake in a preheated oven at 400°F for about 15 minutes. Remove from oven; discard beans and aluminum foil; remove tart shells from the molds and cool completely.

● Quickly rinse the raspberries in ice water; dry. In a cold bowl, whip the cream with powdered sugar. Transfer to a pastry bag fitted with a star tip. In a saucepan, melt the apricot jelly in 1 tablespoon of water. Fill the tartlets with whipped cream. Cover with the raspberries and brush with apricot jelly. Serve immediately.

Grape & fig gratin

Difficulty **average**
Preparation time **15 minutes**
Calories **255**

Ingredients *for 4 servings*

Figs *8*
Grapes *a bunch*

For the zabaglione
Egg yolks *3*
Moscato *1/2 cup*
Sugar *3 oz*

● Rinse the grapes; cut in half and pit. Peel figs and cut in half; mix with grapes. Divide into 4 individual oven dishes.

● Prepare the zabaglione. In a double boiler, whisk the egg yolks and sugar until thick and white. Mix in the Moscato and cook over steaming water until the preparation thickens.

● Pour the preparation over the fruits. Bake in a preheated oven at 425°F for about 3 minutes (or under the grill until golden and bubbly). Serve immediately.

Fruit compote

Difficulty **easy**
Preparation time **40 minutes + resting time**
Calories **205**

Ingredients *for 4-6 servings*

Prunes *1/2 lb*
Dried apricots *1/4 lb*
Green apples *3*
Apple juice *1 1/2 cups*
Grated orange peel *1 tablespoon*
Cinnamon *1 stick*
Walnuts *2 oz*
Lemons *the juice of 1*

● Rinse and dry apples; peel, core and slice. Transfer to a bowl and toss with lemon juice. In a saucepan, heat 1 cup of water, apple juice, orange peel and cinnamon stick. Bring to boil; add dried apricots and prunes.Rinse and dry apples; peel, core and slice. Transfer to a bowl and toss with lemon juice. In a saucepan, heat 1 cup of water, apple juice, orange peel and cinnamon stick. Bring to boil; add dried apricots and prunes.

● Cook for about 15 minutes on medium heat, stirring often with a wooden spoon. Mix in the apple slices and remove from heat, when just tender. Cool the preparation. Cover and refrigerate for at least 1 hour before serving.

● A few minutes before serving, scald the walnuts in boiling water; peel if necessary and toast in a hot oven for a few minutes. Remove compote from the refrigerator; discard cinnamon stick. Place the compote on the stove and heat through, on medium heat. Transfer to a serving bowl; mix with walnuts. Serve hot or warm.

Bananas flambé

Difficulty **easy**
Preparation time **20 minutes**
Calories **360**

Ingredients *for 4 servings*

Bananas *4*
Oranges *1*
Lemons *1*
White sugar *1/2 cup*
Sugar cubes *6*
Vanilla extract *1/2 teaspoon*
Cream *1/4 cup*
Rum *3 oz*
Butter *1/4 cup*

● Rinse and dry lemon and orange; remove peel, if possible in one piece. Peel the bananas and cut in half, and again in half lengthwise.

● In a pan, melt butter on medium heat. Remove from heat and add white sugar, 2 tablespoons of rum, lemon peel and orange peel. Mix well until sugar is dissolved. Add the bananas and stir delicately. Return to the stove and cook on low heat for about 3 minutes, stirring all the times.

● Soak the sugar cubes in 1/4 cup of rum; add to bananas and flambé. Serve while the flame is still going.

Pineapples flambé

Difficulty **easy**
Preparation time **1 hour**
Calories **230**

Ingredients *for 4 servings*

Pineapples *2, medium-size*
Cane sugar *6 tablespoons*
Rum *1/2 cup*

● Wrap the pineapple in aluminum foil. Place the pineapples on a cookie sheet. Bake in a preheated oven at 350°F for 45 minutes. Remove from oven; cool and cut in half lengthwise, with a large knife. Wrap the shells in aluminum foil and heat the grill.

● Sprinkle the sugar on pineapples and pass under the grill for 10 minutes, or until golden. Heat the rum in a small saucepan. Pour over the pineapples and flambé. Serve as soon as the flames are extinct.

Filled peaches

Difficulty **easy**
Preparation time **40 minutes**
Calories **325**

Ingredients *for 4 servings*

Yellow peaches *4*
Sweet wine *1 cup*
Eggs *1*
Amaretti *4*
Peeled almonds *24*
Sugar *2 tablespoons*

● Toast the almonds in a preheated oven at 350°F for a few minutes; remove from oven and cool. Mix in a food processor and transfer to a bowl. Scald the peaches in boiling water for a minute; drain and peel; cut in half horizontally, pit and remove 1 tablespoon of pulp from each half.

● Finely chop the extracted pulp; mix with the almonds, egg, sugar and crumbled amaretti. Use this mixture to fill the peach halves. Place in a baking dish; drizzle with wine and bake in a preheated oven at 350°F for about 20 minutes. Remove from oven; transfer to a serving dish and cool completely before serving.

Cherry soup

Difficulty **easy**
Preparation time **30 minutes**
Calories **205**

Ingredients *for 4 servings*

Cherries *1 lb*
Dry white wine *3 tablespoons*
Sugar *1/4 cup*
Cinnamon *1 stick*
Vanilla extract *1/2 teaspoon*
Lemons *the peel of 1/2*
Oranges *the peel of 1/2*
Vanilla ice cream *1/2 lb*
Mint *a few leaves*

● Rinse the cherries; pit and place in a saucepan. Add wine, sugar, cinnamon, vanilla, lemon and orange peel. Cook on medium heat for 10 minutes, stirring often with a wooden spoon.

● Remove the lemon and orange peels, with cinnamon stick. Transfer the cherries and their syrup in individual bowls. Serve warm or cold, with a scoop of vanilla ice cream. Decorate with mint leaves. Can be served with savoyard cookies.

Oranges with Grand Marnier

Difficulty **easy**
Preparation time **30 minutes**
+ resting time
Calories **240**

Ingredients *for 6 servings*

Oranges *6*
Sugar *3/4 cup*
Lemons *the juice of 1/2*
Grand Marnier *2 tablespoons*
Vanilla ice cream *3/4 lb*

● Rinse, dry and peel oranges; slice horizontally and place on a serving dish. Cut the orange peel in thin strips; place in a saucepan. Cover with cold water and bring to boil; drain immediately. Return to saucepan; cover with cold water and bring to boil again; cook on medium heat for about 10 minutes; drain and transfer to a plate.

● In a high saucepan, melt sugar in 4 tablespoons of water. Cook on very low heat, until sugar is caramelized and golden. Remove from heat and immediately add 1/2 cup of water. (The contact of the water with the caramel will provoke a boiling effect.) As soon as this is finished, return the saucepan to the stove and cook on low heat until the caramel is melted completely.

● Transfer orange peel strips to the caramel. Cook on low heat for 2 to 3 minutes, stirring. Cool for a few minutes; mix in the Grand Marnier, and the filtered lemon juice. Pour onto the orange slices; refrigerate for 2 hours. Serve as is, or with vanilla ice cream.

Filled pink grapefruit

Difficulty **easy**
Preparation time **35 minutes**
+ resting time
Calories **160**

Ingredients *for 6 servings*

Pink grapefruits *3*

Pineapples *1 small*

Peaches *3*

Mango *1*

Raspberries *1/2 cup*

White and red grapes *12*

Lemon juice *2 tablespoons*

Fresh mint *a few leaves*

Pomegranate syrup *3 tablespoons*

Brown sugar *3 tablespoons*

● Cut the grapefruits horizontally; with a grapefruit knife, remove the pulp; refrigerate empty grapefruit shells. Peel the pulp; discard seeds, dice and place in a bowl. Peel the pineapple, core and dice.

● Mix the pineapple with grapefruits, peeled and diced mango, peeled and diced peaches, and the scalded and peeled grapes.

● Sprinkle with sugar and lemon juice; toss delicately and cover with plastic wrap. Refrigerate for 3 hours. Mix in the raspberries.

● Before serving, place some crushed ice, mixed with pomegranate juice, in 6 bowls. Fill the emptied grapefruit shells with the fruit salad. Place on the colored ice and serve, decorate with mint leaves.

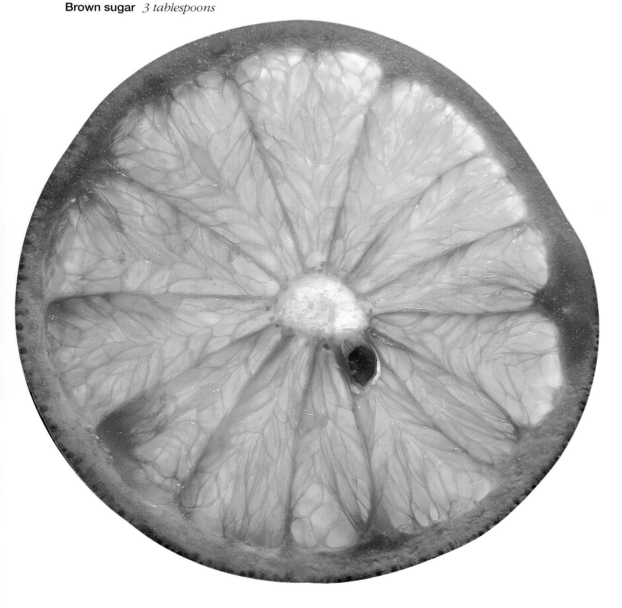

Apple dessert

Difficulty **average**
Preparation time **1 hour**
Calories **145**

Ingredients *for 6 servings*

Apples *5*

Eggs *3*

Sugar *1/2 cup*

Unbleached flour *3/4 cup*

Baking powder *1 teaspoon*

Milk *1/4 cup*

Salt *a pinch*

For the pan

Butter *1 teaspoon*

Unbleached flour *1 tablespoon*

● Break the eggs in a bowl; whisk with sugar until frothy and thick, with an electric mixer.

● Mix in the sifted flour and a pinch of salt. Slowly mix in the milk and finally the baking powder. Mix until the ingredients are well blended and the batter is smooth.

● Peel, core and thinly slice the apples. Stir into the batter. Butter and flour a rectangular cake pan. Pour batter into the pan.

● Bake in a preheated oven at 350°F for about 40 minutes. Remove from oven; cool and cut in pieces to serve.

Grape clafoutis

Difficulty **easy**
Preparation time **40 minutes**
Calories **460**

Ingredients *for 4 servings*

Grapes *2/3 lb*

Eggs *4*

White sugar *1/2 cup*

Powdered sugar *1/4 cup*

Unbleached flour *1/4 cup*

Milk *1 cup*

Vanilla beans *1*

Butter *2 tablespoons*

Salt *a pinch.*

● In a saucepan, boil the milk with vanilla bean. Remove from heat and set aside for 20 minutes. Rinse and dry the grapes; cut in half and pit.

● In a bowl, whisk the eggs with a pinch of salt and white sugar, until thick. Mix in the sifted flour and slowly add to the milk. Stir until all ingredients are well blended and batter is liquid enough.

● Butter a baking dish. Fill with a layer of grapes and the prepared batter. Bake in a preheated oven at 350°F for about 20 minutes. Remove from oven; cool briefly. Sprinkle with sifted powdered sugar. Serve at room temperature.

Grandma's pie

Difficulty **easy**
Preparation time **1 hour 30 minutes**
Calories **410**

Ingredients *for 6-8 servings*

Mixed fruit *2 1/4 lbs (apples, pears, plums, peaches)*
Eggs *4*
Sugar *4 tablespoons*
Savoyard cookies *1/2 lb*
Soft amaretti *1/2 lb*
Lemons *1/2*
White wine *1/4 cup*
Butter *1 tablespoon*

● Crumble the savoyard cookies and the amaretti. Peel the apples and pears; core, dice and toss with lemon juice. Scald the peaches in boiling water; drain, peel, pit and dice.

● In a saucepan, cook the wine, pears, apples and sugar for 5 minutes. Add the peaches and plums; cook for 7 to 8 minutes, stirring often.

● Pour the fruits in a bowl; stir in the remaining sugar, crumbled cookies (keep 2 tablespoons aside), grated peel of 1/2 lemon and eggs; mix well.

● Butter a baking dish. Sprinkle with 2 tablespoons of crumbled cookies. Pour the prepared mixture in the pan. Bake in a preheated oven at 350ºF for about 1 hour. Remove from oven and cool completely before serving.

Plum & Maraschino pie

Difficulty **easy**
Preparation time **40 minutes + resting time**
Calories **700**

Ingredients *for 6 servings*

Frozen pate brisée *for 1 pie*
Plums *1 1/2 lbs*
Maraschino liqueur *1/4 cup*
Sugar *6 tablespoons*
Vanilla extract *1/2 teaspoon*
Lemons *the grated peel of 1*
Biscotti *12*
Butter *a dab*

● Thaw the pie dough at room temperature. Rinse and dry the plums; pit and slice. Place in a bowl with the grated lemon peel, sugar, vanilla and Maraschino liqueur. Refrigerate for 30 minutes.

● Butter a pie dish. Roll out dough and line the dish. Prick the bottom of the pie with a fork; line with the crumbled biscotti.

● Transfer the plum slices in the pie. Bake in a preheated oven at 400ºF for 30 minutes. Cool on a rack before serving.

Pumpkin dessert

Difficulty **average**
Preparation time **40 minutes**
Calories **680**

Ingredients *for 4 servings*

Sugar *1/2 cup*

Eggs *3*

Almond flour *1 cup*

Canned pumpkin *3/4 cup*

Candied citron *1/4 cup*

Lemons *the grated rind of 1/2*

Extra virgin olive oil *1 teaspoon*

Cinnamon *a pinch*

Salt *a pinch*

● Beat the eggs with the sugar; incorporate the almond flour, a pinch of salt, lemon rind and a pinch of cinnamon; mix well. Oil the oven dish. Fill with half the batter by the spoonful. With a wet spoon, give each mound a round shape.

● Arrange over each disk a little canned pumpkin and the diced candied citron; cover it with the remaining batter. Give each mound the shape of a cone, with a round base and a pointed center. Bake in a preheated oven at 400°C for about 20 minutes. The cakes should be golden with a brownish tip. Cool to serve.

Melon & raspberry aspic

Difficulty **average**
Preparation time **50 minutes**
Calories **130**

Ingredients *for 8 servings*

Cantaloupe melon *1 1/2 lbs*

Raspberries *2/3 lb*

Oranges *1*

Dry white wine *2 cups*

Sugar *1/2 cup*

Gelatin *4 teaspoons*

● Horizontally divide the melon in two and remove seeds. With a melon baller, make as many balls as possible with the pulp. Rinse the raspberries. Peel the orange and slice thinly. (All fruit together should weigh 1/2 lb). In a saucepan, boil 2 cups of water with the sugar, for 10 minutes.

● Remove from heat and add the gelatin; stir with a wooden spoon, until dissolved. Cool. Add wine and stir again.

● On the bottom of a mold, place a thin layer of gelatin and refrigerate until set. Add a layer of raspberries, cover with a little gelatin and return to the refrigerator until set. Repeat the same operation with melon balls; continue the same way until you run out of ingredients.

● Before placing the last layer, place orange slices around the edge of the mold, making sure half go over the edge. Cover the last layer of fruit with remaining gelatin. Refrigerate and when the gelatin is nearly set, fold the orange slices that were over the edge. Complete with a thin layer of gelatin and refrigerate for at least 2 hours. Before serving, dip the mold in warm water and turn over onto a serving plate.

Carrot cake

Difficulty **average**
Preparation time **1 hour**
Calories **470**

Ingredients *for 6 servings*

Carrots *1/2 lb*
Sugar *1/2 lb*
Potato starch *1/4 lb*
Walnuts *16*
Grated lemon peel *1 teaspoon*
Powdered sugar *2 tablespoons*
Eggs *6*
Unbleached flour *1/2 tablespoon*
Butter *a dab*
Salt *a pinch*

● Scald the walnuts for a minute in hot water. Drain, peel, dry and chop them. Peel the carrots, wash and grate them.

● In two bowls, separate the egg yolks from the egg whites. Whisk egg yolks with the sugar and a pinch of salt, until frothy and thick.

● Mix potato starch with walnuts; mix into the egg mixture. Add carrots and lemon peel. Stir all ingredients well. Beat egg whites to firm peaks and fold into the batter.

● Butter and flour a cake pan. Pour in the batter. Bake in a preheated oven at 350°F for about 30 minutes. Serve the cake cold, sprinkled with powdered sugar.

Almond cake

Difficulty **average**
Preparation time **1 hour 15 minutes**
Calories **435**

Ingredients *for 4 servings*

Peeled almonds *1/4 cup*
Sugar *1/2 cup*
Pound cake *1/4 lb*
Milk *3 cups*
Eggs *3*
Butter *a dab*

● Scald the almonds in boiling water for a minute; drain, peel and chop finely in a food processor. In a small pot, place milk, sugar and crumbled pound cake and cook on medium heat. Mix in the almonds.

● Cook for 10 minutes; pass mixture through a sieve and transfer to a bowl.

In another bowl, whisk the eggs and add to the batter.

● Butter a rectangular mold and transfer the mixture. Cook in a bain-marie in a preheated oven at 350°F for 40 minutes. Remove from oven, let cool, transfer to a serving plate and serve immediately.

Difficulty **average**
Preparation time **30 minutes**
+ resting time
Calories **160**

Ingredients *for 6 servings*

Strawberries *1/2 lb*
White grapes *1/4 lb*
Red grapes *1/4 lb*
Bananas *2*
Lemons *the juice of 1/2*
Orange juice *2 cups*
Gelatin *4 teaspoons*
Sugar *1/2 cup*

Fruit aspic

● Rinse the grapes; dry, cut in half and pit. Rinse and dry the strawberries; slice. Peel the bananas, slice and toss with the lemon juice.

● In a small saucepan, melt sugar in 2 cups of water. Boil for about 10 minutes. Remove from heat, add the gelatin and stir well with a wooden spoon until completely dissolved. Let mixture cool then add the filtered orange juice and stir again.

● On the bottom of a mold, pour one thin layer of gelatin and refrigerate until it sets. Add a layer of mixed fruits. Cover with a little gelatin and refrigerate again until it sets. Repeat until all ingredients are used. Refrigerate for at least 4 hours. Before serving, dip the mold in hot water; turn the aspic over onto a plate and decorate with a few mint leaves.

Index

A

Almond cake 373
Anchovies filled with spinach 184
Anchovies with fennel 168
Anchovy focaccia 42
Anchovy pizza 69
Anchovy soup 228
Angel hair pasta in tomato sauce 162
Angel hair pasta with curly
        endive salad 147
Apple dessert 370
Apulia-style short pasta 105
Apulia-style sole 168
Artichoke & bean stew 313
Artichoke & carrot salad 18
Artichoke pie, Sicilian-style 313
Artichoke rolls 52
Artichoke soup 160
Artichokes & peas 329
Artichokes & potatoes with herbs 312
Artichokes & vegetables 268
Artichokes cooked with white wine
        vinegar 266
Artichokes with eggs 312
Artichokes with fresh oregano 328
Artichokes with mozzarella 267
Artichokes with pecorino 267
Arugula with black-eyed beans 333
Asparagus & orange salad 322
Asparagus with warm baby
        cuttlefish 25

B

Baccalà with vegetables 182
Baccalà with walnut sauce 198
Baked cauliflower & potatoes 297
Baked eggplant 'caponata' 264
Baked eggplants 265
Baked peppers 335
Baked potatoes & mushrooms 317

Baked stuffed potatoes 282
Baked tomatoes 302
Baked vegetables 272
Baker's salad 336
Bananas flambé 365
Bandiera 320
Barbecued turkey meatballs 251
Barley & black-eyed bean soup 150
Basilicata-style vegetables 272
Bavette with avocado 74
Bean & pasta soup 143
Bean salad 290
Beans & chicory lettuce 290
Beans & potatoes 270
Beans & potatoes 291
Beet green & chili pepper calzone 44
Beet tagliatelle with leek sauce 72
Braided fish with tomatoes 181
Broad bean soup 144
Broccoli Sicilian-style 288
Broccoli with oranges 289
Brown rice with vegetables 123
Bulgur & celery soup 150
Bulgur soup with ditalini pasta 162
Buridda from Genova 230
Buridda of mixed fish with tomato 175

C

Cacciucco 225
Calamari with lemon 207
Cannellini beans & cabbage 271
Cannellini beans with oregano 271
Carrot cake 373
Casereccia with green beans &
        anchovies 100
Cauliflower in tomato sauce 296
Cauliflower salad 297
Cereal & vegetable soup 152
Cherry sorbet 340
Cherry soup 367

Chicken breast pizzaiola 256
Chicken breast with fruit 240
Chicken breast with vegetables &
        herb sauce 242
Chicken chunks 246
Chicken in milk 244
Chicken in salt crust 242
Chicken with lemon 247
Chicken with spinach & ham 246
Chicory tart 318
Chicory, garlic & olive oil 332
Chunky vegetables 320
Ciammotta 274
Ciaudedda 280
Citron & lettuce salad 322
Clam pizza 53
Clams alla napoletana 206
Classic pasta salad 116
Cod salad 208
Coffee granita 342
Cold cream of asparagus &
        rice soup 146
Cold dogfish with lemon 217
Cold stuffed zucchini 292
Conchiglie with zucchini 118
Country-style cauliflower 296
Crab soup 156
Crab with lemon 192
Cream of beet soup 140
Crostata Teresa 50
Crostini with mussels & vegetables 21
Curried chicken with apples 247
Cuttlefish with spinach 172

D

Dogfish & zucchini broth 229
Dogfish in pieces 220
Dressed scampi 172
Dried cod with peppers 176
Drunken rice 132

Duck breast with oranges 252

E

Eggplant & mushroom strudel 60
Eggplant & pepper antipasto 15
Eggplant & pepper pie 58
Eggplant 'peperonata' 334
Eggplant 'Parmigiana' 304
Eggplant compote 304
Eggplant paté 36
Eggplant rolls 265
Eggplant salad 300
Eggplant surprise 327
Eggplants 'capricciose' 326
Eggplants in hot sauce 326
Eggplants in tomato sauce 264
Eggplants in tuna sauce 327
Endive with capers & olives 332
Endives with ricotta 37
Escabeche anchovies 202
Escarole pizza 44

F

Farfalle with artichokes, zucchini &
    leeks 105
Farro soup 158
Fennel & baccalà soup 146
Fennel & pasta soup 142
Fennel with herbs 311
Fennel with pecorino 310
Fennel with vinegar 310
Fennel with walnuts 311
Fettucini with seafood 82
Figs in pastry 358
Figs with walnuts 360
Filled peaches 366
Filled pink grapefruit 368
Filled zucchini, Cagliari-style 276
Fish fricassee 230
Fisherman's soup 229
Focaccia with green olives 57
Four seasons pizza 56
Fresh anchovies 21
Fried peppers 278
Fried potatoes with parsley 274
Friselle alla marinara 22

Frittedda 291
Fruit aspic 374
Fruit carpaccio with mandarin
    sorbet 355
Fruit compote 365
Fruit compote with Grand
    Marnier 344
Fruit salad with pineapples 355
Fruit salad with vanilla ice cream 354
Fruits in gelatin 'bombe' 353
Fruits in jelly 352
Fusilli with caper & oregano sauce 108
Fusilli with fresh tuna 98
Fusilli with herbs 119
Fusilli with squid & spinach 109

G

Garden-style spaghetti 89
Garlic & oregano pizza 65
Gnocchetti with shrimp &
    white beans 109
Gramigna with peppers & pesto 98
Grandma's pie 371
Grape & fig gratin 364
Grape aspic 353
Grape clafoutis 370
Green bean & calamari antipasto 34
Green bean soup 138
Green beans & peppers with
    cheese 299
Green beans with anchovies 298
Green beans with herbs 299
Green beans with tomatoes 298
Green tea granita 343
Grilled eggplant rolls 305
Grilled razor shells 174
Grilled squid on skewers 183
Grilled vegetables 262
Grouper with tomato 170
Grouper with vegetables 220
Guinea fowl with tea 253
Guinea fowl with vegetables 245

H

Hake with anchovies 195
Hake with fennel & onions 198

Hake with herbs 166
Harlequin antipasto 32

J

Jasmine sorbet 346

K

Kiwi sorbet 347

L

Lamb's lettuce & calamari salad 20
Leek soup 142
Lemon rice balls 16
Lemon risotto 135
Lemon yogurt sorbet 347
Lentil soup 152
Ligurian-style spaghetti with
    sardines 83
Linguine with tuna & peas 75
Little neck clams with onions 190

M

Maccheroncelli with sardines 88
Maccheroncini with asparagus &
    mullet 112
Maccheroncini with scampi &
    fresh beans 99
Malfattini & vegetable soup 156
Maltagliati soup 154
Marinated artichokes 328
Marinated sea bass 199
Mediterranean 'crostoni' 37
Mediterranean linguine 92
Mediterranean salad 196
Mediterranean skewers 24
Melon & raspberry aspic 372
Messina-style filled tomatoes 303
Mint granita with syrup 342
Mixed cooked vegetables 306
Mixed cooked vegetables 319
Mixed grilled fish 175
Mixed seafood au gratin 178

Mixed vegetables with tomatoes 319
Monkfish with vegetables 180
Mullet in tomato sauce 216
Mullet with cucumbers 214
Mullet with tomato sauce 190
Mushroom pizza 56
Mussels with lemon 192

N

Neapolitan-style rabbit thighs 256
Nectarine molds 352
Nettle soup 158
Nonna's potatoes 282

O

Octopus in its broth 204
Octopus with sun-dried tomatoes 203
Onion & sweet pepper pie 54
Onion focaccia 64
Onion soup 157
Onions filled with tuna 284
Onions with marsala 284
Orange & carrot salad 26
Orange sorbet 346
Oranges with Grand Marnier 367
Orecchiette with eggplant 119
Orecchiette, garden & sea 106

P

Panzanella 30
Pasta & broad beans in broth 148
Pasta & wild herb soup 143
Pasta alla chitarra with nettles 93
Pasta panzanella 94
Pasta soup with marjoram 157
Pea soup with squid 225
Peach pie 358
Peach sorbet 350
Pears in syrup 354
Penne with herb sauce 108
Penne with squash & radicchio 104
Penne with zucchini 113
Peperonata 279
Pepper filets 335

Peppers with almond sauce 334
Perciatelli with mussels 79
Pineapple & lemon granita 343
Pineapple in puff pastry 359
Pineapples flambé 366
Pinzimonio 330
Pizza all'Andrea 40
Pizza capricciosa 64
Pizza margherita 46
Pizza napoletana 45
Pizza regina 68
Plain pizza 61
Plum & Maraschino pie 371
Potato & herb soufflé 34
Potato & tomato dish 283
Potato crostini 12
Potato pizza 62
Potato tart 283
Potatoes 'all'arrabbiata' 316
Potatoes 'pizzaiola' 317
Pumpkin dessert 372
Purée of beans & chicory 318
Puréed fish soup 224

Q

Quadrucci in fish broth 151

R

Rabbit with olives 257
Rabbit with onions 258
Rabbit with peppers 254
Rabbit with vegetables 257
Radicchio & pasta soup 144
Radicchio pizza 52
Raspberry tartlets 364
Raw artichoke salad 329
Razor shells with tomatoes 206
Rice & parsley soup 163
Rice & zucchini pie 53
Rice crown with vegetables 136
Rice with anchovy filets 134
Ricotta & vegetable tart 66
Rigatoni with baked tomatoes 100
Risotto with fennel 124
Risotto with anchovies &
       pine nuts 126

Risotto with artichokes 126
Risotto with broad beans 130
Risotto with carrots 132
Risotto with herbs & scampi 127
Risotto with lentils 128
Risotto with parsley 135
Risotto with pears & almonds 120
Risotto with peas & basil 122
Risotto with red radicchio 123
Risotto with saffron & shrimp 128
Risotto with scallops & peppers 131
Risotto with squash & spinach 134
Risotto with squid ink 131
Risotto with squid, mushrooms &
       spinach 133
Risotto with tomatoes 127
Risotto with zucchini 130
Risotto with zucchini flowers 122
Roasted lobster 199
Rolled peppers 286
Rosemary focaccia 58
Royal salad 323
Rustic onion & olive pie 69

S

Salad 'deliziosa' 324
Salad with provolone 308
Salmon rolls 216
Sardine pizza 65
Sardine rolls, Palermo-style 202
Sardines with tomato 188
Sardinian gnocchetti with
       fish sauce 96
Sardinian gnocchetti with peppers 99
Sardinian tagliatelle 90
Savory pie with yellow squash 61
Savory potato salad 316
Scallops au gratin 213
Scallops with tomatoes & herbs 221
Scampi & asparagus salad 29
Scampi & squid in their sauce 224
Scampi & zucchini with pesto 179
Scampi with green sauce 33
Scorpion fish with leeks 178
Sea bream carpaccio with olives 194
Sea bream with mushrooms &
       herbs 212

Sea bream with olives 171
Sea bream with radicchio 182
Sea bream with rosemary &
    tomatoes 213
Seafood soup 228
Short pasta with arugula & celery 116
Short pasta with cucumbers 102
Shell pasta with lentils & broccoli 163
Short penne with artichokes 118
Short penne with eggplant 114
Shrimp & asparagus salad 218
Shrimp & fruit salad 30
Shrimp antipasto 14
Shrimp, arugula & carrot salad 33
Shrimp & artichokes 207
Shrimp with avocado & egg sauce 14
Sicilian croquettes 285
Sicilian-style dogfish 222
Sicilian-style tuna 186
Sicilian-style veal kebabs 237
Simply broccoli 288
Skate wings au gratin 221
Small whitefish with zucchini 24
Snapper with herbs 191
Snow peas & potatoes 314
Soft peppers 279
Spaghetti alla marinara 76
Spaghetti with basil sauce 79
Spaghetti with fresh tomatoes 93
Spaghetti with garlic & anchovy
    sauce 84
Spaghetti with herring 75
Spaghetti with lettuce 83
Spaghetti with mussels 82
Spaghettini alla bottarga 84
Spaghettini with shrimp 80
Spaghettoni with tomato sauce &
    eggplant 88
Spicy calamari 217
Spicy chicken 243
Spicy fish soup 226
Spicy mussels on toast 15
Spicy spaghetti 78
Spinach pie 57
Spiral pasta with grouper 110
Squid & artichokes 203
Stewed chicory 333
Strawberries in syrup 348
Strawberry mousse cake 362
Stuffed artichokes 293

Stuffed focaccia 68
Stuffed onions 285
Stuffed peppers 278
Sturgeon with spring onions 194
Sun-dried tomato & vegetable tart 46
Sweet pepper & anchovy crostini 32
Sweet-and-sour artichokes 266
Sweet-and-sour eggplants 305
Sweet-and-sour turkey 238
Sweet-and-sour zucchini 280
Swordfish & mussels 195
Swordfish with basil 171
Swordfish with clams 191
Swordfish with lemon & herbs 179

T

Tagliatelle with chicken sauce 92
Tagliatelle with tuna & herbs 89
Tagliatelle with zucchini flowers 86
Tasty chickpeas 294
Timbal of shrimp, peppers &
    eggplant 28
Timbale of anchovies & curl
    endive salad 184
Toast with clams & eggs 36
Tomato & onion focaccia 45
Tomato baskets 20
Tomatoes filled with eggplants 302
Tomatoes, mozzarella & salad 303
Trastevere-style baccalà 200
Tripoline alla casalese 78
Triumph salad 25
Trout & chickpea salad 174
Tuna rolls 212
Tuna with peppers & tomatoes 210
Tuna-filled zucchini 277
Turbot with peppers & onions 170
Turbot with tomato & kiwi 196
Turkey rolls with pepper sauce 239
Turkey skewers 253
Turkey with olives 238
Turkey with steamed vegetables 239
Turnip tops in red wine 289

V

Veal & vegetable stew 234

Veal chops & artichokes 248
Veal cutlets with capers 250
Veal cutlets with sun-dried
    tomatoes 237
Veal rolls with artichokes 236
Veal rolls with lemon 250
Veal rump with eggplant 236
Veal tidbits with scallions &
    carrots 251
Vegetable 'caponata' 273
Vegetable 'ciambrotta' 273
Vegetable calzone 47
Vegetable pie 60
Vegetable tart 48
Vegetables in sweet-and-sour
    sauce 323
Velouté of cauliflower &
    tagliatelle 147
Venus clams with asparagus 218
Vermicelli & green bean soup 151

W

Warm salad with broccoli &
    kidney beans 270
Wheel pasta with broccoli &
    cauliflower 104
Whitefish with potatoes &
    asparagus 183
Whole wheat plum pie 359
Whole wheat spaghetti with
    anchovies 74
Wild herb tart 47
Wild strawberry surprise 356

Y

Young chicken with anchovies 252

Z

Zucchini & eggplants with basil 277
Zucchini & tomatoes 276
Zucchini, mozzarella & tomato pie 55

Index by section

ANTIPASTI
Artichoke & carrot salad 18
Asparagus with warm baby
        cuttlefish 25
Crostini with mussels & vegetables 21
Eggplant & pepper antipasto 15
Eggplant paté 36
Endives with ricotta 37
Fresh anchovies 21
Friselle alla marinara 22
Green bean & calamari antipasto 34
Harlequin antipasto 32
Lamb's lettuce & calamari salad 20
Lemon rice balls 16
Mediterranean 'crostoni' 37
Mediterranean skewers 24
Orange & carrot salad 26
Panzanella 30
Potato & herb soufflé 34
Potato crostini 12
Scampi & asparagus salad 29
Scampi with green sauce 33
Shrimp & fruit salad 30
Shrimp antipasto 14
Shrimp, arugula & carrot salad 33
Shrimp with avocado & egg sauce 14
Small whitefish with zucchini 24
Spicy mussels on toast 15
Sweet pepper & anchovy crostini 32
Timbal of shrimp, peppers &
        eggplant 28
Toast with clams & eggs 36
Tomato baskets 20
Triumph salad 25

PIZZA, FOCACCIA & SAVORY PIES
Anchovy focaccia 42
Anchovy pizza 69
Artichoke rolls 52

Beet green & chili pepper calzone 44
Clam pizza 53
Crostata Teresa 50
Eggplant & mushroom strudel 60
Eggplant & pepper pie 58
Escarole pizza 44
Focaccia with green olives 57
Four seasons pizza 56
Garlic & oregano pizza 65
Mushroom pizza 56
Onion & sweet pepper pie 54
Onion focaccia 64
Pizza all'Andrea 40
Pizza capricciosa 64
Pizza margherita 46
Pizza napoletana 45
Pizza regina 68
Plain pizza 61
Potato pizza 62
Radicchio pizza 52
Rice & zucchini pie 53
Ricotta & vegetable tart 66
Rosemary focaccia 58
Rustic onion & olive pie 69
Sardine pizza 65
Savory pie with yellow squash 61
Spinach pie 57
Stuffed focaccia 68
Sun-dried tomato & vegetable tart 46
Tomato & onion focaccia 45
Vegetable calzone 47
Vegetable pie 60
Vegetable tart 48
Wild herb tart 47
Zucchini, mozzarella & tomato pie 55

FIRST COURSES
Angel hair pasta in tomato sauce 162
Angel hair pasta with curly endive

salad 147
Apulia-style short pasta 105
Artichoke soup 160
Barley & black-eyed bean soup 150
Bavette with avocado 74
Bean & pasta soup 143
Beet tagliatelle with leek sauce 72
Broad bean soup 144
Brown rice with vegetables 123
Bulgur & celery soup 150
Bulgur soup with ditalini pasta 162
Casereccia with green beans &
        anchovies 100
Cereal & vegetable soup 152
Classic pasta salad 116
Cold cream of asparagus &
        rice soup 146
Conchiglie with zucchini 118
Crab soup 156
Cream of beet soup 140
Drunken rice 132
Farfalle with artichokes, zucchini &
        leeks 105
Farro soup 158
Fennel & baccalà soup 146
Fennel & pasta soup 142
Fettucini with seafood 82
Fusilli with caper & oregano
        sauce 108
Fusilli with fresh tuna 98
Fusilli with herbs 119
Fusilli with squid & spinach 109
Garden style spaghetti 89
Gnocchetti with shrimp &
        white beans 109
Gramigna with peppers & pesto 98
Green bean soup 138
Leek soup 142
Lemon risotto 135
Lentil soup 152

Ligurian-style spaghetti with sardines 83
Linguine with tuna & peas 75
Maccheroncelli with sardines 88
Maccheroncini with asparagus & mullet 112
Maccheroncini with scampi & fresh beans 99
Malfattini & vegetable soup 156
Maltagliati soup 154
Mediterranean linguine 92
Nettle soup 158
Onion soup 157
Orecchiette with eggplant 119
Orecchiette, garden & sea 106
Pasta & broad beans in broth 148
Pasta & wild herb soup 143
Pasta alla chitarra with nettles 93
Pasta panzanella 94
Pasta soup with marjoram 157
Penne with herb sauce 108
Penne with squash & radicchio 104
Penne with zucchini 113
Perciatelli with mussels 79
Quadrucci in fish broth 151
Radicchio & pasta soup 144
Rice & parsley soup 163
Rice crown with vegetables 136
Rice with anchovy filets 134
Rigatoni with baked tomatoes 100
Risotto with anchovies & pine nuts 126
Risotto with artichokes 126
Risotto with broad beans 130
Risotto with carrots 132
Risotto with fennel 124
Risotto with herbs & scampi 127
Risotto with lentils 128
Risotto with parsley 135
Risotto with pears & almonds 120
Risotto with peas & basil 122
Risotto with red radicchio 123
Risotto with saffron & shrimp 128
Risotto with scallops & peppers 131
Risotto with squash & spinach 134
Risotto with squid ink 131
Risotto with squid, mushrooms & spinach 133
Risotto with tomatoes 127
Risotto with zucchini 130

Risotto with zucchini flowers 122
Sardinian gnocchetti with fish sauce 96
Sardinian gnocchetti with peppers 99
Sardinian tagliatelle 90
Short pasta with arugula & celery 116
Short pasta with cucumbers 102
Shell pasta with lentils & broccoli 163
Short penne with artichokes 118
Short penne with eggplant 114
Spaghetti alla marinara 76
Spaghetti with basil sauce 79
Spaghetti with fresh tomatoes 93
Spaghetti with garlic & anchovy sauce 84
Spaghetti with herring 75
Spaghetti with lettuce 83
Spaghetti with mussels 82
Spaghettini alla bottarga 84
Spaghettini with shrimp 80
Spaghettoni with tomato sauce & eggplant 88
Spicy spaghetti 78
Spiral pasta with grouper 110
Tagliatelle with chicken sauce 92
Tagliatelle with tuna & herbs 89
Tagliatelle with zucchini flowers 86
Tripoline alla casalese 78
Velouté of cauliflower & tagliatelle 147
Vermicelli & green bean soup 151
Wheel pasta with broccoli & cauliflower 104
Whole wheat spaghetti with anchovies 74

FISH

Anchovies filled with spinach 184
Anchovies with fennel 168
Anchovy soup 228
Apulia style sole 168
Baccalà with vegetables 182
Baccalà with walnut sauce 198
Braided fish with tomatoes 181
Buridda from Genova 230
Buridda of mixed fish with tomato 175
Cacciucco 225
Calamari with lemon 207

Clams alla napoletana 206
Cod salad 208
Cold dogfish with lemon 217
Crab with lemon 192
Cuttlefish with spinach 172
Dogfish & zucchini broth 229
Dogfish in pieces 220
Dressed scampi 172
Dried cod with peppers 176
Escabeche anchovies 202
Fettucini with seafood 82
Fish fricassee 230
Fisherman's soup 229
Grilled razor shells 174
Grilled squid on skewers 183
Grouper with tomato 170
Grouper with vegetables 220
Hake with anchovies 195
Hake with fennel & onions 198
Hake with herbs 166
Little neck clams with onions 190
Marinated sea bass 199
Mediterranean salad 196
Mixed grilled fish 175
Mixed seafood au gratin 178
Monkfish with vegetables 180
Mullet in tomato sauce 216
Mullet with cucumbers 214
Mullet with tomato sauce 190
Mussels with lemon 192
Octopus in its broth 204
Octopus with sun-dried tomatoes 203
Pea soup with squid 225
Puréed fish soup 224
Razor shells with tomatoes 206
Roasted lobster 199
Salmon rolls 216
Sardine rolls, Palermo-style 202
Sardines with tomato 188
Scallops au gratin 213
Scallops with tomatoes & herbs 221
Scampi & squid in their sauce 224
Scampi & zucchini with pesto 179
Scorpion fish with leeks 178
Sea bream carpaccio with olives 194
Sea bream with mushrooms & herbs 212
Sea bream with olives 171
Sea bream with radicchio 182
Sea bream with rosemary &

tomatoes 213
Seafood soup 228
Shrimp & asparagus salad 218
Shrimp & artichokes 207
Sicilian-style dogfish 222
Sicilian-style tuna 186
Skate wings au gratin 221
Snapper with herbs 191
Spicy calamari 217
Spicy fish soup 226
Squid & artichokes 203
Sturgeon with spring onions 194
Swordfish & mussels 195
Swordfish with basil 171
Swordfish with clams 191
Swordfish with lemon & herbs 179
Timbale of anchovies & curly
        endive salad 184
Trastevere-style baccalà 200
Trout & chickpea salad 174
Tuna rolls 212
Tuna with peppers & tomatoes 210
Turbot with peppers & onions 170
Turbot with tomato & kiwi 196
Venus clams with asparagus 218
Whitefish with potatoes &
        asparagus 183

MEATS

Barbecued turkey meatballs 251
Chicken breast pizzaiola 256
Chicken breast with fruit 240
Chicken breast with vegetables &
        herb sauce 242
Chicken chunks 246
Chicken in milk 243
Chicken in salt crust 242
Chicken with lemon 247
Chicken with spinach & ham 246
Curried chicken with apples 247
Duck breast with oranges 252
Guinea fowl with tea 253
Guinea fowl with vegetables 245
Neapolitan-style rabbit thighs 256
Rabbit with olives 257
Rabbit with onions 258
Rabbit with peppers 254
Rabbit with vegetables 257

Rolled chicken breasts 244
Sicilian-style veal kebabs 237
Spicy chicken 243
Sweet-and-sour turkey 238
Turkey rolls with pepper sauce 239
Turkey skewers 253
Turkey with olives 238
Turkey with steamed vegetables 239
Veal & vegetable stew 234
Veal chops & artichokes 248
Veal cutlets with capers 250
Veal cutlets with sun-dried
        tomatoes 237
Veal rolls with artichokes 236
Veal rolls with lemon 250
Veal rump with eggplant 236
Veal tidbits with scallions &
        carrots 251
Young chicken with anchovies 252

VEGETABLES

Artichoke & bean stew 313
Artichoke pie, Sicilian style 313
Artichokes & peas 329
Artichokes & potatoes with herbs 312
Artichokes & vegetables 268
Artichokes cooked with white
        wine vinegar 266
Artichokes with eggs 312
Artichokes with fresh oregano 328
Artichokes with mozzarella 267
Artichokes with pecorino 267
Arugula with black-eyed beans 333
Asparagus & orange salad 322
Baked cauliflower & potatoes 297
Baked eggplant 'caponata' 264
Baked eggplants 265
Baked peppers 335
Baked potatoes & mushrooms 317
Baked stuffed potatoes 282
Baked tomatoes 302
Baked vegetables 272
Baker's salad 336
Bandiera 320
Basilicata-style vegetables 272
Bean salad 290
Beans & chicory lettuce 290
Beans & potatoes 270

Beans & potatoes 291
Broccoli Sicilian-style 288
Broccoli with oranges 289
Cannelloni beans & cabbage 271
Cannelloni beans with oregano 271
Cauliflower in tomato sauce 296
Cauliflower salad 297
Chicory tart 318
Chicory, garlic & olive oil 332
Chunky vegetables 320
Ciammotta 274
Ciaudedda 280
Citron & lettuce salad 322
Cold stuffed zucchini 292
Country style cauliflower 296
Eggplant 'Parmigiana' 304
Eggplant 'peperonata' 334
Eggplant compote 304
Eggplant rolls 265
Eggplant salad 300
Eggplant surprise 327
Eggplants 'capricciose' 326
Eggplants in hot sauce 326
Eggplants in tomato sauce 264
Eggplants in tuna sauce 327
Endive with capers & olives 332
Fennel with herbs 311
Fennel with pecorino 310
Fennel with vinegar 310
Fennel with walnuts 311
Filled zucchini, Cagliari-style 276
Fried peppers 278
Fried potatoes with parsley 274
Frittedda 291
Green beans & peppers with
        cheese 299
Green beans with anchovies 298
Green beans with herbs 299
Green beans with tomatoes 298
Grilled eggplant rolls 305
Grilled vegetables 262
Marinated artichokes 328
Messina-style filled tomatoes 303
Mixed cooked vegetables 306
Mixed cooked vegetables 319
Mixed vegetables with tomatoes 319
Nonna's potatoes 282
Onions filled with tuna 284
Onions with marsala 284
Peperonata 279

Pepper filets 335
Peppers with almond sauce 334
Pinzimonio 330
Potato & tomato dish 283
Potato tart 283
Potatoes 'all'arrabbiata' 316
Potatoes 'pizzaiola' 317
Purée of beans & chicory 318
Raw artichoke salad 329
Rolled peppers 286
Royal salad 323
Salad 'deliziosa' 324
Salad with provolone 308
Savory potato salad 316
Sicilian croquettes 285
Simply broccoli 288
Snow peas & potatoes 314
Soft peppers 279
Stewed chicory 333
Stuffed artichokes 293
Stuffed onions 285
Stuffed peppers 278
Sweet-and-sour artichokes 266
Sweet-and-sour eggplants 305
Sweet-and-sour zucchini 280
Tasty chickpeas 294
Tomatoes filled with eggplants 302
Tomatoes, mozzarella & salad 303
Tuna-filled zucchini 277
Turnip tops in red wine 289
Vegetable 'caponata' 273

Vegetable 'ciambrotta' 273
Vegetables in sweet and sour sauce 323
Warm salad with broccoli & kidney
    beans 270
Zucchini & eggplants with basil 277
Zucchini & tomatoes 276

SWEETS & DESSERTS
Almond cake 373
Apple dessert 370
Bananas flambé 365
Carrot cake 373
Cherry sorbet 340
Cherry soup 367
Coffee granita 342
Figs in pastry 358
Figs with walnuts 360
Filled peaches 366
Filled pink grapefruit 368
Fruit aspic 374
Fruit carpaccio with mandarin
    sorbet 355
Fruit compote 365
Fruit compote with Grand
    Marnier 344
Fruit salad with pineapples 355
Fruit salad with vanilla ice cream 354
Fruits in gelatin 'bombe' 353
Fruits in jelly 352

Grandma's pie 371
Grape & fig gratin 364
Grape aspic 353
Grape clafoutis 370
Green tea granita 343
Jasmine sorbet 346
Kiwi sorbet 347
Lemon yogurt sorbet 347
Melon & raspberry aspic 372
Mint granita with syrup 342
Nectarine molds 352
Orange sorbet 346
Oranges with Grand Marnier 367
Peach pie 358
Peach sorbet 350
Pears in syrup 354
Pineapple & lemon granita 343
Pineapple in puff pastry 359
Pineapples flambé 366
Plum & Maraschino pie 371
Pumpkin dessert 372
Raspberry tartlets 364
Strawberries in syrup 348
Strawberry mousse cake 362
Whole wheat plum pie 359
Wild strawberry surprise 356